QABALAH

Do what thou wilt shall be the whole of the Law

QABALAH

A Primer

John Bonner

Love is the law, love under will

SKOOB BOOKS PUBLISHING

LONDON

First edition

First published by
SKOOB BOOKS PUBLISHING LTD
Skoob esoterica series
11a-17 Sicilian Avenue
Southampton Row
London WC1A 2QH

Series editor: Christopher Johnson

ISBN 1 871438 57 8

Printed by Ling Wah Press Sdn. Bhd.

To S.E.J

Acknowledgements

Thanks to Geraldine Beskin, Chris Johnson, Ann Kramer,
Charles Newington and Mark Parry-Maddox, who know that ...
"of making many books there is no end; and much study is a
weariness of the flesh".   (*Ecclesiastes 12:12*)

CONTENTS

ILLUSTRATIONS

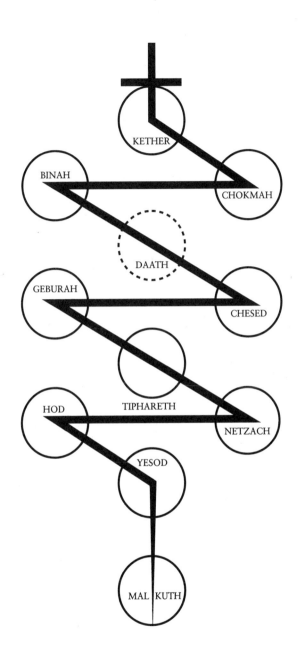

THE DESCENT OF POWER
THE LIGHTNING FLASH OR THE FLAMING SWORD

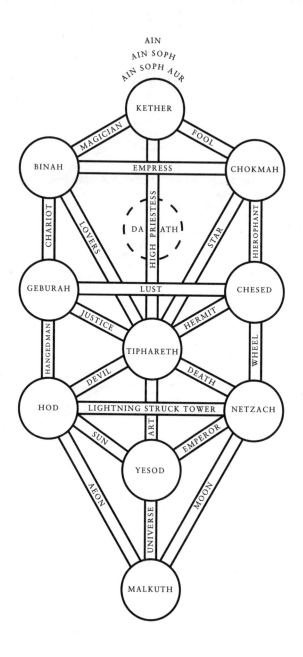

THE TREE OF LIFE

Instead of complaining that God had hidden himself, you will give him thanks for having revealed so much of himself.

(Blaise Pascal, *Pensees* 1670)

Introduction

The Concise Oxford Dictionary defines Qabalah as the "Jewish Oral Tradition, mystic interpretation, esoteric doctrine, and occult lore", which as far as it goes is true enough. Qabalah certainly involves a mystical interpretation of scriptural texts, it does provide an esoteric doctrine, and it undoubtedly represents a substantial body of occult lore. It is much more than any of these however, as over the centuries it has evolved and grown away from its early beginnings as a strictly Jewish oral tradition.

The term "Qabalah" is derived from the Hebrew root-word "QBL", which is itself derived from the closely related language of Aramaic, and means "to receive", signifying particularly "from mouth to ear", emphasising its provenance as an oral tradition communicated by direct teaching. It has also come to have the general meaning of "tradition".

Due to the difficulties of transliterating from Hebrew, which is basically a consonantal alphabet relying on "points" placed below letters to indicate vowels, there are a variety of spellings of Qabalah to be found in the literature. Variants include; Kabbalah, Kabalah, Cabbalah, Cabalah, and Qabbalah.

The version used in the present work is felt to be the one that best approximates the Sephardi form.

Other Hebrew words and phrases are subject to similar difficulties, with a number of possible and equally valid versions in current use. This is in part due to differences between the Sephardi and Ashkenazi dialects. Among those Qabalistic works which are written in Hebrew -some like the *Sepher ha-Zohar* are also in Aramaic- the great majority are in the Sephardi dialect. This form was the one used by Spanish and Portuguese Rabbins who between them produced much of the

Qabalistic canon. The Jewish communities of northern Europe, who spoke the Ashkenazi dialect, contributed comparatively little to the early literature of the Qabalah. Therefore it is the Sephardi forms which have the most common currency in Qabalistic documents, and on which the Hebrew terms used throughout this book are based.

Since the Middle Ages the word "Qabalah" has been used as though it were a synonym for black magic, witchcraft, sorcery, and other supposed evils, while the term has been indiscriminately applied to cover a multitude of occult activities. Even today, apart from its proper technical usage, the word is most likely to be heard in connection with dubious societies, rank superstitions, and indecipherable symbols. As is the case with "Magick", "Qabalah" has come to signify to the uninitiated something very different to its original meaning, and likewise stands in need of rehabilitation.

The current renaissance in Qabalistic studies can be dated from the later half of the last century, when for the first time the central documents of the canon were translated into European tongues. It is to be hoped that this growing interest will continue to help counter the ignorance and superstition with which the subject is unfortunately still identified in the public mind.

We will be looking at the history of Qabalah and that of its primary source material later in this introductory chapter and will therefore confine ourselves here to an attempt at delineating the subject of this work. This is a harder task than it might at first appear, for when attempting to define what Qabalah actually is one cannot help but feel a certain sympathy for St Augustine, who, when asked to give his thoughts on the nature of time, said:

"If no one asks of me, I know; if I wish to explain to him who asks, I know not".   (*Confessions, Book XI*)

The first point to be made is that, in spite of what many people have believed, the Qabalah is not a single book, nor is it a whole library of books. Of course, there is a vast corpus of literature, some ancient, and some relatively modern, that contains much of the essential teachings of Qabalah, but the real heart of the subject is not to be found in any text, no matter how venerable.

Essentially, Qabalah is a practical subject, a discipline that must be *used* in order for it to come alive. Qabalah is a living, growing system of personal development, that provides not only a framework for speculations of the most profound character, but also a means of testing the veracity of those speculations by personal experience.

We will be exploring the "practical Qabalah" in the main body of this work, but it is important to emphasise right from the beginning that although the subject is fascinating from an academic view-point its true value lies in its application and usage.

Qabalah is a metaphysical philosophy, or rather a theosophy, that sets out to answer a series of vital questions regarding the nature of God, His creation, and the place of man in His divine plan.

The pioneering magician and Qabalist, S.L.MacGregor-Mathers, in the introduction to his own translation of Knorr von Rosenroth's, Latin *"Kabbalah Denudata"*, gives the following list as being the ten principle problems that Qabalistic doctrine has addressed:

(a)   The Supreme Being, His nature and attributes
(b)   The Cosmology
(c)   The creation of angels and man
(d)   The destiny of man and angels
(e)   The nature of the soul
(f)   The nature of angels, demons, and elementals
(g)   The import of the revealed law
(h)   The transcendental symbolism of numerals
(i)   The peculiar mysteries contained in the Hebrew letters
(j)   The equilibrium of contraries.

The teachings of the Qabalah are based on a theory of the sequential emanation of God's creation from a condition of unmanifestation to concretion in the physical world.

Although perhaps not a term that would immediately commend itself to all adherents of the Judeo-Christian tradition, the Qabalah could be said to take a fundamentally *pantheist* view of creation. The Creator is not envisaged simply as an architect or artificer, moulding the manifest universe out of pre-existing material, but as one omnipotent and omnipresent being, who creates from His own substance as an act of divine will. Therefore all that exists is necessarily part of the "body of God", matter as well as spirit.

In other words, and with apologies to William Blake;....
"Everything that *is* is Holy".

Qabalists have long recognised that there is a limit to what can be known of the Deity and His attributes, and therefore they have chosen to draw veils across the forever unknowable region of "Negative Existence", which they term the "Ain", and concentrate their main efforts on exploring the mystery of manifestation.

The sequence of this manifestation from "nothingness" to materiality is illustrated by the glyph known as the "Tree of Life", which is usually transliterated from Hebrew as OTz ChIIM and pronounced *Aetz Chiyim.*

The diagram of the Tree of Life is the essential and unique feature of Qabalah, and that which makes its study not only rewarding in itself but also of immense value in understanding other traditions.

With the development of the Tree we have available a magnificently flexible, infinitely expandable tool for investigating virtually any conceivable branch of human interest.

The Tree itself is composed of ten centres or areas of activity, which are termed the Sephiroth, (singular, Sephirah), arranged in three columns and interconnected by twenty-two paths.

The term "Sephirah" has no exact English translation but is taken to mean "numeration" or "emanation", and each represents a distinct and separate stage of the "descent of power" from the God-head to the physical world, usually drawn on the glyph as a lightning flash.(see illustration)

Each Sephirah has a unique character which results from its position in the order of emanation. The creative impulse, which has its roots in Negative Existence, undergoes a sequence of differentiation, specialisation, and concretion in its descent into manifestation.

Each of these stages represents the development of a Sephirah and each Sephirah presents a specific set of qualities and energies defining a particular point in the continuing process of the showing forth of God.

One of the practical benefits of the glyph is that it provides an invaluable system of categorising all phenomena by reference to its Paths and Sephiroth. Indeed, the Tree has repeatedly been described as being analogous to a "filing-cabinet" or "card-index system", as all manner of data and material may be stored and cross-referenced according to an elaborate system of correspondences.

The analogy with a filing-cabinet is a good one, except that such a system is rather lifeless and cannot effectively mimic the dynamic relationships which exist between categories on the Tree.

The pictorial representation of the Holy Tree forms a sort of "flow-chart" which illustrates the manner in which one concept or phenomenon develops as a necessary response to another.

The Tree also offers a form of map by which the individual aspirant, and eventually the entire human race, may navigate the long and arduous journey to (re)union with God.

Although the organisation of the Tree is such that it may be applied to any field of study or sphere of interest, from engineering to human psychology, it is particularly in the areas of Philosophy and Religion that it is found to be most valuable.

A good working knowledge of the Qabalah, and a familiarity with the diagram of the Tree, is a prerequisite for anyone working within the western magickal tradition. One could go so far as to say that without such a background of Qabalistic knowledge their best efforts will be in vain! The vast bulk of available occult literature, magickal, mystical, alchemical, and divinatory, is founded on Qabalistic teaching, however far removed they may be from that source, and is little more than a jumble of confused nonsense without some knowledge of its basic key.

It is not necessary for every occultist to be an accomplished Qabalist however, any more than it is necessary for every Qabalist to be actively involved in what is generally defined as the "occult", but it is important that the fundamentals of Qabalistic doctrine are studied and assimilated before embarking on any specialised study. This is possibly most true for the practical magician, whose work brings him into direct contact with the traditional Qabalah.

It is usual to class Qabalistic work under four main headings, which to return to MacGregor-Mather's scheme are:

(a)   The Practical Qabalah
(b)   The Literal Qabalah
(c)   The Unwritten Qabalah
(d)   The Dogmatic Qabalah

The first category, that of the Practical Qabalah, includes all matters theurgic. This is the branch of Qabalah which is concerned with the art and science of Magick, including divination, talismanic magick, and ceremonial magick, solo or group.

Much of contemporary western magick is based on the work of the Hermetic Order of the Golden Dawn, which flourished in the later part of the last century, and which based its rituals and teachings very firmly in Qabalah. Without a doubt, the Golden Dawn, for all its short and stormy history, has been the single most influential magickal organisation of recent times, and one to whose teachings we shall be returning again and again throughout this work.

The Literal Qabalah concerns itself with the study and manipulation of letters and numbers.

Hebrew, like Greek, has no separate numerals. The twenty-two letters of the alphabet have a dual role, being also used as numbers, thus making each word or phrase an arithmetical as well as a literary expression. (see Appendix for table of letter values).

The Literal Qabalah is itself divided into three main areas, all of which we shall be examining in more detail in later chapters, so for the present we will content ourselves with a brief survey.

The first sub-division is Gematria, an initiated and complex form of numerology in which the number value of words or phrases are first ascertained and then compared, conclusions as to hidden meanings being derived thereby. For instance, two words with the same numerical value would be held to be functionally identical, or at least to have a meaningful, and therefore revealing, relationship.

By skilful use of this technique, scriptural passages may be made to yield a wealth of alternative meanings.

It is important to distinguish between the high art of Qabalistic Gematria and the debased popular forms of numerology which are rightly condemned as superstitious nonsense. To coin a phrase which was once ignorantly used to describe the relationship between astrology and astronomy, the one is the "bastard daughter" of the other.

For the most part Gematria is practised in Hebrew and Greek, but the "order and value" of other alphabets is available, including English and the angelic tongue of Enochian, although with these the student is strongly advised to do their own correlating research.

The second technique to come under the heading of Literal Qabalah is "Notariqon", derived from the Latin, "*notarius*", meaning "shorthand writer". This is a method of word manipulation which has two variants. In the first, the initial letter of each word in a phrase is taken to construct a new word, for example, the God-name "AGLA", is composed of the initial letters of the Hebrew phrase, "*A*teh *G*ibor *L*eolahm *A*donai", which means, "To Thee be the Power unto the Ages, O my Lord".

The second form of Notariqon is the exact reverse of the first. Here the individual letters of a single word are taken as the initial letter of a number of words which then go to make up a phrase. Qabalists, over the years, have expended a considerable amount of energy applying this method to the first word of the Book of Genesis, "Berashith", which has been made to yield all manner of mysteries.

The final technique of the Literal Qabalah is "Temurah", which means permutation, and involves substituting letters according to certain arcane rules, the details of which we will explore in the appropriate chapter.

The Unwritten Qabalah, not surprisingly, is that body of knowledge which has never been committed to paper, or, at the very least, has not been put into general circulation. Certain mysteries of the Qabalah have always been withheld from the uninitiated, or have been purposefully obscured, often by the use of "blinds" or deliberate "misinformation", in published works. The keys to techniques held as being especially powerful and sacred by any given school and only transmitted to the candidate at his initiation constitute an important part of this category.

The Dogmatic Qabalah consists of doctrinal teachings, as contained in the major source works of Qabalistic literature. These include the *Sepher ha-Zohar*, or "Book of Splendour"; *The Sepher Yetzirah*, or "Book of Formation" and the *Sepher Bahir* or "Book of Light". We will have cause to look more closely at these texts during the main part of this work, both in terms of their influence in the development of Qabalah, and as part of the substantial body of the Qabalistic canon.

A Brief History

As the Qabalah developed from an oral tradition which was not committed to paper until at least the time of the destruction of the second temple (AD70), its origins and true antiquity are very much open to question. Also, it has been somewhat eclectic in its later development picking up elements from Neoplatonic, Gnostic, and Pythagorean sources, so making an accurate assessment of its antiquity, in the light of written material, extremely difficult.

Whilst it is true that the Qabalah has been expanded by the addition of elements from other philosophies, it is also true that those philosophies have themselves liberally taken from the Qabalah. Indeed, the degree of cross-fertilisation is such that it is now difficult to say quite which tenet derives from what tradition.

It is possible to divide the history of Qabalah into three main parts; the first being the legendary or mythological accounts of the transmission; the second that long period, which includes biblical times, before the publication of the Zohar; and the third, the period from the *Zohar's* publication to modern times. We may term the second period, "Pre-Zoharic", and the third, "Post-Zoharic".

Inevitably it is of the post-Zoharic period that we have the most knowledge, although even here there are occasional frustrating lacunae.

Some authorities have maintained that the historic root of Qabalah is to be found in ancient Egypt, and that it was Moses, a master of Egyptian magick, who first brought the teaching to the children of Israel. However, apart from legend, it is difficult to find much evidence, certainly in the doctrinal Qabalah, to support this view.

Others suggest that Qabalah in particular, and Jewish mysticism in general, represents a comparatively late development, and one "foreign to the religious genius of Israel" which in part resulted from the philosophical speculations of eleventh and twelfth century Rabbins based largely in Moorish Spain. Although as we shall see the Iberian scholars were most influential in the development of Qabalah, there is no real evidence to suggest that they were the true originators of the teachings and indeed every reason to say that they were not.

In spite of some controversy regarding the date and authorship of the *Sepher ha-Zohar* there is unquestionable evidence for the existence of the Qabalistic tradition to be found in a number of early religious and mystical texts.

The Old Testament, especially in Hebrew and in the Greek of the Septuagint, contains many passages which are inexplicable except by reference to Qabalistic doctrine, as do the books of the Apocrypha, Talmud, New Testament, The Targums, and many other Rabbinical writings.

There seems little doubt that the doctrinal core of Qabalah was at the very least an early manifestation of Judaism, and in all probability pre-dates it by a considerable period of time.

One tradition has it that the secrets of Qabalah were given to Abraham by God through the medium of the Archangel Metatron ("Great Teacher"), traditionally regarded as the first created being.

Another takes the initial transmission even further back and says that God first taught the doctrine to a select company of angels who then passed it on to Adam as a sort of consolation prize for having lost his tenancy of the Garden of Eden. It is said that these angels acted in accordance with the will of the Most High in giving our first father this teaching, for by its use and the exercise of his free will, he, and his children, may eventually return to their previous condition of perfection.

From Adam the teachings were passed to Seth, and then to Noah, and from Noah to Abraham, at which point it was taken into the land of Egypt where Moses first learned of it. Moses is also said to have received additional initiated instruction in the subject from the angels of the Lord during his forty years of wandering in the desert; here again the chief instructor is given as Metatron. Moses, it is claimed, then passed on the teachings to the elders of the tribes; one scriptural justification for this being the Biblical verse which says:

> "And Moses went out, and told the people the words of the LORD, and gathered the seventy men of the elders of the people, and set them round in the tabernacle".   (*Num.* 11:24)

Continuing the chain of initiation we find both David and Solomon claimed as learned Qabalists and with them a whole succession of prophets, including Isaiah, Daniel, and Ezekiel, the later being of particular interest by dint of the profound mystical imagery and Qabalistic symbolism to be found in his visions.

Whilst it is unlikely that this account has any basis in fact, it does suggest a probable course of development for the Qabalah; arising from primitive beginnings, being passed from master to initiate, for the most part slowly evolving in complexity and comprehensiveness but subject to the occasional quantum leap through the insight of those exceptional masters, with the basic structure of the doctrine complete and in place by the time the Pentateuch assumed its current form.

From our own point of view the most important period of Qabalistic history comes at the time when it ceased to be a purely oral tradition and generated a corpus of mystical literature, although, as will be seen, it is difficult to give a reliable date for exactly when this might have occurred.

With the possible exception of the *Sepher Bahir*, the most influential of early Qabalistic publications has certainly been the *Sepher ha-Zohar*, or "Book of Splendour", usually referred to simply as the "Zohar".

The *Zohar* is really a "bible" in the proper sense of the word in that it is comprised of a number of related mystical books, amongst which the following are usually judged the more important: *The Book of Concealed Mystery; Greater Holy Assembly; Lesser Holy Assembly; The House of Elohim*, and the *Book of the Revolutions of Souls*. There are a total of nineteen books classed under the heading of Zohar, which together with the *Sepher Yetzirah*, represent the core of the Qabalist canon, and which provides us with much of the quoted material used throughout the present work.

The *Zohar* has long been the subject of sometimes very acrimonious, dispute regarding its origin. It purports to be the work of the Rabbi Simeon ben Yochai, who lived about 95-190 AD, but some scholars have dated the main body of Zoharic text to the third or fourth century AD, while others insist that textual analysis shows them to be forgeries of the thirteenth century and name the perpetrator as Rabbi Moses de Leon.

The balance of learned opinion on this matter seems to fall in favour of the theory that Moses de Leon did indeed compose the *Zohar* in its present form, but that it may represent the genuine oral teachings of Simeon ben Yochai, preserved both as memory and, just possibly, as scraps of documentation.

Even if it were possible to prove that the *Sepher ha-Zohar* is entirely the work of Moses de Leon it would not necessarily follow that it was intended as a forgery. It was a common literary convention of the time, especially so in the case of mystical texts, for authors to attribute their works to long dead but highly respected scholars, patriarchs, and prophets. This had the two-fold advantage of safe-guarding the real author's anonymity whilst at the same time adding a degree of spurious authority to their essays. It is extremely unlikely that Rabbi Moses de Leon set out deliberately to defraud the scholarly community for as all the available editions must have been copied by hand such a work would have a limited circulation, and then only amongst the more wealthy and dedicated scholars, all of whom would be well aware of such conventions.

The second most important of the early Qabalistic texts, the *Sepher Yetzirah*, is also subject to dispute. It is supposed to have been written by Rabbi Akiba, who lived in the time of the Emperor Hadrian, (circa AD 120.). It has been variously assigned to early Gnostic times, around the third or fourth century AD, and to the period between 700 - 800 AD, but unfortunately, as with the *Zohar*, it is doubtful whether we shall ever know for sure. It is however generally considered to pre-date the *Zohar* and to be the earliest extant Qabalistic text.

For over three centuries Spain was a major centre for the study and dissemination of Qabalistic teaching. The first important school of which we have record is that founded in the twelfth century by Rabbi Issac the Blind in Gerona, Catalonia. Spain was at this time a major focus of the intellectual life of Europe and North Africa. Some of the finest philosophical and scientific minds of the Middle Ages were born in or gravitated towards the Iberian Peninsular during the period of the Muslim ascendancy. This was truly a golden age of learning and cultural cross-fertilisation which lasted until the expulsion of the Jews in 1492, by which time Qabalistic dogma was beginning to exert a profound influence on international Jewry and Christian scholars alike.

During their sojourn in Spain the Jewish community was in a particularly advantageous position because of their knowledge of both Arab languages and culture and those of the European Christians. They were therefore often used as intermediaries in negotiations by both sides and consequently became exposed to a rich variety of cultural experience and intellectual stimulation, which they made full use of in their religious and philosophical texts.

The "School of Segovia" was another extremely important centre of learning. Here the emphasis was on the practice of exegesis; various Qabalistic techniques being developed by which the scriptures could be made to yield up a wealth of hidden meanings. It is in this school that many of the methods of the Literal Qabalah were refined and codified into something like the form they have now.

One of the more notable Qabalists of this early period was the amazing Abraham Abulafia, (b.1240-d.1295) As an example of burning devotion and evangelical fervour Abulafia was without peer. He it was who attempted (unsuccessfully) to convert Pope Nicholas III to Judaism! and who must therefore be accounted the supreme optimist of his or any other age.

Abulafia was possibly the first Qabalist to feel the necessity to publish the previously secret doctrine and practises. He said of himself; "no other Qabalist before me wrote explicit books on this subject", and in this of course he was right, but it was also to be expected that he would suffer the not inconsiderable antagonism of his colleagues as a result of his presumption. In spite of Abulafia's commendable attempts at pursuing a policy of "freedom of information" not one of his thirty-five or more works were actually published until well into the 19th century. However, the meditation practices of which he was a past master and an important innovator eventually came to feature prominently in the work of the practical Qabalah, which we would term Magick.

Abulafia himself undoubtedly had a somewhat quirky personality, and has always been looked upon with a degree of suspicion, due in no small part to his undeniable fanaticism, of which the evangelising journey to Rome in 1280 is one of the more extreme examples.

His cause was further undermined by his claim that Elijah and Enoch had both appeared to him in a vision and gave to him full details of the coming of the Messiah and Millennium, which was to occur in 1285, but which, unfortunately for his reputation, did not.

In the fifteenth and sixteenth centuries a number of Christian scholars saw in the Qabalah the possibility of its being used as a means of converting some of the more intellectual Jews to Christianity, and indeed in this endeavour they were partially successful.

John Stephen Rittengal, the translator of the *Sepher Yetzirah* into Latin, was one such convert, as was Paul Ricci, personal physician to the Emperor Maximilian the First. They, and others like them, were convinced, through the Christian's skilful use of the methods of the literal Qabalah, that the Pentateuch and other sacred texts proved that Jesus was indeed the long prophesied Messiah.

Interestingly there are few examples of Christians being converted to Judaism by Qabalistic study. Why the traffic should all be one way, so to speak, is something of a mystery but is no doubt bound up with the difficult and repressive social circumstances in which the majority of European Jewry have been forced to live during much of the history of the Diaspora.

Of the Christian Qabalists of that time perhaps the most influential was the Geonese nobleman, Giovanni Pico della Mirandola (1463-94).

Mirandola's importance could be said to lie not so much in his own original work, but in his function as a bridge between the Jewish secret tradition and the burgeoning Qabalah of the Christians.

His work entitled *Kabbalistic Conclusions,* even found favour with Pope Julius as a skilful treatment of the Hebrew Torah in the light of the Christian revelation.

An indication of the then lack of knowledge of Qabalah in western seats of learning can be seen in the fact that whilst staying in Rome Mirandola offered by advertisement sums of money to any scholar prepared to dispute with him on this or indeed any other matter.

Mirandola was very much a philosophical Qabalist who had serious reservations about the use of practical magickal techniques, despite the fact that he was an accomplished astrologer and composed a valuable treatise on the subject.

Following on from the work of Mirandola in the Christian tradition, came Cornelius Agrippa of Nettesheim, born in Cologne in 1486.

It was Agrippa who first set about providing a methodical description of the branches of Qabalah. He did much to popularise and make respectable the study of these teachings to the European intellectual community, largely through the publication of his famous opus, "*De Occulta Philosophia*".

It could be argued that it is mainly by the influence of these two scholars that the Qabalah was brought to the attention of men such as: Raymund Lully, Christian Knorr von Rosenroth, Paracelsus, Jacob Boehme, Robert Fludd, John Dee, Francis Bacon, Sir Issac Newton, Spinoza, and innumerable others, including the philosophers Hegel and Schopenhauer.

Two other Jewish Qabalists of the early post-Zoharic period are worthy of special note; the first, Moses ben Jacob Cordovero of Safed, known as the "Ramak", was born in 1522 and died 1570. Cordovero was at the time regarded as "the greatest light of Kabbalism since Simeon ben Yohai", (AE Waite, *The Holy Kabbalah*). He was without doubt the most influential theoretical Qabalist of the period, and was instrumental in founding the Qabalistic Academy of Safed in the Upper Galilee region of Palestine, which subsequently became a major centre of learning. Cordovero was a prolific writer who produced a great many erudite works including the abstruse but seminal *Pardes Rimmonim* or "Garden of Pomegranates".

Whereas Cordovero's work was chiefly philosophical, that of Issac Luria was primarily mystical.

Luria was born in Jerusalem of Ashkenazi German parents in 1534 and died at Safed in 1572, at the early age of 38.

He developed a very idiosyncratic style of Qabalah which was to gain widespread popularity after his death He engaged for much of his life in the practice of a form of meditation which afforded him a great many illuminating visions, upon which his mystical interpretations of sacred texts were largely founded. In contrast to Cordovero, Luria based his work on revelation rather than scholarship. Although obviously learned (in his youth he had studied Rabbinical Law in Egypt) he was by no means a literary figure and, apart from a handful of poems in Aramaic, published nothing. When asked by one of his disciples why he did not publish his revelations he is said to have replied

> "It is impossible because all things are interrelated. I can hardly open my mouth to speak without feeling as though the sea burst its dams and overflowed. How then shall I express what my soul has received, and how can I put it down in a book?"
>
> (Gershom G Scholem *Major Trends in Jewish Mysticism*)

It has therefore been left to his students to preserve his teachings, and it is by their writings only that we have any knowledge of this extraordinary man and his work. In spite of this, Lurianic concepts exerted a powerful influence on the subsequent development of Qabalism, all the more remarkable when one realises that, even by the standards of sixteenth century Palestine, its more adventurous speculations are bizarre in the extreme.

One of Luria's best known pupils, Rabbi Chayim Vital, produced a truly monumental work, based on the master's teachings, entitled *"The Tree of Life"*, which was to influence generations of Qabalists and still stands as a classic in its field.

From the Europe and North Africa of the sixteenth century we now move to eighteenth century Poland. It was here that Rabbi Israel (1698-1760), known as the "Baal Shem Tov", or "Master of the Name", established the fundamentalist sect of the Hassidim, ("The Devout").

The practical Qabalah was central to the early form of this spiritual revival movement, with the *Zohar* taken as its primary text. They are said to have rejected much of the *Talmud* and concentrated instead on powerful meditation practices and internal prayer, also engaging in those practices which we would term magick, as a means of spiritual development.

At the movement's peak, in the nineteenth century, it could claim hundreds of thousands, perhaps millions, of followers, mainly among the eastern European Jewry.

A large number of Qabalistic texts were published during the great years of the Hassidim, often for the first time, and its Rabbis became highly influential, not only amongst their co-religionists but also in the intellectual life of Christian and secular Europe.

Much of the knowledge of the Hassidic communities is thought to have been disseminated by the travels of peregrinating Rabbis known as the "Tsadikim", ("righteous ones") who were committed students and exponents of the practical Qabalistic arts.

Coming now to nineteenth century France we encounter the extraordinary figure of the Abbé Alphonse-Louis Constant, who styled himself "Eliphas Levi Zahed". With Levi we have at last arrived at the age of the modern magician, of which breed he may certainly be accounted the first. Levi's contribution to magick and Qabalistic studies is immense, mainly by virtue of his published works which presented for the first time a (relatively) clear and concise treatment of magickal theory and practice, predicated of course on the Qabalah. His best known works are; *"Le Dogme et Rituel de la Haute Magie"* (1852), and the *"Histoire de la Magie"* (1860). Both works are still in print and in English Translations.

Towards the latter end of the nineteenth century a number of talented scholars applied themselves to the ancient mysteries, most notably the London coroner, William Wynn Westcott, whose translation of the *Sepher Yetzirah* is used throughout this work; and Samuel Liddell MacGregor Mathers, a founder member of the Golden Dawn and translator of portions of the *Zohar* and the *"Sacred Magic of Abramelin the Mage"*.

We might also mention here, Arthur Edward Waite, amongst whose voluminous literary output is *"The Holy Kabbalah"*, a comprehensive, if at times rather pompous, account of the development of the secret tradition in Israel.

The towering figure of Aleister Crowley dominates twentieth century magick, indeed it was he who rehabilitated the term and gave to it its current spelling. It is probable that there has been more invective, and equally, more praise, heaped upon this one man than upon all the other occultists of previous centuries put together.

To the majority of the uninformed public he was "The Wickedest Man in the World", to his followers he is, quite simply, "The Prophet of the lovely Star", who through his reception and promulgation of *Liber AL vel Legis*, the "Book of the Law", in 1904, ushered in the Aeon of Horus.

Regardless of one's attitude to Crowley it is undeniable that his influence on magick will be felt for a long time to come.

Although most of his prolific output concerns the practical side of Qabalah, the doctrine, according to his own interpretation, permeates his entire work. Crowley has often been accused of placing deliberate, and dangerous, "traps" in his written work, to mislead the unwary. Quite apart from the fact that these"blinds" have a long and honourable provenance in occult literature, a reasonable knowledge of basic Qabalah will be more than sufficient protection against them. In any event, as Crowley would I am sure agree, persons without such knowledge would do well to avoid not only his books, but all of the more advanced occult material.

As far as our present study of the Qabalah is concerned the most important of his published works is undoubtedly *Liber 777* which was based on the pioneering work of Alan Bennett, Crowley's mentor in the Golden Dawn who later became a Buddhist monk in Ceylon and took the name Ananda Metteya. Other contributors included George Cecil Jones, Crowley's proposer for Golden Dawn membership and VictorNeuburg, poet and occasional magickal partner of Crowley whose life has been documented in a biography by J.O.Fuller.

777 represents the most complete tabulation of Qabalistic correspondences ever to be published and is unique in the history of occult literature. Basically the book is arranged as pages of tables, with each Sephirah and path being assigned a large series of corresponding concepts. The categories range from the Orders of Qliphoth (the "demons" of Qabalah) to the typical diseases of each path, with useful supplementary lists appended to the main body of the work. Many of the major categories of attribution are discussed and elaborated by Crowley in his explanation of the tables.

Liber 777 is an invaluable reference work for anyone interested in exploring the practical Qabalah and forms the basis for the Sephirothic attributions used throughout this work. Its early acquisition and constant study is earnestly recommended to all serious students of practical Qabalah.

The twentieth century has seen the publication of a number of guides to basic Qabalah, which although rarely contributing to the development of the subject itself have served to bring it to the notice of a wider range of people than had hitherto been reached.

Amongst those modern Qabalists we should mention two outstanding writers; Dion Fortune, a former member of the Golden Dawn and founder of the Society of the Inner Light, whose excellent "*Mystical Qabalah*" is still, over fifty years since its first publication, one of the classic books on the subject; and Israel Regardie, formerly Crowley's secretary, whose "*Garden of Pomegranates*" and "*Tree of Life*" are both valuable contributions to the dissemination of Qabalistic knowledge.

Plainly a detailed history of the development of the Qabalah from its ancient origins to the present day is a mammoth task, and one that would require many volumes to do the subject full justice.

Even an abbreviated version of such a history would be beyond the scope of the present work. What we have tried to do however is to suggest something of the background of the subject in hand, and to highlight, as far as is possible in the space available, some of the more important developments and personalities in the strange and convoluted tale of the evolution of this ancient and, until comparatively recently, all too secret tradition.

1

OTz ChIIM

THE TREE OF LIFE

In this chapter we will attempt to gain an "overview" of the glyph which lies at the very heart of Qabalistic teaching.

The Tree is composed of four distinct elements. These are; the three Pillars of Manifestation, the ten Holy Sephiroth, the "Paths" which run to and from the Sephiroth, and the "Veils", which includes the great Abyss below the Supernal Triad. (see illustration)

What we have described is the basic traditional Tree in its simplest configuration. It is possible to extend the glyph to illustrate such concepts as the four worlds and their multitudinous correspondences, but here we shall restrict ourselves to the most commonly seen form. As the various models of the extended Tree were developed to deal with some of the more arcane Qabalistic speculations they are hardly suitable for inclusion in a "primer" such as this. However, armed with a thorough understanding of the structure and dynamics of the basic glyph, plus a good general knowledge of Qabalistic philosophy, even the more outlandish outcroppings of Qabalah become accessible, for they are all ultimately founded upon this one simple design.

It will be noticed that we have referred to the Tree as having but ten Sephiroth, and not the commonly seen eleven. This is because we are viewing the Tree in its original version before the concept of the "pseudo-Sephirah", Daath, was introduced.

One of the earliest of Qabalistic documents, the *Sepher Yetzirah*, or "Book of Formation", is quite specific about the number of Sephiroth to be assigned, for it says:

"Ten is the number of the ineffable Sephiroth, ten and not nine, ten and not eleven. Understand this Wisdom, and be wise in the perception".

(*Rittangelius edition 1642.* trans. Wm.Wynn Westcott.)

This message is reiterated throughout the first chapter of the book. However, Daath is now fully established in mainstream Qabalah as a legitimate, if somewhat enigmatic, Sephirah and in many ways it is possible to argue that this "invisible" sphere is now the one of greatest importance to us in the present century.

We shall deal with Daath throughout this work as a proper and accepted emanation, whilst taking care to recognise both its unique character and its relative modernity as a fully fledged Sephirah.

Even the most superficial of glances at the diagram of the Tree of Life will be sufficient to suggest that it contains a number of repeating patterns, the most obvious being that of the triangle.

Apart from the arrangements of Sephirothic "Triads" that can be seen grouped on the Tree, the other noticeable feature is that the design is based around three vertical columns, which contain the Sephiroth. These columns, or Pillars as they are more often termed, are of the greatest importance to the functioning of the Tree, and to our understanding of it.

The Pillars of Manifestation

Before discussing the pillars as such it might be wise to briefly explain the "handedness" of the Tree as it is usually drawn.

In most cases the glyph will be found with the positive or masculine column to the viewer's right, and the negative column to his left. This representation is that of the macrocosmic Tree.

The microcosmic Tree, as we would apply it to our own bodies, is the exact reverse, rather as though we have backed on to the diagram. The columns, and the Sephiroth they contain, would therefore read as, the masculine or positive pillar on our left, and the feminine or negative pillar on our right. The matter assumes its greatest importance when it comes to tracing the outline of the Tree on the body, as for example, during the Qabalistic Cross, which opens and closes the Lesser Banishing Ritual of the Pentagram.

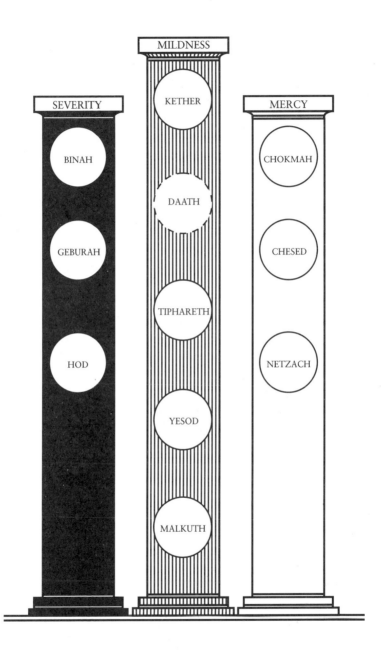

THE PILLARS

All that has existed, exists, or will exist, arises from the union of the masculine and feminine principles.

"All that which exists, all that which has been formed by the Ancient, whose Name is holy, can only exist through a male and female". (*Zohar*)

The combined potencies of the masculine and feminine in nature results in a new state, which is one of balance. The conditions of force and form which these potencies represent come to their final equilibrium in the product of their union.

As all created things derive from an interaction and combination of polarities it is natural that one of the first patterns to be discerned on the Holy Tree is the one that best demonstrates this eternal truth, the three "Pillars of Manifestation".

The three columns or pillars on the glyph represent the positive and negative potencies and the central state of equilibrium.

It is important that it is understood from the beginning that terms such as "positive" and "negative" are used to distinguish states or modalities of "being" or "doing", and do not carry the judgmental connotations that they might possess in everyday speech.

The usage of these terms in the context of this work is purely technical, somewhat after the manner of the definitions of electrical science, and have *no* other implications.

The positive or masculine pillar is termed, "The Pillar of Mercy", whilst the negative or feminine side is called, "The Pillar of Severity". The Middle Pillar is usually called just that, "The Middle Pillar", but is occasionally referred to as the "Pillar of Mildness" or "of Equilibrium".

The first objection that newcomers to the system of Qabalah raise is in regard to the titles of these pillars, and in particular that of the feminine potency. How can it be, they ask, that the column which represents all the attributes of the female principle is called the "Pillar of Severity" and the masculine column is called, (of all things!), the "Pillar of Mercy"?

Actually these attributions are entirely in keeping with the functions of each column and the nature of the principles that each expresses. It is not intended that we should spend overmuch time dealing with this matter now, as the accuracy of the titles will become much clearer as we progress down through the Sephiroth on the Tree and see there the different aspects of each principle in action.

But, briefly; the feminine column represents restriction and containment. It "captures" and "incorporates" the dynamic kinetic energies of the masculine potency, and in so doing condemns them to a period of "imprisonment" in the bonds of form.

This process is one which Qabalists call "severity", the imposition of discipline and structure upon unrestrained force.

These two conditions are absolutely essential to one another for form cannot exist other than as patterns of interlocked energy, and energy itself is valueless and ephemeral unless conditioned by the principles expressed by the negative pillar.

The following table, detailing the principle characteristics of each column, may provide a starting point for understanding their qualities and the manner in which they must therefore interact.

SEVERITY	MILDNESS	MERCY
Form		Force
Matter	Spirit	Energy
Negative	Balance	Positive
Passivity	Rest	Activity
Feminine	Androgynous	Masculine
Restraint	Equilibrium	Expansion
Static Force	Stability	Kinetic Force
Antithesis	Synthesis	Thesis
Receptive		Inceptive
Destructive		Constructive
Catabolism		Anabolism

This table should amply demonstrate that the outer columns represent not merely opposed but complementary principles. They are, as it were, two sides to the one coin.

This then is the first triplicity of the Tree, the pattern of which will be seen repeated again and again as we progress further into the teachings of the Qabalah.

The negative column or "Pillar of Severity", bears three Sephiroth; Binah, the third Supernal; Geburah, the fifth Sephirah; and Hod, the eighth. All these spheres are essentially feminine in function, although two of them, the fifth and the eighth, may superficially present themselves as male.

In order to understand why this should be it is necessary to remember that polarity is determined by function and not appearance. These are the receptive Sephiroth of the Tree, which accept the energetic impulse from their opposite numbers on the Pillar of Mercy and add to them the extra dimension of form.

Form in any tangible sense does not appear until Malkuth, the last emanation, although the concept is inherent in each. In Binah, at the head of the negative pillar, the concept of form is first developed as a necessary response to the dynamism of Chokmah. In the central Sephirah of the column, Geburah, stringent discipline is imposed on the energies emanating from its opposite, Chesed. While in the pillar's basal sphere the concept of form is further concreted and brought into the area of human cognition.

It must be remembered that all the spheres are in a sense bi-polar or bi-sexual. Each responds in a different manner according to the position of the sphere with which it is interacting. For example, Binah, the archetypal feminine Sephirah, is negative or female to Chokmah, the sphere that preceeds it in the descent of power, but is positive or masculine in its relationship to Chesed, which is the subsequent Sephirah in the order of emanation.

The potency of each sphere is variable according to its position relative to other Sephiroth, but nevertheless each retains a primary polarity.

The God-names of the Sephiroth of Severity give us an indication of how they might best be considered in the light of this bi-polarity. Each of the spheres on this column contain, as part of its name, the word "Elohim", which in Hebrew means God. This name is composed of two elements and, as a feminine noun with an attached masculine plural, encompasses both polarities. This is the God who says:

"Let *us* make man in *our* image, after *our* likeness", and therefore; "male and female created He them".   *(Gen 1:26/27)*

The name itself will be explored in the appropriate Sephirothic chapters, but its mention here should be sufficient to illustrate how important an understanding of the Qabalistic interpretation of gender is to our present study.

Another factor to be kept in mind is that each Sephirah contains the "seed" or "imprint" of the one that follows after it. Therefore, until we arrive at Malkuth, every Sephirah necessarily holds within itself the potency of the sphere which will eventually emanate from it, and which is always the opposite to its own presenting polarity.

The Pillar of Mercy, the positive and constructive column of the Tree, also bears three Sephiroth. These are; the second Supernal, Chokmah; the fourth Sephirah, Chesed; and the seventh, Netzach. The triplicity of Sephiroth which constitute this column are energetic and expansive in character, in contrast to the restriction of the opposite pillar.

Whereas the modality of the negative column is determined by the powerful brooding presence of Binah, here it is the explosive effervescence of Chokmah which imbues the triad. Each of the three spheres of this column expresses an aspect of the masculine creative drive. In Chokmah this is the primary impulse of Kether being sent outward on its journey to eventual manifestation, raw creative power, as yet untamed and undisciplined by interaction with the feminine current. In the central sphere of Chesed this power is more balanced and controlled, although still highly vigorous in its expression.

After the primary impulse has been subjected to the strictures of Geburah and the gentle mediating influence of Tiphareth it is shown-forth in Netzach in the typical qualities of Venus, its "mundane chakra" or planetary correspondence, as emotion and the drive to union.

In a sense, the Middle Pillar, or Pillar of Mildness, is as much a result of the interaction of the two opposed outer columns as it is is a direct conduit of the power of Kether. Here is found harmony and balance, the outer pillars brought to reconciliation and equilibrium, a place of rest and repose.

This pillar contains four Sephiroth and the "Invisible Sephirah" of Daath. At the head of the column is the "Primal Glory" of Kether, first of the emanations and the interface with the Unmanifest.

Below Kether lies the mysterious area of Daath, astride the great Abyss. In the very centre of the Tree, below Daath and above Yesod, is found Tiphareth, the heart of the glyph even as it represents the subtle heart of man. With Yesod we have the first concentration of the total energies of the Tree, for below, in Malkuth, there is no new factor or quality to be added.

The Middle Pillar is sometimes referred to as the "Pillar of Consciousness", as opposed to the two outer pillars of "function".

The middle pillar Sephiroth are then taken to represent different levels of consciousness. To borrow Dion Fortune's extremely useful classifications these are: Malkuth, "sensory consciousness"; Yesod, "astral psychism"; Tiphareth, "illuminated consciousness"; Daath, "conscious awareness or apprehension"; until in Kether is found "union with God", a level of consciousness inexplicable to those who have not so attained.

It is the way of the magician to journey (through initiation in its proper and full sense and not by the ersatz rites propagated by some occult orders) up the ladder of the Tree, following the paths and Sephiroth described by the image of the Serpent upon the glyph. (see illustration)

The way of the mystic however is very different, for he follows the "Path of the Arrow", ascending the planes of consciousness, represented by the Middle Pillar Sephiroth, from Malkuth to eventual union in Kether.

This path is, of course, considerably more direct then that of the circuitous travels and adventures of the magician. But it is one that does not lay open to all. Although the gate may indeed be strait, and narrow the way that leads unto it, it requires a combination of qualities rarely found in the West to successfully negotiate this path without falling prey to delusion or despair, the especial dangers that await the mystic.

The magician, needless to say, has his own problems, not the least being a constant and all too often unsuccessful guerrilla war with his own ego.

The Sephirothic Triads

Looking at the graphic representation of the Holy Tree it is clear that the Sephiroth fall into a series of triadic groups.

Each of these triads is composed of a positive sphere, a negative sphere, and a point of balance and reconciliation. In this way they resemble the pattern of the Pillars of Manifestation.

The first, and most obvious, triad is that of the Sephiroth above the Abyss. These three spheres are referred to as the "Supernals" and

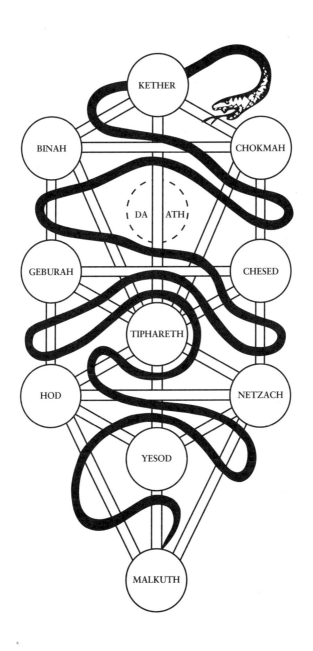

THE SERPENT ON THE TREE

therefore this grouping is known as the "Supernal Triad".

They are also termed, in Hebrew, *Olam-ha-Mevshekal*, which has the approximate meaning of the "Intellectual World".

Describing this particular triad as the "Intellectual World" is somewhat misleading however, for the intellect as such has no place above the Abyss. Another name, although less common, for the Supernal triad is "The Intelligible World", but again this does not convey the true essence of the triad.

The Sephiroth above the Abyss are the prototypes of the forces to be found below. In a sense all the subsequent Sephiroth are but particular, specialised, expressions of the principles contained in the Supernal Triad.

Kether is the point at which the Unmanifest first begins the process of manifestation and is the conduit for the *Mezla*, the creative energy which courses through the Tree. The second Sephirah, Chokmah, or "Wisdom", represents the first differentiation of Kether's homogeneous flux. The asexual impulse is transformed in Chokmah into positive, masculine force. In the following sphere of Binah, the creative impulse is again intercepted and is now rendered into a negative, feminine current.

So, above the Abyss is thereby established a stable triad which is to be the model for all others on the Tree.

All the necessary components are in place; positive and negative energies, represented by Chokmah and Binah respectively, and the balance point of Kether.

These three Supernal Sephiroth combine to make one creative unit, the "Three-in-One" or "The One Head which are Three Heads", to quote just two of Kether's many subsidiary titles.

The major difference between the Supernal Triad and the two other triadic arrangements below the Abyss, is that here the apex is upward. In the case of the two subsequent triads the apex of the triangle points down the Tree. Kether is not only the equilibrating sphere in the arrangement, it is also the fount of the Tree's sustaining energy.

As it is indeed the case that the focus of the Supernal Triad is upwards, unlike that of the two lower groupings, we must assume that here the emphasis is somewhat different. The lower triads focus their energies down through the Tree, the negative and positive forces combining in the third sphere to transmit their, now equilibrated, influence to the next level, which in the case of the final triad is the pendent sphere of Malkuth. Kether, although effectively the balancing sphere in the Supernal Triad,

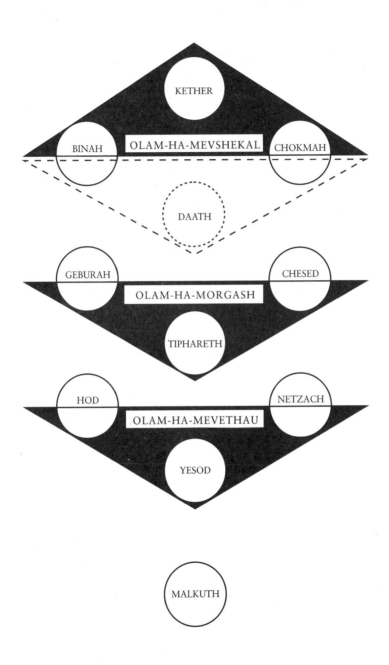

THE TRIADS

does not of course transmit the combined energies of Chokmah and Binah out to the Ain, but rather is the collector and receiver of energies *from* the Ain. In this way the Supernal triad is very different from those below the Abyss. Nevertheless, the principle of the creative trinity, which is to be found repeated throughout the glyph and even within the Ain, is first clearly demonstrated on the Tree by the Supernal Sephiroth.

It is also possible to discern another triad based above the Abyss; in which Daath represents the inverted apex and Chokmah and Binah the base line. Daath is said to be the product of the combined Supernal influence and in this light may be viewed as an alternative focus for the first triad, one that now directs the current down through the Tree. This secondary triad is, in a sense, a reflection of the Supernal Triad, but one that is perhaps more accessible to human consciousness. It is through the agency of Daath that access may be gained to the Supernal realm, as the "invisible" or "mystical" Sephirah functions after the manner of a bridge. As Kether is the interface between the manifesting Tree and the Ain, so Daath may be visualised as a similar interface between the very different conditions that obtain above and below the Abyss.

A fuller reflection of the first triad is found in the second. This grouping consists of Chesed, Geburah, and Tiphareth, and is called, *Olam-ha-Morgash*, the "Moral" or "Sensuous" world.

As is the case in all these triplicities we find a male and a female potency, initially discreet, combining in the third sphere. Chesed is the masculine vibration in this arrangement, with Geburah as its complementary opposite, coming to union in the sixth Sephirah, the "Mediating Intelligence" of Tiphareth.

This triad occupies a most important position on the glyph, for Tiphareth is not simply the focus of Chesed and Geburah it is in a very real sense, the focus of the whole Tree.

Tiphareth is poised equidistant between Kether and Malkuth, on the Middle Pillar, and is the central Sephirah of several possible sub-divisions of the Tree; such as the *"Sephiroth-ha-Benyin"* or "Spheres of Construction", and the "Ruach", or intellectual faculty.

It is literally the pivotal point of the Tree, both functionally and geographically. As the Middle Pillar is the equilibrating element in the vertical axis, so Tiphareth, whose name means "Beauty" or "Harmony", extends that function into the horizontal axis. A great cross is therefore formed at this point with the Tiphareth at its centre, emphasising the sixth Sephirah's function as the mediating Christ-centre of the Tree and as the sphere of the sacrificed gods.

Dion Fortune has termed the second triad the "Ethical Triangle", which in is many ways a more accurate title than the traditional "Moral World", and certainly more so than "The Sensuous World", favoured by Issac Myer. This triad is composed of the principles of love, justice, and reconciliation, qualities that would seem to amply justify Fortune's alternative appellation.

The final triad of the Tree is that of "Olam-ha-Mevethau", the "Material World". Strictly speaking this is not the material world at all, for that title rightly belongs to the pendent Sephirah of Malkuth. An alternative title given by Issac Myer, (*Qabbalah 1888*) is "The Natural World", which is a only slight improvement on the more usual rendering, but does at least suggest a degree less tangibility. For what is meant by "material" in this context is the supporting structure of the Astral realm which underpins, and to a certain extent precipitates, physical reality.

This is the penultimate stage of the process of manifestation. Out of this triad develops the realm of physical matter. Here is the "densest" possible pre-manifest expression of the creative impulse, preparing for its imminent impact in the world of form. And yet there is a sense in which those "forms" are already existent, for all the components are now at hand. We have seen that it is in Binah that the concept of form was first developed, and also that throughout the descent of power down the Tree that concept has been growing steadily more tangible. Now, in this last triad, the influence of Netzach and Hod (the positive and negative potencies of the triad) provides the "finishing touches" to the work begun in the third Supernal.

These two Sephiroth are described by the Qabalists as being "like unto the arms of God". The *Zohar* states that: "All the energies, forces and increase in the universe proceed through them".

As in the other triads the twin polarities are united in a third sphere, in this case Yesod, the "Foundation", and appropriately for the penultimate Sephirah, also called the "The Treasure House of Images".

Myer says of this triad:

"Together they (the three Sephiroth) represent the Deity as the universal power, creator and generator of all the existences"

(Qabbalah)

The Paths

There are a total of twenty-two "Paths" that link together the Sephiroth of the Holy Tree. Each of these paths may be referred to a letter of the Hebrew alphabet, and to a Tarot trump.

Care should be taken to distinguish between the "paths" proper, that is the interconnecting lines shown on the glyph, and the Sephiroth or Emanations, which are also, rather confusingly, called paths in the *Sepher Yetzirah*.

The paths can be said to represent subjective experience, as opposed to the objective "reality" of the Sephiroth, although they are a function of the interaction of the emanations and are therefore to be seen as part of the Tree proper.

The character of each path is determined to a large extent by the two Sephiroth which it links. They are, in a sense, both the equilibrium and synthesis of the interconnected spheres, and demonstrate thereby a new aspect of the divine powers.

It is by means of the paths, *i.e.* by experiencing the specific states of consciousness which are characteristic of them, that progress is made around the Tree.

It is not enough however merely to experience the qualities of the paths, each one must be mastered and thoroughly assimilated. There are a number of techniques available to achieve this end, varying from ritual magick to intense meditation. The individual student's assessment of both himself and his final goal must be used to determine which method is deemed most appropriate.

The Hebrew alphabet is in effect the magickal language and sacred tongue of the West, holding a somewhat similar position to that of Sanskrit in the East, for it is written that:...

"He hath formed, weighed, and composed with these twenty-two letters every soul, and the soul of everything which shall hereafter be" *(Sepher Yetzirah. Chap.2:2)*

Each of the twenty-two letters has a numerical as well as a phonetic value. We will come to see the importance of this fact when we explore the mysteries of the "Literal Qabalah", and in particular that arcane science of Qabalistic numerology termed "Gematria". As well as the value assigned to each letter by virtue of its alphabetic position, it holds another number derived from the Hebrew spelling of its name. (see list. Appendix 2)

Furthermore, each letter carries a host of traditional meanings which are partly derived from their pictographic designs, their number value, and their association with the Tarot Trumps.

Even by this brief account of the alphabetic correspondences it can be seen that there is a wealth of occult lore hidden in these twenty-two letters, for as the *Sepher Yetzirah* says:....

> "The twenty-two sounds and letters are the Foundation of all things".

The major arcana of the Tarot deck are an important source of Qabalistic knowledge, indeed it is difficult to arrive at a full understanding of the nature of the paths without reference to the "Book of Thoth", to give it its alternative name.

Each of the twenty-two Tarot trumps is a pictorial representation of one of the paths. In the esoteric decks the symbolism, colours, and general composition of the cards are not only useful as an aid to intellectual appreciation of the paths, but are also a means of gaining access to them by meditative techniques. In this way the trumps function both as a kind of "doorway" and as a map of the terrain we wish to explore. Tarot arcana are also used in a temple setting, often placed upon the central altar, to symbolise the forces with which the ritualist is working.

Without a doubt the most common use of the Tarot pack is for the purpose of divination. In order for the exercise to be worthwhile it is necessary that the diviner understands, both intellectually and intuitively, not only the meanings of the individual cards but their relationship to Qabalistic philosophy as it is presented by the Holy Tree. Likewise, constant study and use of the pack can only enhance our understanding of the dynamics of the Tree.

The Abyss and the Veils

On some versions of the Tree will be discovered a number of fine, or dotted lines, drawn horizontally across the glyph. These mark the

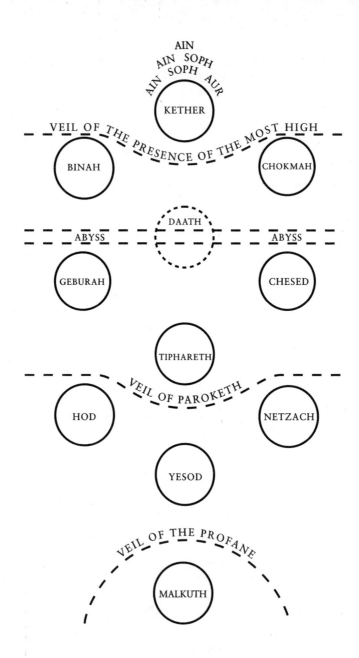

THE VEILS

position of the Veils, and of the Abyss. On most modern versions of the diagram it is only the Abyss, below the Supernal Triad, that is shown, and occasionally not even that. The great gulf of the Abyss is the boundary between the Supernal world of Atziluth and Briah, and the worlds of Yetzirah and Assiah below. This is the barrier which divides the Macroprosopos from the Microprosopos, God from God's creation, or to be more accurate, Man from his own God-head, for is it not written:....

"I have said, Ye are gods; and all of you are children of the most High", *(Psalm 82:6)*

The Abyss bisects the whole Tree, covering all three pillars, and is straddled by the "Mystical Sephirah" of Daath, which stands as a bridge between the upper and lower Sephiroth.

Conditions above the Abyss are radically different to those existing below and this gulf marks the border between what can be understood by mentality and that which is incapable of comprehension or expression by the intellect.

In some earlier Qabalistic writings the Abyss is considered as a sort of rubbish dump for the flawed creations of the Deity, for although He may create only perfection, being Himself perfect, man, His greatest and most complex product, has the capacity to make of himself what he will, and therefore provides more than occasional fodder for the dog-faced demons of the great pit.

In these early works the Abyss is called *Masak Mavdil* or the "place of rejection", and is presided over by the angel Mesukiel whose name means the "Veiler of God".

Some Qabalists suggest that the Abyss represents the barrier referred to in the third chapter of Genesis, between the Garden of Eden (symbolised by the Supernal Triad), and the rest of creation; guarded by the:....

"flaming sword which turned every way" and Cherubims which together "keep the way of the tree of life". *(Gen.3:24)*

However, the Christian concept of the Prime Deviation or "Fall" maybe taken on a number of levels, for as there is an Abyss in the model of the macrocosmic Tree, so there is an Abyss in the microcosmic Tree of man. This is the chasm that has arisen between the highest element of man's nature, comprising those god-like attributes which in Hebrew are

17

called *Neshemah*, and the lower faculties of the *Ruach* and *Nephesh*, the intellect and "animal soul" respectively.

It is the central work, and perhaps the only justification, of magick to reunite these dissociated faculties and in so doing become again the perfect eidolon of the God whose creation we surely are.

As well as being the "cosmic rubbish dump" of early Qabalism into which bottomless pit is cast the failed and the impure, the detritus of previous creative enterprises and rejected archetypes, the Abyss is said to have a second function, one which equates it with another Christian concept, that of Limbo. It is here that the unbaptised or otherwise unworthy souls await the "ending of days" when, to mix our mythologies, they too will see their hearts balanced against the feather of truth.

The Veils on the Tree can for the most part be considered lower analogues of the great Abyss as they serve much the same function of "borders" between different modes of existence and states of consciousness. Whereas the Abyss is an actual part of the Tree proper, the veils described here are perhaps more subjective in their presence and effect, and operate in a manner that is more consistent with their description. That is to say they obscure but do not necessarily prohibit access to those other realms. Nor are they possessed of the powerful sanctions which the Abyss may bring to bear on the unwary or the ill-prepared traveller. Whilst any effort to effect a major change in consciousness, be it temporary or permanent, is bound to entail some risk, the penalties for failure at the level of the Abyss are far in excess of those found in the lower veils.

The Abyss is the line of demarcation between the combined Atziluthic and Briatic worlds and the worlds below. There are two other veils, rarely mentioned in modern Qabalistic literature, which also serve as borders between worlds. The first is sometimes termed "The Veil of the Presence of the Most High", and lies above the spheres of Chokmah and Binah, but below Kether; between the world of Atziluth and that of Briah, the Archetypal world and the world of Creation.

Very little can be said about this veil as it is accessible only to those preparing to undergo the ultimate spiritual experience of "Union with God". This is the veil that protects the impure from glimpsing the face of The Most High, and protects Him also from the presence of the unperfected.

The second of the veils serving as barriers between worlds is that known as the "Veil of the Profane", which is positioned across the lowest three paths of the Tree, separating Malkuth from the lower triad. In this case the barrier is between the worlds of Yetzirah and Assiah, which are respectively the worlds of Formation and Action. Plainly there is a considerable difference in condition between these two states, as might be surmised by the veil's title.

The "profane" are those who are rooted in earth and whose only experience of God's creation is that of the "sphere of the elements" in Malkuth, and who have yet to develop even a vague awareness of the astral realm that inter-penetrates the material plane.

Paroketh, (which actually translates as "veil", making any further description redundant) is far more frequently encountered in the literature and shown on the glyph than is the Veil of the Profane. It lies below the central Sephirah of Tiphareth, the focus of the second triad, and above Netzach and Hod, the positive and negative poles of the third.

It will be noticed that all the veils protect the third point of each triad, where the typical energies that each expresses are concentrated and brought to equilibrium. This is true even in the case of the Veil of the Profane which is drawn under the primal glory of Kether, although here it is the Abyss which provides the ultimate protection of the mysteries of the Supernals and which encompasses Daath, the alternative focus of the first triad.

In this manner every major leap in consciousness, signified on the Tree by the triads, is achieved only after one of these obscuring veils is penetrated.

Paroketh's exact position on the Tree is subject to some dispute. Here we have used the traditional Golden Dawn arrangement of the Tree and placed it below Tiphareth. However, some authorities, notably Dion Fortune and Gareth Knight, have placed it above Tiphareth, forming the border between the sixth Sephirah and the spheres of Chesed and Geburah. The justification for this seems to be the belief that Tiphareth is the highest sphere achievable by strictly human consciousness, and therefore that Paroketh represents the demarcation line between two radically different states. There is some biblical evidence to support this view, for three of the four evangelists claim that at the moment the Rabbi Jesus "gave up the ghost";

"the sun was darkened, and the veil of the temple (Paroketh) was rent in the midst"   *(Luke 23:45)*

As the crucified Christ is assumed to be already active in the sphere of Tiphareth it is taken that the veil was rent as a result of his ascending the Middle Pillar on route to union with his father in the upper reaches of the sphere of Kether, and that therefore the veil must lie beyond the sixth Sephirah, and not below.

However Paroketh, "The Veil of the Temple", is assigned it does mark an important frontier on the Tree. Once this veil is penetrated the aspirant becomes an adept in the proper meaning of the word. It marks the limit of the outer order of the Golden Dawn, and the beginning of the adept's progress through the grades of the Rose Cross. Having attained to Tiphareth he now has the Knowledge and Conversation of his Holy Guardian Angel to assist him in his work upon the Tree.

Until the second great milestone of magickal progress, the adventure of the Abyss, the adept may rely on the relationship forged in Tiphareth with his HGA for guidance and succour.

That the Veil of Paroketh is a true analogue of the great Abyss can be seen by the changing relationship with the adept's Angel, which is gained after the opening of the Veil of the Temple and lost during the crossing of the Abyss, these two experiences being the most critical of the magickal progression.

Some writers suggest that below Tiphareth, and parallel with the "Veil of the Profane", lies yet another veil, called "Qesheth", which is symbolised by the colours of the rainbow and is the "bow of promise" set as a sign in the sky; the colours resulting from the refraction of Kether's ineffable light through the mediating sphere of Tiphareth. Strictly speaking Qesheth is not a veil at all but an image relating to the Bible flood story. It takes its name from the three paths ascending from Malkuth which it bisects. The designated Hebrew letters of these paths, *"Tau"*, *"Shin"*, and *"Qoph"*, spell *QShTh*, Qesheth, which means "Rainbow".

2

The Four Worlds

OLAHM Ha-ATZILUTH   OLAHM Ha-BRIAH

OLAHM Ha-YETZIRAH   OLAHM Ha-ASSIAH

Qabalists conceive of four "worlds", which represent the four stages of manifestation.

These they call; Atziluth, or the Archetypal World; Briah, or world of Creation; Yetzirah, the world of Formation; and, finally, the plane of materiality, Assiah.

The four worlds illustrate the sequential development of the primary creative impulse. This sequence might be characterised thus: first there is Intention; then there is Conceptualisation; followed by Composition; finally culminating in Presentation.

Or, to put it another way; in the beginning is the will to do "something", secondly comes the creative visualisation of what that "something" should be. Thirdly the "something" is manufactured,and finally the newly-made "something" is shown forth to the world at large. All productive processes are analogous to the model presented by the four worlds, be they industrial, social, personal, or indeed, divine.

Each world signifies a separate development in the process of the showing-forth of God. And in each He can be seen to perform His works in a different manner. It is however only in the first world of Atziluth that he works directly; in the remaining three He works through the medium of His appointed agents. Therefore it is the Atziluthic world that must best express the nature of God, for here He could be said to be in His own "element".

Although the world of Atziluth is the natural realm of the manifesting God, it would be a mistake to consider it to be more "holy" or more "important" than the other three worlds.

He is necessarily present in all His worlds and at all times, the last even as the first. Throughout this work we shall be returning to the theme that all of God's creations are of equal holiness as all ultimately have their roots in His will. The degrees of "concretion" which are evinced in the Sephiroth and illustrated by the four worlds, are not to be seen as degrees of relative holiness, but as denser, more tangible aspects of a continually creating omnipresent Deity. The four worlds merely represent developmental stages of the creative process at work. Although the origination of the creative impulse is to be found in Atziluth it must be "processed" through Briah and Yetzirah before it may come to its fruition and fulfilment in Assiah.

There are a number of Biblical passages which are taken by Qabalists to refer to the doctrine of the four worlds. One such occurs in The Book of the Prophet Isaiah, where God says;

"Even every one that is called by my name: for I have created him for my glory, I have formed him; yea, I have made him".

(*Isaiah* 43:7)

This verse describes the actions of the Deity in each of the worlds. At first He says that he has "called" by His name. As the names of God are the highest expression of His power this may be taken to refer to Atziluth. Next He says that He has "created him", which immediately refers us to Briah, the World of Creation. Then He says "I have formed him", an action which corresponds with the mode of Yetzirah, which is the World of Formation. And finally, He tells us that He has "made him", which brings us into the world of Assiah. Another example occurs at the very beginning of the Old Testament, in Genesis 1 verses 3-5, where the image of "light" is used five times in succession. In this instance Qabalists take the first two references to mean just one form of light, making a total of four separate stages of production. The expressions "Let there be light: and there was light" refers to Atziluth; "And God saw the light, that it was good" to Briah; "and God divided the light from the darkness" to Yetzirah; and finally, "And God called the light Day, and the darkness he called Night" to the physical realm of Assiah.

This process recalls the invocational hierarchy of "Name of God", Archangel, Angel, and Element or Planet, which bears heavily on the teachings regarding the four worlds.

As well as what has become a common method of applying the doctrine of the four worlds to the Holy Tree, by referring the Sephiroth to each world either singularly or in groups, it is also possible to view the worlds as different levels of operation of the Tree as a whole. That is to say each version of the Tree may be conceived as having four arcs of activity ranging from the most sublime (Atziluth) to the most mundane (Assiah). In its highest level of manifestation the Tree, and each of its constituent Sephiroth, is operative in the realm of archetypes and in its lowest in the world of physical existence. There is therefore an Atziluthic form of Malkuth even as there is an Assiatic form of Kether and it is to these levels that the hierarchy of God-name, Archangel, Angel and Element applies.

This four-fold classification of the Qabalah may be considered as reflection of the Divine Name, IHVH, Yahweh, or "Tetragrammaton", usually translated as LORD or God in the English versions of the Bible. This name, which will be further considered under the heading of Chokmah, whose God-name it is, contains a formula of progressive manifestation which is applicable throughout the Tree.

Each of the four letters of the Tetragrammaton in Hebrew represents a degree of "unfolding", from initial creative impulse to final manifestation. The first letter, *Yod*, is the creative impulse itself, and may be related to the first world of Atziluth. The second letter *Heh*, is both the reception and conception of that impulse and corresponds with the Creative World of Briah. The third letter in this "mighty name" is Vau and refers to the next development of the creative principle, the formative world of Yetzirah. In the final letter, which is a repeat of the second and termed *Heh (final)*, we enter the plane of actual manifestation which Qabalists call Assiah.

Through the common factor of this four-fold division, the worlds may be related to a great number of correspondences. These might well include; the four elements, the animals which appear at the Merkabah or Chariot Throne in Ezekiel's vision, the cardinal directions, the Tarot suits and court cards, the four heads of the river which flowed out of Eden, and the triplicities, which are formed by dividing the Zodiacal signs into groups of four.

We now have some idea of how the four worlds function together as a developmental process, and we have seen that they represent stages or levels of the unfolding of the Most High.

Now we will turn our attention to each world individually, examine them in more depth, and relate them to the doctrine of Qabalah as it is expressed by the glyph of the Tree of Life with particular reference to the way in which the Sephiroth are commonly allocated.

Atziluth

The world of Atziluth (from the Hebrew root, meaning "Proximity") is, a World of Archetypes. It is also known as the "World of Emanations", for this is the world in which the Sephiroth first come into existence. Another version of this title is *Olahm Ha-Sephiroth*, the "World of the Sephiroth". Issac Myer says of Atziluth,

> "This is the most exalted of all the Conditions (ie the Four Worlds) and is considered as containing only the Holy Upper Ten Sephiroth; the highest round of the ladder of Intermediaries (again, the Four Worlds), which are nevertheless only an Unit, and are between Ain Soph, the Primal Cause of All, and the inferior emanations which develop the existences".

> (Issac Myer, *Qabbalah 1888*).

Atziluth is the level of existence closest to that state of unmanifestation which Qabalists term the Ain. It is close both in terms of its position, as the first emanation from the Void, and in terms of its own condition, which closely approximates but does not equal that of the Ain. Atziluth may also be termed the "World of Origination", for it is on this level that the Will of the Deity first expresses itself, and it is here also that He acts without intermediaries.

In the world of Atziluth there is but one Sephirah, Kether, and in that Sephirah may be found a complete Tree. This Tree represents the highest octave of the emanations - or the "Holy Upper Ten Sephiroth" - the sphere of "Kether of Kether" being the point of contact with the Ain.

Throughout the Qabalistic texts the student is constantly reminded that there is a special and particular relationship existing between Kether and Malkuth, for it is said that, "Kether is in Malkuth, and Malkuth is in Kether, but after another fashion". One of the many parallels between the first and last Sephiroth is found in the fact that each of these spheres is the sole tenant of its world, in the case of Malkuth this is the world of Assiah. In Malkuth too is contained a complete Tree, and therefore, as with Kether in Atziluth, the only Tree of its level.

Each of the Sephiroth contains a model of the Holy Tree, the number of Trees in a given world depending on the total of Sephirothic tenants. The Kether of any Sephirothic Tree is emanated by the

Malkuth of the Tree contained in the preceding Sephirah. Therefore that Malkuth stands in relationship to the Kether which develops from it as the local equivalent of the Ain.

Throughout the Tree, on all its levels, we will find relationships which are analogous to those first expressed in the Atziluthic world.

As Atziluth is the level at which God is active in a direct manner it is therefore the sphere in which are found the ten forms of the Divine Name. Each of the Sephiroth has attached to it one of these names, which represent the highest, most transcendent quality of each sphere.

Briah

This level of existence is a continuation of the world of Atziluth, but now is a stage further removed from the primal source of the Ain.

The Briatic World is called the "World of Creation", or "Khorsia the Throne", which is also a title of Binah, the third Supernal.

It is in this condition that the process of creation, as it might be understood from below the Abyss, begins. However, at this high level the act of creation involves a purely spiritual vibration for there is no material element in the process. All is achieved in terms of force and principle, the ideal "forms" are established, the patterns evolved, the "designings" are completed, but nothing tangible has yet been produced, for materiality must wait on the emergence of the fourth world.

Contained within the world of Briah are two Supernal Sephiroth, and therefore two complete Trees. The two Briatic spheres are Chokmah and Binah, which represent the highest level of the masculine and feminine principles respectively. Without the development of these potencies no further act of creation would be possible, for all must now proceed from their union.

Briah is the abode of pure spirit and is the realm of the Archangelic forces, the first of the ministering agents of God. This is the sphere of the "Great Presence Angel of the Covenant", Metatron, the sum of all the angels of the Tree, whom we have already met as the putative first teacher of Qabalistic lore.

Yetzirah

The world of Yetzirah is the World of Formation, as it is here that the constructive phase of the process of creation is undertaken. This level contains the greatest concentration of Sephiroth in the four worlds.

All the spheres below the Abyss, with the exception of Malkuth, are encompassed by Yetzirah. As this world contains six Sephiroth, so it must also contain six Sephirothic Trees.

These six Sephiroth; Chesed, Geburah, Tiphareth, Netzach, Hod, and Yesod, are termed the *Sephiroth ha-Benyin*, or "Sephiroth of Construction". They represent six discreet stages of development in the work preparatory to manifestation. The formative spheres have been compared to the six days of creation described in Genesis; the pendant sphere of Malkuth being considered as the Sabbath, a day of rest and passivity after the labours of construction have ceased.

The world of Yetzirah is a complex one in comparison with those which proceed it. Here the simple ideal designs of Briah are manipulated and modified, each of the Yetziratic Sephiroth contributing a little of their unique essence. Rather than being mere eidolons or images of the perfected "forms" of the second world, the product of Yetzirah is rich in its diversity and pregnant with the hope of imminent manifestation.

Yetzirah is the home of the angelic beings who are the constructive workers of the Lord, labouring to bring into actuality the potentials of the Briatic world.

The Angels work under the guidance of the Archangelic beings of each Sephirah, the relationship being akin to that between a labourer and his foreman.

Assiah

The world of Assiah, the last of the four levels, is the place of materialisation. It is here that the creative forces loosed in Atziluth come to fruition, for this is the world of actions.

In Assiah we encounter the phenomena of matter for the first time. The kinetic energy of Yetzirah is now bound in the solidity of the manifest world.

We have already seen that the sphere of Malkuth is the single Sephirothic inhabitant of Assiah, but below Malkuth in Assiah is postulated another world, pendent to and dependent upon the tenth Sephirah, outside of the original creative scheme but responsive to it.

This world Qabalists call *Olahm Ha-Qliphoth*, the realm of the "shells", the demons of the Qabalah. The denizens of this world necessarily view Malkuth as though it were Kether for it is from the tenth Sephirah that the demonic realm is emanated.

The inferior pendent tree is a distorted reflection of the Holy Tree itself, having three "supernal" emanations - *Tohu* ("the formless"); *Bohu* ("the void") and *Chashek* ("the Darkness") representing the negative principles of the Supernal Sephiroth proper.

Below the upper triad are seven spheres which form seven different forms of hell.

In the world of Atziluth the Deity performs His work unassisted; in Briah He creates through the medium of His Archangels; while in Yetzirah it is by the unceasing labour of His Choirs of Angels that His work proceeds. In Assiah it is said that He works through the agency of the "Mundane Chakras" of each Sephirah. Most of these Chakras are planetary bodies within our own solar system, and are accepted by occultists as being centres for the expression and dissemination of specific forces. They are viewed as having the same relationship to the "body" of interstellar space, as the chakras or subtle power centres with which most people are acquainted have to the human body.

3

The Sephiroth

CORRESPONDENCES AND ATTRIBUTIONS

Each Sephirah of the Tree of Life has applied to it a considerable number of attributions and correspondences. Some of these constitute part of the original body of knowledge we call Qabalah, while others are of more recent origin.

One of the major benefits that accrue to those who are prepared to make a study of the Tree is that it provides an amazingly flexible "filing system", which they may then apply in any area of interest. Many of the later attributions to the Sephiroth and Paths are the result of the Tree being used in this manner. The individual spheres may act as "pigeon-holes" in which to place any experience, concept, or phenomena likely to be encountered in this, or indeed any other, world. Likewise, the structure of the Tree, and the relative positions of the Sephiroth, can be used as a schematic diagram to assist the student in establishing relationships between items seemingly unconnected.

To the student of myth it is obviously a great boon to have a recognised system of classification in which it is possible to relate the pantheons and mythologies of very different cultures one to another.

For practical magicians it is imperative that they have a reliable method of assessing and interpreting the phenomena encountered in their work, as well as having available a scheme by which they may judge their own progress.

For astrologers too the Tree offers a method by which they can relate the principles expressed by the planetary forces to a vast selection of other correspondences.

For students of the Judeo-Christian tradition, a knowledge of the correspondences of the Tree of Life is indispensable if they are to extract the maximum benefit from scriptural teachings.

In fact the list of uses, and therefore of categories of attribution, is endless.

In this chapter we will discuss and, as far as is possible, explain, the most common correspondences, their usage, what they mean, and their history. It is by no means a definitive list, as such a thing is neither possible or desirable, given that each person's approach and needs regarding this ancient glyph will be different, but it will at least cover those categories which are touched on in the following chapters.

The Titles

These are part of the original Qabalah, their origins lost in the mists of time. Each title, be it in the original Hebrew or in their English translations, can be said to express the basic idea of the Sephirah to which it is applied. At times it will be found that there are several alternative titles which may be used. These are different from what might be termed "subsidiary" or "secondary" titles which expand, often in paradoxical or poetic language, particular aspects of a sphere's nature. The alternative titles are those, such as *Pachad* (Fear) for Geburah, or *Gedulah* (Glory or Magnificence) for Chesed, which are in common use in place of the more orthodox versions. However, very often these alternative titles may be found to have, as it were, crossed over and become through usage accepted as subsidiary titles themselves.

The Yetziratic Text

These quotations, often obscure and somewhat gnomic, are to be found at the head of every chapter for which such a text is available. They are taken from an appendix to the *Sepher Yetzirah*, and may have been the contribution of the seventeenth century scholar-convert Rittangelius, for no earlier Hebrew versions of the verses are known. Although not part of the original work these commentaries on the Sephiroth and paths are occasionally of great value in expanding our understanding of the Tree, and are therefore frequently quoted in occult literature.

The *Sepher Yetzirah* proper is possibly the oldest extant treatise on the Qabalah. It discusses in detail the "three Sepharim of Numbers, Letters and Sounds", and lays out the whole schema of creation in a matter of thirty odd pages in its English translation. The particular translation used throughout this work, and quoted verbatim, is that of William Wynn Westcott M.B. one of the original founders of the Golden Dawn who died in 1925. This version of the sepher was first published in 1887, and is based on the text of Joannes Stephanus Rittangelius, published in Hebrew and Latin at Amsterdam in 1642.

Although Wynn Westcott's translation has been criticised as being somewhat unscholarly we have decided on its inclusion because it is the most common version and therefore the one most likely to be encountered by the average student.

It should be noted that the *Sepher Yetzirah* describes both the ten Sephiroth and their inter-connecting channels as "paths", making no distinction between them; hence there are thirty-two verses in the supplementary text, one for each of the Sephiroth and the paths proper.

The Names of God

The God names applied to the Sephiroth are part of the original body of Qabalistic knowledge.

These divine names cannot be held to be descriptive of the God Himself, for to adequately describe even a fraction of Him is patently impossible. They should rather be seen as references to His various modalities, each one being descriptive of a particular manner of His manifestation. The names are necessitated by the inability of the human mind to comprehend the totality of God, for without resorting to such devices we could not hope to further our understanding of His nature.

> "The Names of the Deity are only abstract symbols and ideas necessary to man's mind in our matter-world so as to grasp in his thought that a Deity exists. They do not describe God's essence or content".   (Issac Myer, *Qabbalah*)

The use of such names should not be thought to imply that God is anything other than One, nor is He in any sense diminished by their use for He may have many names and yet still be One. In fact the Unity and Oneness of God is a fundamental Qabalistic teaching, for this is a cosmology which is predicated on the doctrine of His sequential emanation, in which diversity springs from and returns to the one source. The Sephiroth, and therefore the God-names applied to them, do not represent divisions of God, but suggest the order of His unfolding manifestation, which occurs without diminution of His substance.

Each Sephirah has a distinct god-name assigned to it, which may act as an aid to greater understanding of the sphere. Many of these names are to be found in the Pentateuch, but unfortunately the richness and variety of them has been largely lost in translation from their original tongue.

Knowledge of the name under which the God was deemed to be operating in any given instance constitutes a major key to the understanding of the Old Testament. In the English Revised Standard Edition of the Bible, the reference is usually simply to "God" or to the "Lord".

With the exception of a handful of cases where the Deity is spoken of in terms that most readers would consider to be mere poetic licence, but which are actually often the remnants or corruptions of Hebrew names, much of the original teaching has been excised. In spite of this, the importance of God's name to the Old Testament Jews is apparent in a number of places, as for example in Exodus, where God gives Moses the name, AHIH, (pronounced Ee-He-Yea) "I AM", which is a God-name of Kether, the first Sephirah of the Holy Tree.

The Mundane Chakra

This rather confusing term refers to the physical correspondence traditionally attributed to each Sephirah. For the most part these "chakras" are celestial bodies within our solar system, but there are three exceptions to this rule; four if you count Daath.

To Kether is assigned the principle of the Primum Mobile or "first swirlings", the initial movement of the developing universe; to Chokmah, the entire wheel of the Zodiac; while to Malkuth, the final Sephirah of the Tree, is assigned the "sphere of the elements".

In the case of the pseudo-Sephirah, Daath, the mundane chakra is actually not of this solar system, although in galactic terms it is quite a near neighbour, being the "Dog Star", Sirius.

To each of the remaining Sephiroth is assigned one of the seven traditional planets; the correspondences having been established before the discovery of the extra-Saturnian bodies.

There have been many attempts to incorporate the outer planets into the scheme of the Tree; most notably by Kenneth Grant who assigns Pluto to Kether, Neptune to Chokmah, and Uranus to Daath whilst keeping the traditional attribution of Saturn to Binah.

Throughout the present work it is the traditional correspondences which are applied but the serious student could do worse than to devote some time to meditating on these and other alternatives. There is nothing immutable about the attributions of the various elements of the glyph and the individual must at all times be guided by his or her own experience and understanding.

These, mainly astrological, correspondences are of great help in understanding the nature of the Sephiroth and their manner of interaction, as each chakra can be said to represent, or at least to approximate, the typical energies expressed by the emanation to which they are assigned.

Particular emphasis has been placed on discussing the mundane chakra of each sphere, not simply because they are important in themselves, which they undoubtedly are, but also because experience has shown that they represent a useful means of approaching the essence of a Sephirah, via a system that is often more familiar to the student.

It is worth remarking that although astrologers use the term "planets" to describe all celestial bodies, including the Sun and Moon, they do so, not in ignorance, but in the original sense of the word, which is derived from the Greek and means "wanderer".

The Gods and Goddesses

One of the most useful sets of correspondences which may be applied to the Tree is the category of gods and goddesses.

Each Sephirah, and indeed each of the twenty-two interconnecting paths, displays a unique set of characteristics which have developed in response to their position in the order of emanation, and to their relationship with neighbouring spheres.

The deities of many, if not all, of the worlds religions can be easily related to one or more of these paths, providing a useful "database" for cross reference. The attributions are based on corresponding characteristics; for instance in the dynamic, martial Sephirah of Geburah one might place the great warrior gods such as Ares or Mars, whilst to the Lunar sphere of Yesod might be assigned Selene and Diana.

It can readily be seen that by this system the deities of quite different cultures can be related to each other by virtue of their shared Sephirothic correspondence. Of course one reason why the application of god-forms to the Tree is so successful is that the world's mythologies and their divine pantheons are as much a response to the great philosophical and metaphysical questions that beset man as the system of Qabalah itself.

As with the astrological correspondences, the gods and goddesses on the Tree will be discussed in some detail. Again, the reason for this is that many people find that they can better understand the nature of a Sephirah if it is explained in the more accessible terms of a colourful mythology.

It may be found that a number of the gods are assigned jointly to two or more spheres. This does not mean that there is some error in their attributions for many of these deities have undergone considerable metamorphosis in their long careers, in some cases even changing their original character into something close to its opposite. Others are complex forms that do not lend themselves to a single classification. This is perfectly in order, for the gods are assigned to each Sephirah by virtue of particular aspects of their function or history. For example Tahuti, or Thoth, may be placed in both Yesod, as a god of the Moon, and in Hod, as the Egyptian Mercury figure. In all cases it will be made clear which aspect of a given god-form is the qualifying criterion for inclusion.

Archangels

The Archangels represent the organising function of the Sephiroth. It is through them that the typical forces of each Sephirah are directed throughout the Tree. These beings exist only in the world of Briah, the Creative Realm.

It is solely in the world of Atziluth, the Archetypal Realm, that the Deity chooses to perform His work directly. In the three succeeding worlds He works through His appointed agents, the Archangels, the Angels, and in a certain sense, the Mundane Chakras.

The world of Briah is a realm of "pure spirit" and is closer in its nature to the Atziluthic world than it is to the Yetziratic; proceeding from the first world as if a continuation of its essence rather than as an entirely new development.

This is the sphere of the "Great Angel" Metatron, the first created being of God, who has responsibility for all the angelic orders of the Tree, for the Deity "has given him dominion over all His hosts". Of Metatron it is said that he alone constitutes the entire angelic world, and is therefore to be considered the sum of all the angelic forces. He, and only he, is the *direct* agent of the will of God.

Although Metatron is the principal Angel of Qabalistic tradition, and he within whom is subsumed the totality of angelic forces, there are other Archangels which correspond to the individual Sephiroth.

This does not undermine Metatron's primacy as each of these entities may be seen as functional aspects of the "Great Angel".

Some of the Angels assigned to the emanations may be familiar to the student, others less so. The Christians, by and large, admit to few such beings. With the obvious exceptions of Gabriel, Angel of the Annunciation and the Archangel Michael, the Holy Bible is curiously reticent about naming its angels. This is despite the fact that there are nearly three-hundred separate references to angelic beings to be found in the combined Old and New Testaments! In most cases the angel referred to is simply described as an "Angel of the Lord" or an "Angel of God", although we can often deduce which particular being is in operation from their descriptions, behaviour, or the context in which they appear. Many of these references to angelic beings are in fact allusions to Metatron himself, or to the Shekinah, a feminine form of the Holy Spirit, which we will be discussing in the chapters devoted to Binah and Malkuth.

The names of the various Archangels feature quite heavily in magickal operations. It is usual in ritual work to "work from the top down", first placing oneself under the protection of the God by calling upon Him in the name that is deemed most appropriate for the work in hand, and then progressing on through the Archangel of the sphere, down through the order of Angels, and so on, to the chosen level of operation. A good example of this hierarchical approach is found in the lesser banishing ritual of the pentagram, where the names of God are given to the four cardinal points, followed by invocation of the Archangels of those same directions.

It is the angels Raphael, Michael, Gabriel, and Uriel, who are most commonly invoked in ordinary ritual work, as these have presidency over the cardinal points and, most importantly, the four elements.

It is advisable for the student to invest a good deal of time in building up appropriate visual forms for these beings, concentrating particularly on their colours and weapons.

A basic description of the Archangelic forms is given in the appendix dealing with the Lesser Banishing Rituals.

The Orders of Angels

We have left the creative world of Briah, home of the Archangels, and are now entering the realm of Yetzirah, the world of Formation, in which are found the Orders or Choirs of Angels.

Angels operate under the presidency of the Archangels, as though the former were the private soldiers, and the latter the upper echelons of commanding officers.

There are many forms of angel; the term is often indiscriminately applied to virtually all forms of disincarnate being, but the ones that are of interest to us here are those that are deemed to be the constructive powers of the Sephiroth.

The Orders or Choirs of Angels are those who actually carry out the work commanded by the Supreme Deity, the orders for which are transmitted to the Archangels, who then organise the labour on the shop floor, as it were. However, analogies such as this, though useful, are not perfect models of the relationship between the angelic and archangelic forces, for between the two groups there is (literally) a world of difference. That difference is not only one of function but of kind, for they were created separately and inhabit separate worlds. Qabalistic teaching has it that the first chapter of Genesis may be read as a description of the creation of both orders of beings. For it is written that on the fifth day God created the fowl of the air and the fish that swim in the sea.

The fowl are taken by some Qabalists to refer to the Archangels in the world of Briah, whilst the creatures of the sea are considered to represent the orders of Angels of the formative world of Yetzirah. Whether such an interpretation is valid or not need not concern us overmuch here, what is important, and what this doctrine emphasises, is that these beings were indeed created separately, and that they were destined to perform different services for the Creator, and to inhabit different realms.

All angelic beings are lacking both in physical functions and in individual will. They are ultimately specialised, carrying out the will of the Most High, if not mindlessly then certainly, amongst the lesser angels, automatically.

Unlike man, angelic beings are not true microcosms of the Holy Tree. They are fully developed in their limited specialised function; no further evolutionary progress is possible, for they were created without potential, the willing slaves of the Most High.

An angel is strictly limited to his one sphere of operation and is incapable of functioning outside this narrowly defined area.

The Great Archangels are not quite so limited in their faculties as the Angels, for although they too are lacking man's full potential, they do show evidence of individual will. It was after all the Archangel, Lucifer, the "Light Bringer", who refused the express command of the Deity to submit himself to Adam, and in consequence was branded "Samael", the "Poisoner of God" (Sam=poison, al=god), and expelled from His holy presence.

Although the story of Lucifer is one which conceals many mysteries, and is by no means the simple moral tale that some would have us believe, it is a sobering thought that even the greatest of the Archangels can fall from grace.

The Orders Of Qliphoth

The name "Qliphoth", (singular "Qliphah") occasionally to be found spelt "Klippot", means "shells" or "harlots". These are the "demons" of Qabalah; destructive forces constantly at work in the universe.

The Qliphoth are not independent of the Holy Tree, although they may be said to inhabit a second, inverse, Tree below the world of Assiah. Some Qabalists consider this Tree to be a fifth "world", and equate it with the Biblical conception of Hell.

> "Above in the Tree of Life exist no strange Qliphoth for it is said: "With Thee dwelleth no Evil", but in the Tree Below exist the strange Qliphoth"   *(Zohar)*

> "Above are not any Qliphoth for no one can enter in the Gate of the King in a rough garment, but the Qliphoth are below".
> *(Zohar, Rayah Me'hemnah)*

In general terms the order of Qliphoth assigned to each Sephirah represents the adverse of the principles that the sphere expresses, being a perversion of its essential qualities. The manner in which a Qliphothic order functions is determined by the sphere to which it is attached, and is commonly its perverse mirror image, or, often even more destructive in its effect, is an exaggeration of a sphere's virtues. Usually the names applied to the orders themselves give us a clue as to their *modus operandi*; for instance in the sphere of Kether, where all is Unity, we find the Qliphoth to be *Thaumiel*, the "Twins of God", who by their duality and their contention deny the unity of the Primal Glory, while in Yesod the Qliphah is *Gamaliel*, the "obscene ass", a perversion of the sphere's sexual function.

There are two main, although not necessarily mutually exclusive, theories to account for the presence of the Qliphoth. One, perhaps in modern times the most widely held, suggests that they are the result of momentary periods of imbalance, brought about by the process of successive emanation. The Tree, although stable above the Abyss, is not fully equilibrated until the establishment of the final Sephirah of Malkuth, when all is brought to a point of balance. It is during this unstable stage of the Tree's development that the stray energies which go to form the Qliphoth become detached from the pattern of emanation and begin to aggregate into the "shells" of Qabalistic tradition.

An alternative theory suggests that the demonic forces are in fact little more than the detritus of an earlier cycle of creation. It is said that the remains of the previous universe, both physical and subtle, are still in existence and it is from this that the Qliphoth were formed and from this also that they draw a portion of their sustenance.

A very different theory to account for the presence of evil in the world was developed by Issac Luria and his followers.

This highly involved doctrine, called *Shevirath-ha-Kelim*, or the "Breaking of the Vessels", describes a catastrophic sequence of events in the first creation. Stripped to its essentials Luria's theory is that the Sephiroth were developed to contain the ineffable light of the manifesting Ain. The three Supernal Sephiroth were able to perform this office well enough as they were formed from the highest vibration of this light, but the remaining six spheres (excluding Malkuth which is the *place* of manifestation) shattered under the impact of the unbalanced descending power. But Luria does not suggest that these fragments of the original Sephirothic vessels are the substance from which the Qliphoth were formed. He says that the roots of the Qliphoth existed *before* the vessels were broken, and that they were an integral part of the original Sephiroth, and therefore the breaking was a necessary act of "purification" on the part of the manifesting Light. With the fragmentation of the vessels evil in general, and the Qliphoth in particular, was externalised and achieved an identity separate to that of the Sephiroth. Evil was thus excised from the Tree itself, and now dwells in a place apart. Some authorities suggest that this shattering of the Tree took place on the level of the fifth Sephirah,

Geburah, whose difficult and complex character we shall be exploring in some detail later.

If one does not accept that evil is an inevitable by-product of the creative act the question that must then arise is, why does the Deity allow such forces to inhabit His perfect creation?

It is said, in answer to this question, that the Qliphoth have the function of "tempters and testers" of mankind, to challenge his morality and prove it sound. The *Zohar* says of the *Malakha-Meth*, the Angel of Death who is at one and the same time, Satan, Deceiver, and Accuser, that he performs his work "because the Holy, Blessed be He! orders it through his love to His children"; and that the activities of the orders of Qliphoth are therefore in accordance with the Will of the Most High.

These workers of apparent wickedness are as essential to the proper functioning of the Tree as the angels, for all are ordained by God, and each is necessary to the existence of the other. After all we should not forget that in Isaiah the Deity says:

"I form the light, and create darkness: I make peace, and create evil: I the LORD do all these things". *(Isaiah, 45:7)*

Although it may be accepted that the Qliphoth are as much a part of the divine plan as any other order of being, and like any other being will be redeemed and re absorbed into the God-head at the end of this cycle of creation, it is nevertheless wise to treat them with a considerable degree of caution. The student is therefore strongly advised to master the basic banishing rituals of both pentagram and hexagram as well as the more complex "Star Ruby", which may be found in *Magick in Theory and Practice*, before attempting any other magickal operation.

Magickal Powers

Also called "The Spiritual Experience", these are the powers which accrue to the magician or mystic with each successive attainment to a path or Sephirah.

The magickal powers are best considered to be specialised enhancements of the adept's consciousness and extensions of his range of operation. With each Sephirothic attainment is associated a "Vision", such as the "Vision of Splendour", found in Hod, or the "Vision of Power" in Geburah. Unlike the Sephiroth, the powers of the paths are not described as "Visions".

The visions are typical of the essential characteristics of the Sephiroth to which they are attached, and result from a complete understanding on the part of the adept of that sphere's true nature, both internally and in relation to the other Sephiroth.

As the individual ascends the ladder of the Tree, so at each stage a new level of consciousness is awakened. Each of these newly gained expansions of consciousness equip the seeker with the necessary armoury to essay the next stage of the ascent. The powers of the paths proper - those which connect the spheres one to another - tend to confer more immediately practical benefits than do the Sephiroth themselves, whose own powers are more abstract but, equally, more profound.

The final magical power of the Tree is that found in Kether, namely "Union with God", not in this case described as a "vision", whilst the ultimate achievement is re-absorption into the Ain, which is unsurprisingly titled "The Supreme Attainment".

The Virtue and the Vice

Each Sephirah is assigned a "Virtue" and, with the exception of Kether and Chokmah, also a "Vice".

Plainly these do not emanate from the Sephiroth themselves but arise from the reactions of those who make contact with them.

In this sense they represent human rather than Sephirothic qualities.Both categories are fairly self-explanatory; the virtue, embodying the finest aspects of a sphere, at least in so far as they can be translated into terms of human activity, and the vice, representing a perversion or exaggeration of the sphere's principle attributes.

For example in the fifth Sephirah of Geburah, a sphere of intensely energetic activity which encompasses matters martial and judicial, the virtues are "courage" and "energy", while the corresponding vices are "cruelty" and "destruction".

The Magickal Image

These are mental images built up by the individual to represent, as best he can, the nature of a given sphere.

Whilst each person working with Qabalah will develop his or her own "personalised" version of the traditional images, according to their orientation and abilities, there is a lot to be said for working with the traditional models, at least to begin with.

When any given image is used over a long period of time by a large group of people, and especially when it is used within such a powerful system as the Qabalah, it effectively becomes an autonomous entity. Constant visualisation of, and meditation upon, the image will vitalise and sustain it, making it easier to access and more potent in use. Generally the older and more accepted an image the more effective will be its usage. Although carrying certain dangers which require the student to exercise some discrimination, for there is always the possibility that a long-standing form has suffered some corruption, using a magickal image that has been in general circulation for some time can confer considerable benefit on the beginner.

The Magickal Grades

To each Sephirah is assigned a magickal grade which indicates the level of attainment reached by the adept.

Each of the grades is suffixed with a dual figure, separated by an equals sign, which describes a position on the Tree. The first figure is always suffixed with a superscript zero while the second is followed by a square. Hence, the highest grade achievable, that of Ipsissimus, is designated by the suffix $10°=1^{\square}$, while the first Sephirothic grade is numbered $1°=10^{\square}$. Each set of numbers adds to eleven, that being the total of full grades on the Tree proper, and the number of the Great Work completed.

There are also preparatory and linking grades which do not relate directly to Sephiroth and which are therefore unnumbered.

The system used throughout this work is that of the order known as the A∴A∴, and is based on the structure of that order as described in the essay, *"One Star in Sight"*, by Aleister Crowley.

The grades themselves may be considered to be fully functional only when the adept has achieved the full power of a given sphere, that is to say, in almost all cases when the adept is about to move forward into another sphere.

It cannot be overemphasised that attainment of grades is not necessarily carried out in strict sequential order, nor are they necessarily attained in full by every aspirant.

The individual grades will be discussed in the appropriate chapters, but it will be understood that, particularly above the Abyss, the nature and duties of such achievements are incapable of explanation and description to those who do not themselves hold similar rank.

Many occult groups use the grade system of the A∴A∴ as a model and award grades to its members in accordance with their own rules. Hence one may occasionally find occultists who profess to hold the most exalted of grades, but who in actual fact are not properly entitled to any. While it is perfectly reasonable for such groups to award their own grades, care must be taken that there is no confusion between these and their true Sephirothic models.

The Magickal Weapons and Symbols

It is often the case with magickal symbols and weapons that there is some dispute, not only about which category any given item might belong to, but also how each category should be defined to begin with.

Often the symbols of a given Sephirah are actually used as magickal weapons in ceremonial ritual. Equally, the weapons of a sphere may, on occasion, do double service as appropriate Sephirothic symbols.

Indeed, some authorities make no distinction between the two categories. It might be less confusing if we distinguish those items which have an important and active place in any given ritual working, from those that having a more peripheral role. In this way we may decide to which category an item should be assigned by the function it has in a particular circumstance, rather than be held to a fixed system of classification. That is to say, any given item may be equally a weapon or a symbol depending on the use to which it is put.

Throughout this work it will be made clear what is to be considered a weapon and what a symbol in the context of each sphere.

The symbols of a sphere are those things that seem to the student to best represent its qualities, and to suggest something of its inner nature. To a certain extent these symbols are arbitrary, their validity and usefulness depending entirely on the response they evoke from the viewer. There are many examples of appropriate symbolic forms to be found in the literature, and specimens will be given of the more common variants in each chapter, but there is no reason why the student should feel constrained to use the traditional symbols. It is far better to use a system which has personal relevance, no matter how idiosyncratic it might seem to others, than to attempt to work with classical images which do not truly engage the imagination.

The matter of weapons is somewhat different, for these are the "tools of the trade" and are designed for specific tasks. To use an inappropriate weapon in ritual work is as foolish as attempting the same in any other sphere of activity. As one would not by choice use a pickaxe when repairing a chair, so one would be equally careful in selecting the proper weapons for a magickal working; to do otherwise would at best be inefficient, and at worst downright dangerous.

The difference between a weapon and a symbol might be summed up by saying that whereas the symbol is merely suggestive of a particular energy, the weapon will allow the ritualist to control and manipulate that energy.

Therefore choice of weapon, although sometimes extensive, offers less scope for personal preference than does the choice of symbols.

The Divisions of Man

Qabalists believe that man is composed of three major elements, which they term the *Neshemah*, *Ruach*, and *Nephesh*.

The first of these three-fold divisions is itself subdivided into three components, one for each of the Supernal Sephiroth.

The *Neshemah* is the Triad of the Immortal Man in that this is the essential "self" of the individual which transcends bodily death,

> "the most simple, subtile, and sublime, of all the substances, (which) is not attached to the corporeal body".
>
> (Issac Myer *Qabbalah*)

The highest arc of *Neshemah's* triad is termed *Yechidah*, "The Unique One", the essential spark of immortality to be found in every man and woman and described in *Liber AL vel Legis* as the *Khabs*, the "Star" or "Inmost Light", as distinct from the *Khu*, or "magickal garment", which provides a vehicle through which it might incarnate:....

> "The Khabs is in the Khu, not the Khu in the Khabs. Worship then the Khabs, and behold my light shed over you!". *(AL 1:8/9)*

There is a school of thought that classes *Chiyah*, the "Creative Impulse", (under our scheme, the second sub-division of *Neshemah* and the one corresponding to Chokmah) as a separate "sub-soul" in its own right. It is true that there is a certain attraction to this arrangement as it then becomes possible to establish links with the four worlds and a number of other four-fold correspondences.

However, the arrangement used throughout the present work is the one most commonly encountered in general occult literature, and also has the benefit of corresponding to a number of equally important tri-partite arrangements.

The third aspect of *Neshemah* takes its name from the triad as a whole and is attributed to Binah, being the highest possible level of Intuition and Spiritual Understanding.

The second element of man's subtle constitution is termed the *Ruach*, which may be loosely described as his "intellectual" aspect, incorporating the mind and its functions, including the faculties of perception and sensation.

Like the *Neshemah*, the *Ruach* too is subdivided, but into five parts, one for each of the Sephiroth below the Abyss, excluding Yesod and Malkuth. Each of the Sephiroth represent an aspect of the intellect. In the order of emanation these faculties are: Memory, Will, Imagination, Desire, and Reason. Of these Qabalists consider Reason to be the lowest and the least as its usefulness is strictly limited to the lower paths of the Tree.

The final element of man's make-up according to this method of classification, is termed the *Nephesh*, the "animal soul"; that which Israel Regardie has described as the "gross side of the spirit".

The *Nephesh* is not divided in the same manner as the two preceding elements, but it is considered to be of a dual nature. The first part is something akin to the Prana of the Eastern tradition, "the breath of life", the vital, electric principle of the life-force which animates the body. The second element, and the one which immediately relates it to the sphere of Yesod, its correspondence on the Tree, is that of the "Astral Body", one of the "subtle" forms of man's extended being.

Malkuth is the only Sephirah of the Holy Tree which does not have a corresponding subtle principle, although it could be argued that its higher reaches contact and to a certain extent participate in the life of Astral Realm. The corporeal body as such is called by Qabalists *Guph* and is the means through which is experienced the physical world manifested by the tenth Sephirah.

There are a number of classification systems based on the extended being of man. As it is written that man, alone of all creation, is the very image of God, made in His likeness, it is unsurprising that Qabalists have tried over the centuries to expand their knowledge of Him through their knowledge of themselves, and to apply their understanding of the dynamics of the Holy Tree to the only created creatures that are truly microcosms of it.

Many of these systems and theories are based on the Qabalistic concept of the "Divine Man", Adam Qadmon, whose body is comprised of the ten Sephiroth. Adam Qadmon is considered by Qabalists to be the first manifest reflection of the Deity, not in the sense that Metatron is held to be the first created being, but rather as though he is, himself, the very Atziluthic world where God's manifestation begins. For this reason he is sometimes termed "The Atziluthic Adam", as distinct from the Briatic Adam, the created "Man of Dust" of Genesis.

The Chakras

Indian esoteric physiology postulates the existence in the human body of subtle "power centres", which are said to be the seats of particular forms of psychic energies. These centres, termed "Chakras", meaning "wheels", have a certain relationship with physical organs, but are not located in, or dependent on, them.

It is held to be possible to activate or "open up" the chakras by various techniques, including formal initiations and intense meditation, in order that one might thereby function to the limit of one's true potential.

The Eastern chakras do not however correlate exactly with the Sephiroth on the microcosmic Tree of the human body.

There have been innumerable attempts to devise a system whereby the seven main chakra centres can be related to the Sephirothic glyph without doing too much violence to the fundamental principles of both schemes.

The three best known systems are those of Crowley, Major-General J.F.C.Fuller, and Dion Fortune. Of these it is the method advocated by Crowley which is used throughout the present work.

This is not the place to rehearse the arguments over correct or incorrect attributions; in each case where there is a serious clash between the system used and one or both of the alternative methods of attribution attention will be drawn to the fact, but in order to help clarify the main areas of disagreement at the outset a comparison table is shown below.

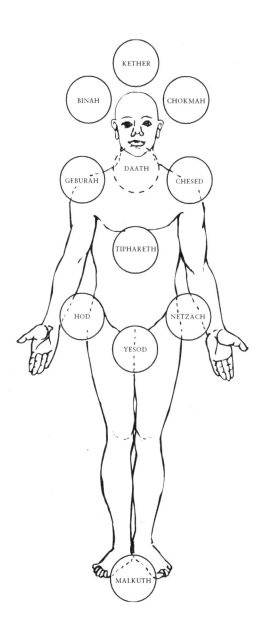

THE TREE IN MICROCOSM

Even though the chakras themselves do not entirely match the Sephiroth on the Tree there is nevertheless a great deal of information to be gained from them. They do at least cover the same ground as the Sephiroth, and express in their own terms the same general principles.

Indeed it would be surprising if it were otherwise, for the traditions from which both systems spring represent the zenith of philosophical speculation of two of the world's greatest cultures, struggling to find answers to the same basic questions.

Three Methods of Allocation Compared

	FORTUNE	CROWLEY	FULLER
Sahasrara	Kether	Kether	Kether
Ajna	Daath	Chokmah	Chokmah
Vishuddha	Daath	Binah	Binah
Anahata	Tiphareth	Chesed, Geburah, Tiphareth	Chesed
Manipura	Tiphareth	Netzach	Geburah
Svadisthana	Yesod	Hod	Yesod
Muladhara	Malkuth	Yesod	Malkuth

The Colours in the Four Worlds

Each Sephirah has associated with it a set of colours; one for each of the worlds of Atziluth, Briah, Yetzirah, and Assiah. They are useful aids in contacting individual Sephiroth and Paths, both as a tuning device, to create an appropriate level of receptivity, and as a means of determining one's current position on the Tree.

In the latter case the colours offer a valuable "map" which, along with other path-specific symbols, enables practitioners to pin-point their precise location and to navigate purposefully around the glyph.

The four colour scales correspond with the Hebrew letters of the God-name IHVH, the Tetragrammaton, which will be analysed in the chapter dealing with Chokmah, the second Supernal Sephiroth, to which it is assigned.

The first colour is that of the Atziluthic or Archetypal world, and is assigned to the letter Yod, the initial letter of the Tetragrammaton. Here is found the root of all colour, the purest possible expression of each Sephirothic hue.

As this is the plane in which God performs His work directly, without the intervention of His mediating agencies, the colour should be visualised as a pure radiant light which is projected out of the primordial darkness.

The next corresponds to the Briatic, or Creative, world and *Heh* the second letter of IHVH. Here the light is degraded from the purity of Atziluth, and is now seen to be a reflection of it. Consequently the colours of this scale, although intense, do not quite evince the brilliance of the first.

The third colour is assigned to formative world of Yetzirah, and is always composed of an admixture of the Atziluthic and Briatic scales. The Yetziratic colour is referred to *Vau*, the penultimate letter of the Mighty Name.

In the fourth scale, corresponding with *Heh final*, we enter Assiah, the world of actions and plane of materiality, where the hues are at their maximum degradation. The colours in this range are far less pure than those that precede it, and are all admixtures of two or more others, most of which are derived from the previous scales.

The Book of Thoth

The origins of the Book of Thoth, or Tarot pack, are obscure to say the least. It has been variously ascribed to the priests of ancient Egypt, and to the late middle ages. Whatever the cards' actual history, and it need not concern us overmuch here, they have long been considered part of the authentic Western magickal tradition.

This enigmatic set of images is considered by many occultists to represent another strand in the ancient body of Qabalistic knowledge. It is said to contain within its mysterious symbolism the complete teachings of the Secret Doctrine which were deliberately kept separate from the written and oral sources by presenting them as a harmless and inconsequential parlour game. Tradition has it that this was done in order to ensure the survival of this knowledge in an uncertain world, to function as a sort of "ark" of ancient teaching.

Whatever the truth of this, it is undoubtedly the case that each of the seventy-eight cards of the Tarot pack are closely related to either the Sephiroth, or the Paths.

In our present study it is the minor cards which are of most interest, the position of a sphere in the order of emanation determining which four cards are assigned to it. Hence to Geburah, the fifth Sephirah, is assigned the four fives, and to Yesod, the ninth emanation, the four nines, so that each of the ten original Sephiroth is assigned one card of each suit.

The four suits correspond to the letters of the Tetragrammaton, the four worlds of the Qabalah and to the elements.

The Wands are assigned to the world of Atziluth, and to the element of Fire; the Cups are referred to Briah, and Water; Swords correspond with the Yetziratic world and elemental Air; while the suit of Disks relates to the element of Earth and Assiah.

The sixteen court-cards, like the suits themselves, may also be correlated with the letters of the Tetragrammaton, and with the four worlds. These attributions are as follows: Knights, Atziluth and *Yod*; Queens, Briah and *Heh*; Prince, Yetzirah and *Vau*; Princess, Assiah and *Heh final*.

Each of the four court-cards of a suit also represents a sub-division of an element; for example, the Princess of Wands describes the earthy part of Fire; and the Queen of Swords, the watery part of Air. The elements themselves, along with the sub-elemental divisions, will be covered in the appropriate chapters, and in particular in the one devoted to Malkuth, whose Mundane Chakra is *Cholem Yesodoth*, the "sphere of the elements".

The serious student is strongly recommended to study Crowley's *Book of Thoth,* and to become familiar with its associated pack, as this is the version Thelemites consider best describes the conditions we may expect to meet as we progress further into the Age of Horus.

Other Correspondences

Under this heading we shall look at some of the more common minor attributions of the Sephiroth.

These categories, and very many others, are to be found tabulated in Crowley's indispensable work, *777*, an absolute "must" for all serious students. *777* is a unique reference work, but it should be considered only as a starting point and as a model, for there is nothing more valuable to the student than to develop his or her own individual list of correspondences.

Animals

Each Sephirah and path has assigned to it a corresponding animal, whose nature, real or imaginary, seems to best epitomise its qualities.

These may be natural or mythical beasts and range from a "god" to a tortoise. In all cases it will be made clear why a given creature is applied to the path in question, as with some the connection may not at first be apparent.

Plants

Plants may feature in a list of Sephirothic correspondences under a number of different categories. They may be symbols of a sphere or path, the basis of its allocated drugs, or deemed to typify certain Sephirothic qualities.

The latter group is essentially based on the ancient doctrine of "signatures", which supposes that if a thing, in this case a plant, is sufficiently like any other thing in appearance or behaviour then those two things must belong to the same class, and should therefore be treated of in the same manner.

Drugs

The drugs assigned to each path and sphere may be of vegetable or mineral origin. These drugs are selected because they either produce states of consciousness that are analogous to those experienced in the spheres to which they relate, or their effect is in some other manner typical of a given path; for example all heart stimulants are assigned to Tiphareth, which is itself the heart centre of the Tree.

It is possible to use the appropriate drugs as an aid to path-working, but this is an advanced form of magickal work that requires considerable skill to master. As certain of the drugs listed in the main body of the text are dangerous, illegal, or both, the student is not encouraged in their use, but in this, as in all else, "thou hast no right but to do thy will".

However, it must be clearly understood that there are few occasions in which the use of such drugs can be magickally justified. In many situations their consumption may be an actual hindrance to productive work, and in all cases they presents a real danger to the psychic, mental, and physical well-being of the user.

4

Ain

Ain Soph   Ain Soph Aur

"Mighty was the draught of Voidness to draw Existence in."
(William Blake, *Vala, or The Four Zoas, Night the Second*)

"The most secret of mysteries is that which is called Nothing, the Most Holy Ancient, from whom the light flows forth".   (*Zohar*).

This is the realm of the unknown and unknowable God, "The Ancient of All Ancients", the unmanifest Deity of whom it is said:

"Before the universe was made, the Most Blessed One and its Name, were One....Before the Most Blessed One made Its world, It was, and Its Name was hidden in It".

(*Midrash Ha-Neelam, Zohar*)

Prior to the emanation of the Sephiroth there obtained a condition termed by Qabalists, "Ain", or "Negative Existence".

"It is so named (Ain) because we do not know, and also it cannot be known, what was in this principle as this, to our understanding, yea, even by our Wisdom! is unattainable".... "Therefore the Sacred Ancient is called No-Thing, since No-Thing hangs on it".

(*Zohar*)

The state of "*No-Thingness*" is a very different condition from that of "*nothingness*", for here it is not simply a matter of an "absence of things", which would imply that there were in fact "things" to absent themselves, and indeed some "where" from which they might be absent. Nor can "Negative Existence" be considered as a mere lack of complexity, for it contains all possibilities and potentialities, as ultimately all emanate creation derives from its mysterious heart.

It has however yet to manifest itself in any form, for to quote the *Sepher Yetzirah*:

"And from the non-existent He made Some Thing; and all forms of speech and everything that has been produced; from the empty void He made the material world, and from the inert earth He brought forth everything that hath life. He hewed, as it were, vast columns out of the intangible air, and by the power of His Name made every creature and everything that is; and the production of all things from the twenty-two letters is the proof that they are all but parts of one body". *(Chap.2:6)*

Until this creative act which willed into existence the first concretion of its essence, the Ain was alone and "face beheld not face", therefore the "He" referred to in the *Sepher Yetzirah* created out of His own substance when He desired to make "Some-Thing".

It is important to realise that this verse does not refer to a creative deity taking pre-existing but separate material and from it manufacturing the worlds; rather the Deity has extended Himself, and has caused a portion of Himself to become manifest.

It is our inability to comprehend the true nature of such a state that leads us to describe it as "Negative Existence", for a more accurate term might be "Pure Existence"; an existence which is not limited by any category of expression.

As the condition of Pure Existence is necessarily stable, all being encompassed and equilibrated, it therefore requires a conscious act of will on the part of the Unmanifest to disrupt its ageless balance and allow itself to extrude a manifesting point.

Referring back to the earlier Zoharic text in which it was said that the principle of the Ain is unattainable by "our understanding, yea, even by our Wisdom!", it may now be worthwhile considering quite what was meant by that peculiar but very particular phraseology. "Understanding" is the title of Binah, the third Supernal, and "Wisdom" that of Chokmah, the second. What the passage seems to suggest is that even these exalted attainments are insufficient to enable a comprehension of the nature of the Unmanifest. However, the sphere of Kether is not so mentioned, and therefore one may assume that from the vantage point of the first Supernal, which is after all dependent from the Ain, some small notion of its essential qualities may be gained.

The achievement of Kether is the final stage of the ascension of "Jacob's Ladder", the magickal power of which is "Union with God". In fact those who do so attain are effectively gods themselves.

It would seem then that the Ain is truly unknowable, even from the supra-normal level of the Briatic world which is comprised solely of Binah and Chokmah, but that a "god" may indeed look upon the face of the "God and very God".

The Ain is limitless and timeless so that all that issues forth from its bosom does so without in any way diminishing its substance. Actually, in a sense there *is* nothing outside of this condition, even that which we see and recognise as the physical universe is so only because the Ain has chosen to extend a portion of itself into materiality.

The material universe might be likened to an ice-cube, floating in a chilled glass of water, it is created of the same material and will return to the state of the "mother" element in due time, but for the duration it exists as a discrete island in the sea of its birth.

In the same way that our ice-cube has not diminished the total quantity of water in the glass, merely effected a temporary change of state in a small portion, the Ain suffers no loss through the coalescence of an aspect of itself into tangible form.

A Jewish prayer illustrates this well; "Thou wast the same before the universe was created, Thou hast been the same since the universe hath been created, Thou art the same in this universe, and Thou will be the same in the universe to come".

The Ain is considered to consist of three parts or stages of potential manifestation. These stages are referred to as the "Veils of Negative Existence". The Ain proper, which is the most abstract of the veils, is the condition of negative existence itself, the other two stages developing from the Ain represent a "solidifying" of the original principle. Ain Soph, the second of the veils, is termed "The Limitless", where out of the nothingness has formed a "some-thingness" which now has sufficient feature (at least in comparison with the Ain) to be defined by the expression "Limitless".

The third veil or stage is that of Ain Soph Aur, or "The Limitless Light", suggesting that the immanent God is preparing to become an emanant God, for another dimension of the Ain has now been activated. Light is the most subtle and rarefied of all possible external expressions of the manifesting Deity, the first creative act that impinges on our perceived universe, the others being, as it were, merely preparatory.

It will be noticed that each of these successive stages is characterised and confirmed by an additional title. To the "nothingness" is added "limitlessness", the "Soph". Whilst to the "limitless nothingness", is added the Light, "Aur".

This triadic arrangement foreshadows the Trinities and Triads which will be met with again and again as we continue our study of the Tree.

The process that we may infer to be occurring in the Ain, as it prepares to manifest a portion of itself, can best be termed, "coalescence", or "crystallisation". The Unmanifest God is in the process of "concentrating" a centre, which is both unlocated and lacking in dimension. This position-less focus becomes the first Sephiroth, Kether, the point at which the primal force of light ceases to be noumenal and becomes phenomenal.

Although Kether is indeed the concentrated "centre" of the Ain, it is equally true that the Ain is at the centre of Kether. This unapproachable core may be equated with the Christian concept of the "Transcendent God", while the final stage, Ain Soph Aur, becomes the endless and limitless light of the Primal Glory itself.

In the opening verses of the Book of Genesis may be found a formula which is applicable to a number of aspects of the Tree, including the establishment of the Supernal Triad.

Although the same general principles of increasing concretion and specialisation are to be found in action throughout the emanating worlds the initial verses of Genesis are also, and perhaps primarily, an expression of the development of the Ain prior to its eventual manifestation.

"And the earth was without form and void; and darkness was upon the face of the deep", would seem to apply to the condition of negative existence, the Ain proper. The point at which "The Spirit of God moved upon the face of the waters", can be readily equated with the second development of Ain Soph, the "Limitless", for now there is a suggestion that the original unity of the Ain is no longer, and that the Deity has differentiated Itself, moving as a separate "Spirit" across the face of the unmanifest. In verse three we find: "And God said, Let there be light: and there was light", which can be taken to refer to the initial development of the "Limitless Light" of Ain Soph Aur whose concentrated flux establishes and invigorates Kether.

The three stages or gradations of the Unmanifest, culminating in a fourth stage which represents the development of Kether, may also be related to the four worlds of Atziluth, Briah, Yetzirah, and Assiah.

The archetypal world of Atziluth equates with the Ain, for it is above human consciousness and exists prior to manifestation, "perfect but unrealised"; containing within all future possibilities.

The world of Briah, the Creative realm, "the abode of pure spirit" and the point at which the Spirit of God moves across "the face of the waters" is comparable with the Ain Soph. The Yetziratic world, where the first development of form is foreshadowed as the Deity calls forth Light to disperse the "darkness upon the face of the deep" is an equivalent condition to the Ain Soph Aur. And finally, the moment of manifestation itself, the emergence of the first Sephirah from the Limitless Light, which from the "point of view" of the Ain represents a state of gross materiality, and can therefore be compared with the physical world of Assiah.

Some Qabalists have postulated a "hidden Tree", beyond the veils of negative existence, which has Kether as the equivalent of Malkuth.

The entire Sephirothic structure, depending backwards from Kether, would in this case be contained within the Ain Soph Aur.

One could then go on to speculate on the nature of the Tree which has its equivalent of Malkuth in the Kether of Ain Soph Aur. Fascinating though such conjectures are they are rather outside the scope of an introduction to Qabalah but they do serve to remind us that the Tree is a universally applicable glyph and one which provides a sturdy framework for all manner of imaginative adventures.

Naturally there have been a number of speculative models developed to account for the initial establishment of the Tree. Indeed given the crucial importance of the matter it would be surprising if this were not the case. Although the doctrine we have outlined is undoubtedly the most generally accepted today, an alternative developed by Issac Luria in the sixteenth century has some very attractive points and gained considerable currency among his fellow Qabalists.

Luria's theory literally stands the more accepted accounts of the cosmological process on their heads. He says that, instead of the Unmanifest projecting its creative will to develop the Sephiroth, quite the opposite happened. The unmanifest god first *withdrew* into Himself, and that therefore the universe was made possible as a result of His *contraction* rather than by His expansion.

This doctrine, which is called *"Tsimtsum"* (best translated as "withdrawal" or "retreat") suggests that God could only make room for His creation by "stepping inside" of Himself and thereby establishing an area which was no longer part of His holy being.

He could then return to it in the role of Creator, rather than, as would otherwise have been the case, simply as a manipulator of His own substance. God's creation in this manner exists outside of Him.

His presence still imbues the universe of course, and it will, at the ending of days, return to its source and be re-absorbed but for the duration that universe is not properly speaking part of the divine "body".

One aspect of this model of creation which has been especially attractive to some Jewish Qabalists is that it ameliorates their natural concern over the pantheism implied by the expansive theory of emanation and which is particularly evident in the *Zohar*.

It is a matter for some debate as to whether one would be justified in attempting to assign any gods to the Ain. However it is a useful exercise which can go a long way towards helping us achieve a greater understanding of the nature of the Unmanifest, and on that basis alone is well worth the effort.

Perhaps the first god-form we may reasonably assign is that of the goddess Nuit, the Egyptian "Queen of Heaven".

Nuit describes herself, in *Liber AL vel Legis*, as "Infinite Space, and the Infinite Stars thereof" (*AL 1:22*), thereby presenting an excellent image of the Ain. In the same revealed document she is found referred to as "continuous"; omnipresent and without bound, in other words "Limitless", but she is more (or less!) than this, for the relevant verse goes on to say:

> "O Nuit, continuous one of Heaven, let it be ever thus; that men speak not of Thee as One but as None; and let them speak not of thee at all, since thou art continuous!" *(AL 1:27)*

Nuit then is both "continuous" and "None", and she is also "not"; all terms that are equally appropriate to describe the Ain.

To the Egyptians, Nuit personified the "vault of heaven", which should be seen in its widest sense as the great Unmanifest realm, and not in the more limited sense of the visible sky.

From the body of Nuit emerged all the heavenly bodies The stars are her children and also her sustenance, hence the Egyptians sometimes referred to her the "female pig who eats her piglets"; the stellar bodies being born from her womb after being swallowed by her mouth in a continuous process of construction and destruction.

This constructive/destructive cycle is typical of the activity which takes place at the interface of Ain Soph Aur and the upper Kether and this aspect of the goddess is therefore best considered as representing the point at which the first Supernal becomes manifest on emerging from the densest part of "The Limitless Light".

Crowley suggests Hoor-paar-Kraat (Harpocrates), as the "Silence", and Amoun the "Concealed", as correspondences of the Ain. Both these gods are also, and perhaps with slightly more justification, assigned to Sephiroth; Amoun, as the creative *Chiyah*, to Chokmah; Harpocrates as the Child and Centre, to Tiphareth.

Another Egyptian deity who might be thought appropriate is Atum, primary creator god of Heliopolis. Atum came "into being of himself; before Heaven and Earth were separated". Being alone in the created universe he had no option but to create by copulating with himself, he achieved this remarkable feat by the vigorous use of his hand; "I have copulated into my fist" he says, and by his essence created Shu, the god of Air, and Tefnut, goddess of moisture.

The story of Atum, self-created, emerging from the primeval chaos to bring forth the stuff of the universe, is most instructive in the light of what we already have learned of the Ain.

This small selection of gods from the Egyptian pantheon should be sufficient to illustrate the criteria by which the gods of any other tradition may be assigned to the Ain. It must be borne in mind however, that these correspondences are merely an aid to understanding the general principle of the Ain. There can be no god conceivable by the human mind whose nature even approaches the totality of the mystery of the Unmanifest.

5

Kether

THE CROWN   THE PRIMAL GLORY

"The First Path is called the Admirable or the Hidden Intelligence (the Highest Crown): for it is the Light giving the power of comprehension of that First Principle which has no beginning; and it is the Primal Glory, for no created being can attain to its essence."
(The Yetziratic Text)

Kether is the first Sephirah of the Tree of Life and is positioned at the head of the Middle Pillar, the pillar of equilibrium. It is the apex of the Supernal Triad, and the balance point of the Triad of *Olam-ha-Mevshekal*, the "Intellectual world". Unlike the triads which define the "Moral" or "Sensuous" worlds and the Material world, below the Abyss, here the focus is upward, as Kether is both the source and equilibrating power of the initial triad.

It is here also that the world of Atziluth is located, with Kether as its sole Sephirothic inhabitant.

This is the point at which the Unmanifest begins the process of manifestation. Herein are contained all potentials of force and form. It is pure existence, undifferentiated and undivided.

Kether is the primal fount, all subsequent Sephiroth, and hence all creation, have their roots in this, the first emanation.

"Kether is the principle of all principles, the Secret Wisdom, the Most Exalted Crown, with which all Crowns and diadems are adorned". *(Zohar)*

The first Supernal is the point at which the Light first manifests at the divine command;

"Let there be Light", and therefore represents the "Will of the Absolute" to reveal itself, for:....."Until Elohim created the

57

universe, it was alone, and then it went forth from its Will to create the universe", *(Zohar)*

Although Kether is the purest and most transcendent of all the Sephiroth, whose brilliance is unapproachable, indeed inconceivable by any incarnate being, from the "point of view" of the Ain it is a sphere of solidity and darkness. Compared with the ineffable light of the Unmanifest, Kether is but a shadow, a dense reflection of the concealed, the "Absolute Indivisible Unity" from which it emanates. It represents a concentration of the Ain to a point of "Perfect Form and Individuality".

"When the Unknown of all the Unknown wished to manifest itself, it began by producing a point, for as long as that Light point did not appear through its energy, the Infinite was still completely unknown and did not spread any Light. *(Zohar)*

Using any kind of analogy as an aid to explaining the concepts involved here is necessarily fraught with difficulty as the mechanisms involved (in so far as we can understand them) are not, strictly speaking, paralleled elsewhere. However, with that caveat in mind, the emergence of Kether from the void of the Ain might be likened to the sudden development of a crystal in a saturated solution of sugar. Alternatively, it may be compared to the effect of warm breath upon a cold pane of glass, the appearanceof liquid condensation forming from the initial stage of haziness, being somewhat reminiscent of the mode of Kether's coalescence from the amorphous mists of the Ain.

Due to Kether's dependence on the Unmanifest it is said to be but partly revealed (and in this it may be compared to the Earth's moon, which likewise is partly revealed and partly concealed) for the roots of Kether reach far into the vast emptiness of negative existence.

As Malkuth is the densest and most tangible of the sequential numerations that proceed from Kether, so might Kether be seen to be the "Malkuth" of the Unmanifest, a crystallisation of its Limitless Light. Once again this analogy of Kether with Malkuth must not be taken too far, for whilst Malkuth is the product of a series of increasingly specialised and concrete emanations, Kether is manifested by the Ain Soph Aur without preliminary.

Nor should it be thought that the "concentration" or "coalescence"of the Ain which signifies the manifesting point of Kether is in any sense "central" to it, for there is no centre, nor can there be, given that the Ain is by definition limitless. The Ain by a purposeful concentration of its essential quality generates the first Sephirah which thereby becomes an unlocated focus in its infinite sphere.

"In the sphere I am everywhere the centre, as she, the circumference, is nowhere found". *(AL.2:3)*

Kether is androgynous, containing within itself the principles of both the male and female potencies, but expressing neither.

The complementary polarities, without which no further evolutionary development can occur, do not emerge as discreet elements until the second and third Supernals respectively.

The first Sephirah is sometimes identified with the "monad" of Pythagoras, for it represents the number, one.

"In this number are the other nine hidden, it is 1 by itself and it still remains 1, multiply 1 by itself and it is still 1 and unchanged, Thus it is a fitting representative of the great unchangeable Father of All". (S.L.MacGregor Mathers *The Kabbalah Unveiled*)

The God name attributed to Kether is AHIH, *Aleph, Heh, Yod, Heh*. It will occasionally be found transliterated as EHEIEH, and is pronounced "Ee-He-Yea".

This name has been variously translated as "I", "I will be", "I will become", and "I am"; the last being the more accepted version.

Occasionally it will be found rendered erroneously, "I Am that I Am".

The scriptural provenance of this first tetragrammic name is to be found in the passage from Exodus in which God gives it to Moses in answer to his plea:

"...Behold, when I come unto the children of Israel, and say unto them, The God of your fathers hath sent me unto you; and they shall say to me, What is his name? what shall I say unto them?."
"And God said unto Moses, I AM THAT I AM; and he said, Thus shalt thou say unto the children of Israel, I AM hath sent me unto you". *(Exodus 3:13/14)*

Strictly speaking only the second rendition of the name is accurate for AHIH, the expanded first version being properly, AHIH AShR AHIH, which also has the meaning of "Existence of Existence", another of Kether's many titles. The *Zohar* has much to say about this important name and it is worth quoting at least one passage at some length:

"The secret of this word AHIH, I Am, comprises everything, when the ways are hidden and not separated and together in one place, then it is called AHIH, I am, all hidden and not revealed; but after it goes out from its defined line and that river bears in its bosom all things, then He is called AHIH AShR i.e. That I Am, that means; I Am, prepared to bring forth all and after He revealed and brought forth all He is by that name."

With this passage from the *Zohar* we now have a third variant on the basic name to add to the two mentioned in Exodus. The three names fall into the common triadic pattern which we meet so frequently in Qabalah. It is possible to view the progression of the first name of God as a reflection of the development which takes place prior to manifestation. It requires no great effort to equate the unfolding name with the developmental stages of Ain, Ain Soph, and Ain Soph Aur.

Each stage is a successive degree of manifestation. It could also be said that the first name AHIH, "I Am", represents the innermost heart of Kether, being in effect projected directly from the Ain Soph Aur. The second name AHIH AShR, "That I Am", could then be considered to represent the actual establishment of the first Supernal; while the final variant AHIH AShR AHIH, "I Am That I Am", signifies the power of Kether moving out to form Chokmah and Binah, and eventually the remaining seven Sephiroth below the Abyss.

Concealed within the name AHIH is an interesting formula for our meditations on Kether and one which prepares the way for the second tetragrammic name, IHVH, which is assigned to subsequent Sephirah of Chokmah.

The initial letter of the name, *Aleph*, is also the first of the Hebrew alphabet, and signifies the "beginning of things". Its shape is somewhat reminiscent of the fylfot cross or swastika (an important Kether symbol) which expresses very well the manner in which the first emanation whirls out of the void. The second letter, *Heh*, represents the reception of the primal force symbolised by *Aleph*, whilst the third, *Yod* may be seen as the male creative drive, the fertilising principle, alike in shape and function to the spermatozoon. The final *Heh* of the name is receptive, as is the first, but now offering an additional element of stability. We find then, hidden in this name, the principles of the "coming forth", the initial reception and incorporation, and the two polarities of positive and negative, male and female, arising from the condition of the newly incorporated primal movement.

The very sound of the name, when correctly vibrated, demonstrates that essential quality of equilibrium which characterises Kether, for it consists of a balance between inhalation and exhalation.

Kether's mundane chakra is the *Rashith-Ha-Gilgalim*, called variously the "commencement of whirling motions", "First Swirlings", or the Primum Mobile. These are the first intimations of imminent manifestation, foreshadowing creation, the development of the inscrutable monad from which the entire structure of the Holy Tree is developed.

Unlike the mundane chakras that appear at later stages of the Tree, the Primum Mobile cannot be related to any known place or principle. It is clearly a unique occurrence. Its descriptive name gives us an excellent visual image on which to meditate however, for here is the picture of the void giving birth to the first principle, which comes spinning out of the vacuum. This is the point where negative existence becomes positive existence, the very instant of creation where:...

"the shadow of thy Light hast made the generation of all that which is". (Solomon Ben Yehudah Ibn Gebirol *Kether Malkuth*).

The titles applied to Kether fall into two main categories; the first expresses its primal quality as the first crystallisation of the Unmanifest in terms of its great antiquity; the second stresses the vastness and mystery of the conception.

It may be found in older Qabalistic writings that Kether is referred to as "Wisdom", which is properly the title of the second Sephirah, Chokmah. The form of wisdom that is appropriate to Kether is that termed *Chokmah-illa-Ah* or "Heavenly Wisdom", as distinct from that suggested by the name of the second emanation which means simply "wisdom", and refers to a lesser, although still transcendent, manifestation of that quality.

Kether is called by Qabalists, "Arik Anpin" or the "Long in Face", sometimes rendered as the "Vast Countenance", and more commonly as "Macroprosopos". On occasion these titles are applied to the Supernal triad as a whole, in which case they may be taken to be references to God as the "Three in One", with Chokmah and Binah being considered as the positive and negative aspects of the triune deity initially expressed in Kether.

The six Sephiroth below the Abyss, excluding Malkuth, are termed "Zeir Anpin", "Short in Face", the "Son of Arik Anpin" and, more rarely, the "Young One". They are the "Microprosopos" to Kether's Macroprosopos, and are the product and reflection of the Supernal.

The pendant sphere of Malkuth is sometimes called the "Bride of Microprosopos", for it is here that the potentials of the preceding Sephiroth are harmonised and brought into the material realm in a mystical marriage of Heaven and Earth.

A number of titles use the image of the "point" which, having no dimension but only position, illustrates Kether's condition extremely well. Variants include; "The Small Point", "The Smooth Point", "The Primordial Point" and "The Point within a Circle". The latter is descriptive of one of Kether's symbols and reminds us once again that Kether exists within the Unmanifest, "everywhere the centre".

The image of Kether as a "head" occurs frequently; some notable examples being: "The White Head", "that has no beginning nor end"; "The One Head which are Three Heads", referring (on one level at least) to the combination of Sephirothic powers above the Abyss, and "The Head which is Not", again suggesting the combined Supernal Triad. The latter title also gives a clue as to the nature of Kether's dependence from the Ain, for the word "Not" as used in this context suggests a state of being rather than of absence, making it particularly apposite for the concept of "negative existence".

The titles, "Lux Simplicissima" and "Lux Occultus", refer to Kether as the point source of all light in the universe, to its purity and its ultimate mystery.

Kether being the first of the emanations is also the oldest sphere and for this reason is called, "The Ancient of Days", "The Long of Suffering", and the "Ancient of Ancients", although care must be taken with this last title as it is easily confused with "The Ancient of *all* Ancients", which is only properly applicable to the Ain.

As Kether is essentially unknowable, "for no created being can attain to its essence", its mysterious aspect is found suggested in such titles as; "Inscrutable Height", "Concealed of the Concealed", and "Existence of Existences", which are more of the nature of Zen koans then explanatory descriptions, and do indeed serve something of a similar function in Qabalistic meditation.

The primary creator gods of most world religions, and especially those who were self-created, can be easily assigned to Kether, although many have additional correspondences elsewhere on the Tree, including, as we have already seen, the Ain.

Ptah, the principle creative god of Memphis, is the first of the Egyptian pantheon to be referred to this sphere. He was usually represented in human form, wrapped as a mummy without obvious gesture. As Crowley has commented, this "signifies that Kether has no attributes". (777) Kether, of course contains all attributes in embryo, but as these are not yet differentiated or manifested in any way, Crowley was perfectly correct in his assertion.

Ptah was the "ancient one" of the later Egyptians, the god who created by means of his "heart and his tongue", a phrase that is also used by Nuit when sending outward the "kiss" that regenerates the "little world my sister",   (AL 1:53)

Ptah, though presenting as a male, was actually androgynous for he contained within himself both a male aspect, "Nun", and a female aspect "Naunet". Although in late Egyptian mythology he becomes a composite figure as Ptah-Sokar-Osiris, it is by virtue of his earlier form that he is assigned to Kether. Ptah was thought by his worshippers to have been self-created and to have made the world and its denizens on a potters wheel.

Crowley also suggests Asar-un-Nefer, the highest form of Osiris; and Horus, as Heru-Ra-Ha, for he;

"contains the twin forms of the Lord of the Aeon. He is Kether to us in this time and place as being the highest positive conception of which we are capable".   (777)

Zeus, as the creator of the Olympian dynasty and supreme god, is an obvious Kether correspondence, although one must be careful to distinguish between his creative form and that of the son of Cronus, in which capacity he banished his father to eternal captivity.

Zeus is particularly a god associated with high places which is fitting for one assigned to the first and "highest" of the Sephiroth.

Jupiter, as a Roman form of Zeus, is similarly qualified for his inclusion under Kether. He was, during his long career, the recipient of a number of epithets which bear upon the first Supernal, such as "Terminus" (boundary), "Conservator Orbis" (preserver of the world) and the marvellous "Optimus Maximus", ("the biggest and the best"!)

The Hindu universal creator, Brahma, can also be attributed to Kether, although some authorities specify that "Parabrahma" is the correct form. Crowley gives this in 777 but then goes on to say, rather cynically it might be thought; "or any other whom one wishes to please"!

Bramah was born from a seed formed by the "Great Unknown" (Ain) and was also called Narayana, "dweller in the waters", a reference to his early condition as the sole created being. He is credited with the creation of the universe and its contents, including both gods and men, and therefore would seem in every way to be an admirable correspondence for the Primal Glory.

The Archangel of Kether is Metatron, "Great Angel of the Presence", "Angel of the Covenant" and "World Prince". Metatron is said to be, "Above all and infinitely superior to all other angels" and that he represents "the sum of all the angelic forces or ministering energies" (Myer *Qabbalah*), having rulership therefore over the entire Tree. He is also considered to have been the first created being and is the one referred to in Genesis as "Abraham's servant", the "eldest servant of his house, that ruled over all that he had" *(Gen 24:2)*. As the *Zohar* explains; "The oldest of his house, because he (Metatron) is the first of the creatures of (Elohim), who governs over all that belongs to Him! For the Holy, Blessed be He! has given him dominion over all His hosts".

Tradition also avers that the "flaming sword" which guarded the way of the Tree of Life in Eden, was Metatron himself; and that this Great Angel was the very being who gave to Abraham the core of that body of knowledge which came to be termed Qabalah.

Metatron has also been identified with the Biblical Enoch; with the active principle of the Shekinah (the feminine form of the Holy Spirit); with that river which went out of Eden to water the Garden, and with the ultimate leadership of the exiled children of Israel in the desert.

We shall be looking further at the Great Angel in the chapter dealing with Malkuth as he is also the traditional Archangel of the final Sephirah. In this fact alone can be seen the truth of the axiom that "Kether is in Malkuth and Malkuth is in Kether, though after a different fashion".

The order of angels assigned to Kether are the *Chayoth-ha-Qadesh*, the "Holy Living Creatures" of the Merkabah, or Chariot Throne. These are the Bull, the Lion, the Eagle, and the Man, each symbolising one of the fixed elemental signs of the Zodiac.

The Bull represents the element of Earth as expressed through the sign Taurus; the Lion is the symbol of the sign Leo, and represents the element of Fire; the Eagle is symbolic of the higher aspect of Scorpio and is of the nature of Water; and finally the Man, corresponding with the Air sign, Aquarius. These are the Kerubim, or Cherubs, of the Prophet Ezekiel and of the vision of St.John. They are also the heraldic emblems of the four Evangelists, which in the order given above are; Luke, Mark, John, and Matthew.

It should perhaps be pointed out that, in terms of the Christian belief system, Kether, as the focus of the Supernal Triad, does not correspond with the Evangelists themselves but with the Trinity.

As the Holy Living Creatures each represent the root of one of the four elements a vast range of potential correspondences is opened up. One such classification, among many, is found in Jungian psychology, where the four functions of Sensation, Feeling, Intuition, and Intellect, can readily be applied to the *Chayoth-ha-Qadesh*, again in the same order as above.

Kether's symbols are in their own way as descriptive of the sphere as its titles. We have already seen that the Swastika suggests in a graphic form the principle of the First Swirlings, but care must be taken to differentiate between the symbol as a glyph representing the Primum Mobile, and its more usual application as a solar cross, in which case it is properly assigned to Tiphareth.

Again, the "point" and the "point within the circle" are equally both visual symbols and titles of Kether. They illustrate both its emergence from the void and its situation as an unlocated focus within a sphere of infinite size.

The *Sepher Yetzirah's* supplementary text describes Kether as being the "Highest Crown", so it should come as no surprise to discover that the crown is indeed one of its major symbols. In some of the older representations of the OTz ChIIM, Kether is drawn surmounted, or even replaced, by a stylised crown. In point of fact the Sephiroth as a group are often called "crowns" in older works, but Kether is clearly the "Most Exalted Crown", and is placed above all others.

The crown of Kether should on no account be confused with that applied to Chokmah, "The Crown of Creation", which refers to the second emanation's mode of action, for the Highest Crown is in every respect more splendid.

In the traditional three-fold division of man, the Supernal Triad as a whole is referred to *Neshemah*, that being the highest aspiration and the "supreme self" of the individual. *Neshemah* itself is subdivided into three categories, *Yechidah* being that which is assigned to Kether. *Yechidah* translates, very loosely, as "The Unique One", the eternal spark of divinity at the centre of every man and woman. It is often described as the "real ego" of the individual, which is somewhat misleading for regardless of what is actually meant by such an inexact term, the concept of ego as such has no place above the Abyss. Israel Regardie describes the *Yechidah* far more usefully when he says;

> "It is the quintessential point of consciousness making man identical with every other spark of divinity, and at the same time, different with reference to his individual point of view".

> (*A Garden of Pomegranates*)

When the Tree of Life is applied to the human body Kether is seen to be situated slightly above the head with the lower circumference of the sphere just touching its crown. This is also the approximate position of the chakra which corresponds to Kether, the "Thousand Petalled Lotus" of the *Sahasrara*, the final chakra in the system.

This is considered to be the most important such centre of the body, and is said to be the collecting point and reservoir of a "heavenly dew" that is drawn from the aether and transmitted down through the spinal column into the genital area.

This elixir, the "exalted tincture", which is both the ambrosia of life and the essence of mystical illumination, has parallels in a number of traditions. Techniques for its acquisition and application are part of the secret teachings of mystery schools in both east and west.

The *ros*, as it is sometimes termed in the European tradition, is referred to in both Bible and, extensively, the *Zohar*. In the Song of Songs it is mentioned thus;

> "I sleep, but my heart waketh: it is the voice of my beloved that knoweth, saying, Open to me, my sister, my love, my dove, my undefiled: for my head is filled with dew, and my locks with the drops of the night". *(5:2)*

In the Zoharic book called *"The Greater Holy Assembly"* concerning the "Dew, or Moisture of the Brain of The Ancient One", we read that;"...from that skull distilleth a dew upon Him which is external, and filleth His head daily...And from that dew which floweth down from His head, that (namely) which is external, the dead are raised up in the world to come", and further; "The dew of the lights (Sephiroth) is Thy dew"... And by that dew are nourished the holy supernal ones".

This most mysterious of substances much exercised the minds of medieval physicians and was the subject of considerable interest even into the mid eighteenth century when Emanuel Swedenborg speculated at length upon its nature. Perhaps the most accessible and practicable teachings regarding the collection and manipulation of the *ros* are to be found in the Chinese Taoist texts, where a variety of exercises are described to this end. The meditation techniques of the Shaolin Brocades may be found especially useful in this regard.

The Spiritual Experience or Magickal Power of Kether is "Union with God", whilst its Virtue is "Completion of the Great Work, the Attainment" which is at one and the same time both obvious in its meaning and utterly inconceivable in its effect.

The magickal grade of one who has attained, in fullness, to the "Most High", is Ipsissimus 10°= 1□. The Ipsissimus is effectively a god, whose condition and modality is "beyond all comprehension of those of lower degrees". (*"One Star in Sight"*) This being so, it is prudent to remember that the grade sign of an Ipsissimus is that of Harpocrates, the sign of silence, and to respect that exalted state by saying no more.

There is not, nor can there be, any Vice associated with Kether, except in so far as the corresponding order of Qliphoth can be said to represent a negative effect resulting from a contradiction of the sphere's essential qualities.

The order of Qliphoth assigned to Kether is the *Thaumiel*, The "Contending Heads" or the "Twin Heads of God", which by their divisive duality deny the Primal Glory's fundamental characteristic, that of perfectly balanced unity.

Kether's magickal weapons are sometimes given as being two in number - the Crown and the Lamp. Strictly speaking only the crown is properly a weapon of the sphere. The lamp is an additional symbol

67

representing the divine Light to which the magician aspires, and which both illuminates his work and acts as a beacon to guide him to his goal.

The crown of Kether symbolises the Supreme Divinity towards which the Great Work is directed, and represents the fully activated *Sahasrara* chakra, making the adept heir to the "gift of dew".

The magickal image is of an "Ancient bearded king seen in profile", emphasising the fact that Kether can never be fully revealed.

Another possible image for Kether is a huge bearded head rising up out of the waters, reflected down onto the calm sea. Here we have the "Vast Countenance" appearing out of the Unmanifest, and transmitting its eidolon down through creation.

The colours of Kether in the four worlds are, as one might expect, variations on the theme of "white brilliance". This is the pure white light that contains all the other colours of the spectrum. As with all else connected with this Sephirah, the conception is that all potentialities are present but as yet undifferentiated. This light is not, however, an optical phenomenon but the Light of the Spirit.

The Atziluthic colour is Brilliance itself, the colour that is not a colour but a spiritual force of light, uncorrupted and utterly pure. The colour of both the Briatic and Yetziretic worlds is "pure white brilliance", as through these two worlds of creation and formation the ray of brilliance begins to become more tangible with the addition of the "pure white".

The light from Kether only starts to resonate on an optical level in Assiah, the world of material form, where it is now a white flecked with gold, the "physical perfection of Kether made manifest," tinged perhaps by the mediating influence of Tiphareth.

There can be no doubt about the correct "animal" correspondence for Kether, which is a "god", but Crowley also gives the Hawk and the Swan as being appropriate for the sphere. The Hawk because its high vantage point, motionless in the uplifting thermal current, enables it to look down and observe all creation spread out below; the Swan because it is said to symbolise the divine word AUM.

The plant attributed to Kether is the "Almond in flower" which represents the budding rod of Aaron and is a popular wood for certain types of magickal wand.

The vegetable drug (if indeed such it be) is the "Elixir Vitae"; to quote Crowley "the attribution to Kether is due to its omniform virtue". (*Liber 777*) This elixir may be identified with the above mentioned "ros" and many another thing beside, from mothers milk to mythological ambrosia.

The perfume is Ambergris, which in itself is all but odourless but has the unusual power (unfortunately for the Sperm Whale) of intensifying the scent of any other perfume mixed with it, for this reason it is often used by perfumeries as a base.

The diamond is Kether's precious stone, as it is formed from pure carbon, the basic material of life on earth, raised under tremendous heat and pressure to the highest degree of hardness and clarity.

The word "diamond" comes from the Greek *Adamas* which means "invincible" and it is the gemstone attributed to Libra, the sign of balance and equilibrium.

A diamond, when well cut, also has an unequalled ability to both reflect and refract light, making it an ideal stone to represent the sphere of "Lux Simplicissima".

As Kether is the fount and root of the elemental powers it has assigned to it the four aces of the Tarot, which are themselves the root of the powers of the four elements;

"not the elements themselves, but the seeds of those elements"

(*Book of Thoth*).

6

Chokmah

"The Second Path is that of the Illuminating Intelligence: it is the Crown of Creation, the Splendour of the Unity, equalling it, and is exalted above every head, and named by the Qabalists the Second Glory".   *(The Yetziratic Text)*

Chokmah is the second of the three Supernals, and is the positive potency in the Triad of *Olam-ha-Mevshekal*, situated at the head of the Pillar of Mercy, the "masculine" column of the Tree.

From the "smooth point" of Kether has extended a line, the first movement of the Primal Glory's spiritual force outwards on its journey into eventual manifestation.

"As the point extends and thickens into a line, the line into a plane, and the plane into the expanded body, so God's manifestation unfolds itself". (Issac Ibn Latif, 1220-1290 AD)

With the establishment of Chokmah comes the first differentiation of the androgynous force of Kether. It is the positive, masculine power that stimulates the universe and directs the forces of the Ain, as first expressed in Kether, down through the Tree, and may be termed the "energising principle" behind creation.

Chokmah is a Sephirah of force, as is Kether, but now that force becomes more specialised and directed. The Unity has allowed Itself to become a duality, the second phase of the unfolding of the Most High.

Chokmah is negative to the first emanation, from whence it receives its impetus, but is positive to the opposite sphere of Binah, at the head of the Pillar of Severity, and to Chesed, the central Sephirah of the Pillar of Mercy.

"Chokmah" means Wisdom, and it is by this English title that the second Supernal Sephiroth is most commonly known.

In Chokmah is found the creative word of God, that which was in the beginning, the word that was with God, and the word that was God. One Talmudic exposition of the first line of the book of Genesis suggests that the word *Bereshith,* usually considered to mean "In the Beginning", should properly be translated as "By (or In) the Principle", which is taken to refer to Chokmah.

The opening verse would then read "By the Principle (of Chokmah) Elohim (God) created the height and the depth of the universe", or, more simply; "Through Wisdom the universe was emanated".

The *Zohar* tells us that "Wisdom generates all Things", and on several occasions describes Wisdom as the "Divine Word", clearly identifying it with the creative power loosed upon the universe by the initiating utterance of God.

Chokmah, being the second emanation, is also called by Qabalists "the First Born of Elohim", and the "Only Begotten Son", as it alone proceeds directly from the primal essence of Kether.

The god-names assigned to the "Second Glory" are "Yah", and its expanded form of Yahweh, which is usually transliterated as IHVH but may also be found as YHVH, or even JHVH.

"Yah" carries the meaning "Father" and is comprised of two Hebrew letters, *Yod* and *Heh*. In spite of the obvious masculine potency of the sphere, and of the image of the father implied by "Yah", within this name both polarities are combined, *Yod* representing the fertilising principle of fatherhood, and *Heh* the receptive principle of the mother. The dynamic energies of Chokmah contains the seeds of their incorporation in Binah even as they rush forth from the second sphere, for it is axiomatic that above the Abyss every idea contains its own opposite.

IHVH is the second and most common name applied to Chokmah. Often referred to as "Tetragrammaton", this four-lettered "ineffable name" was considered so holy by orthodox Jews that it was never pronounced in full for fear of violating the third commandment, save once a year by the High Priest in the "Holy of Holies" in the Temple at Jerusalem. There is also a tradition which asserts that the correct pronunciation of this name would result in the total destruction of the universe! There is a not dissimilar taboo regarding the Hindu god

71

Shiva, constant repetition of whose name is also looked upon with some disquiet.

An orthodox Jew, for reasons of piety rather than fear, would have to substitute another name for IHVH, usually Adonai (Lord), when reading aloud, and employ certain devices to overcome the problem of actually writing the "Mighty Name". There are two main conventions which allow the name to be indicated in texts; the first is to substitute it with its Aramaic form, Yeya; and the second, which is perhaps more common, is to place under it the vowel-points from "Adonai", thus producing a word which is impossible to pronounce.

This cannot be regarded as mere superstition, nor even as a simple matter of proper respect, for the names of God are potent magickal "words of power" which have been vitalised by the veneration of countless generations and it pays therefore to treat them with a degree of caution.

IHVH is generally accepted as meaning "To Be". In all of the twelve possible permutations of spelling, known as the "Twelve Banners of the Mighty Name", this meaning remains constant. Each of these "Twelve Banners" demonstrates a modality of the One God in his variety, and can be related to, amongst many other correspondences, the twelve tribes of Israel, and the signs of the Zodiac; the last being of particular importance as it is the mundane chakra of the sphere of Chokmah itself.

IHVH is composed of the Hebrew letters; Yod, signifying the "means of action" and representing the father, self-begotten and eternal; Heh, the principle of receptivity referred to the mother; Vau the son, both as heir and ultimately redeemer; and Heh final, representing the daughter, who is both future bride and mother. The pattern of relationships within the name may be illustrated thus: the son is the fruit of the union of the father and the mother, he in turn is mysteriously both brother and father to the daughter, whom he redeems by making her his bride and placing her upon the mother's throne, the daughter, now in the place of the mother, becomes that mother by her union with the father, and so the cycle repeats.

We can see that implicit in the Tetragrammaton is a formula which is especially apt for Chokmah, given that its mundane chakra expresses the cyclic nature of creation within the continuous wheel of the Zodiac.

The letters may also be taken to correspond with the four elements

72

and therefore, by extension, to a whole range of occult references,including of course the Tarot. The elemental attributions are:.... Fire, *Yod*; Water, *Heh*; Air, *Vau*; and Earth, *Heh final*.

The accuracy of these correspondences will become clearer as we progress down through the Tree. In the Tarot deck the four suites may be assigned thus: Wands, to *Yod*; Cups, to *Heh*; Swords, to *Vau*, and the Disks to *Heh final*.

The letters of the Tetragrammaton can be applied to the Holy Tree in a number of instructive ways. The most common method is to assign one to each of the four worlds: *Yod* to Atziluth; *Heh* to Briah; *Vau* to Yetzirah; and *Heh final* to Assiah.

Another common method is to apply the letters to certain Sephiroth, a traditional arrangement being as follows: *Yod* to Chokmah; *Heh* to Binah; *Vau* to Tiphareth; and *Heh final* to Malkuth.

Chokmah's many titles include, "The Power of Yetzirah", and "The Yod of Tetragrammaton". The second of these auxiliary titles has already been touched on in connection with the mighty name, IHVH.

The letter *Yod*, as we have seen, represents the creative male element, and is itself rather reminiscent of the shape of the spermatozoon, in fact Crowley describes it as being, "the polite equivalent" of the male seed which is the "true glyph".

Its traditional association is with the hand, and can here be visualised as the "hand of God" (recalling the manner in which Atum brought forth the worlds) reaching out to set the wheel of the Zodiac in motion. The letter suggests the vigorous out-rushing of primal energies, the very image which characterises the sphere.

"The Power of Yetzirah" refers to that aspect of Chokmah which is identified with the dynamic principle of the Creative Will, the energising factor in the eventual establishment of the world of formation.

Two other titles are commonly given to Chokmah, although these two are in essence, one. Ab and Abba, as with Yah and Yahweh, both have the meaning of "father". They are each composed of the first two letters of the Hebrew alphabet, *Aleph* and *Beth*. In both cases the two letters signify the development of a second principle, symbolised by *Beth*, arising out of the primary impulse, symbolised by the initial *Aleph*. In the case of Abba however, the expansion into four letters, as a mirror image of the original name, suggests a continuously reflecting cycle as the first creation views itself.

Ab, like Yah and Tetragrammaton, also posits the existence of another polarity for *Beth* means "the house" and is essentially feminine in character, foreshadowing the balance which is to stabilise the Supernal Triad with the development of the third Sephirah.

Chokmah remains however the "Supernal Father" as this is the first sphere in which that principle is differentiated for in Kether it exists only in embryo.

The mundane chakra of Chokmah is the "Sphere of the Zodiac" which is termed in Hebrew, *Mazloth*. The literal meaning of "Zodiac" is a "circle of animals". It is defined as a band around the heavens extending eight to nine degrees north or south of the ecliptic, the line traced by the apparent yearly path of the sun.

Within this band is found the orbits of all the planets of the solar system, with the exception of Pluto, the most distant and most recently discovered of the major planetary bodies. The Zodiac itself is divided into twelve segments of thirty degrees of longitude each.

When any planet, including the Sun, is said to be in a particular sign it is a reference to its relative position within this great wheel, each division being one of the twelve signs of the traditional Zodiac, from Aries through to Pisces.

The twelve signs are themselves divided into "triplicities and "quadruplicities". In the first case the circle is divided by three to produce four groups of three signs each; each of these groups corresponding to one of the four elements, and therefore to the letters of Chokmah's god-name. In the case of the quadruplicities, the division is by four, producing three groups of four signs, each representing a "quality" or modality of action; these being termed, "Cardinal", Fixed" and "Mutable".

Within the twelve-fold cycle of the zodiacal signs is traced a glyph of the successive stages of evolutionary development, which may be applied on a personal, historical, or cosmic level.

The planets themselves represent specific principles, modified by their angular relationship to other planets and by the sign currently occupied. The planetary influences as individualised forces only begin to manifest themselves in Binah, the third Sephirah.

Even after such a brief description it is clear that Mazloth is a very complex sphere indeed. Not only does it contain all of the planetary forces which will manifest during later stages of the unfolding of the

Tree, it contains them in all their possible modes of expression and interaction. Yet even this complexity does not encompass the breadth of the sphere because Mazloth is not merely the physical wheel of the Zodiac, but is also the very evolutionary process that the wheel is said to symbolise.

There have been many attempts to assign a planetary body to Chokmah in place of its traditional correspondence. Crowley for instance suggested Neptune as a possibility as at the time of his writing it marked the outer boundary of the solar system. He has also advanced Uranus as an alternative, as it represents the "will of the magician".

Kenneth Grant agrees with Crowley's attribution of Neptune but places Uranus in Daath and Pluto in Kether.

Both Neptune and Uranus have much to commend them, and as yet do not have entirely satisfactory correspondences on the Tree, but they are in fact already represented in the sphere of Chokmah by virtue of their inclusion within the Zodiac. The same cannot be said for Pluto, the outermost of the trans-Saturnine planets, which is outside the band of the Zodiac as strictly measured, and may prove to correlate to the "Invisible Sephirah" Daath, currently associated with Sirius.

The gods appropriate to the sphere of Chokmah fall into three distinct categories, Father gods, Messenger gods, and those who represent "divine wisdom".

The "Father gods" include those of fertility, viewed in their highest aspect, some of whom may not be considered as ideal "father figures" themselves but are well qualified by virtue of their undeniable generative powers.

In the first group the Christian conception of "God the Father" is an obvious correspondence, as is the paternal deity of any other religion.

The Egyptian creative deity Amun, the "King of the Gods", is assigned to the second emanation in his original form of ithyphallic fertility god and also in his later conceptions as "the hidden one" and "he who abides in all things". Amun developed from a Thebean air god of purely local importance to eventual identification with the Sun god Ra, in which aspect he was worshipped as Amun-Ra. About the time of the eighteenth dynasty he became generally accepted as the national god of Egypt but during the reign of Akhenaten his worship, like that of the other great gods, was effectively banned and was only resumed on the monarch's death. Akhenaten's successor was the boy king Tut-ankh-aten, who signaled to the world that the old gods were once again in the ascendant by changing his name to Tut-ankh-amun.

Amun eventually became widely adopted throughout the ancient world - to the extent that even Alexander the Great thought it politic to assume the title, "Son of Amun".

The Roman god Janus is triply qualified to represent Chokmah. He was the "god of beginnings", after whom the initial month of the year is named, and to whom is the first day of every month held sacred. He was also "Janus Pater", creator and supreme father of the Roman pantheon, and considered by his more devout worshippers superior to Jupiter himself. As "the god with two faces" he was held to represent the dyad, his twin aspect looking both up into the Supernal realm and down into the microprosopos below the Abyss.

For the same reason he is also assigned to the "invisible" Sephirah of Daath, which bridges the great gulf.

All the priapic gods, once again when viewed in their highest aspects, may be assigned to Chokmah. Although many of them will be listed as correspondences for other Sephiroth, they all have their roots in the archetypally masculine second Sephirah. Included amongst this category is of course Priapus himself, the Hellespont fertility god from whom this group takes its generic name.

Virtually any of the multitude of male fertility gods can be included here as expressing the masculine generative drive; one such example from many being "the great god" Pan. He was originally a god of herds and flocks, although due to his rutting behaviour he soon came to be recognised as the embodiment of male sexuality.

It is Pan's libidinous aspect that commends him to Chokmah, and it is important that a distinction is made between Pan as a god of fertility and fecundity, and Pan in the fullest sense of the word which means "All". Crowley with some justification assigns him to the Ain, as he both represents the All and is deemed capable of destroying all positive manifestation.

Certain of the "messenger gods", such as Hermes and his Roman equivalent Mercury, although obviously applicable to Chokmah, may be jointly assigned to Hod, the eighth Sephirah, and will be considered under that heading.

There are also several female deities which may legitimately be referred to Chokmah, in spite of the sphere's powerful masculinity.It must be understood that in this case the attributions are based on modalities rather than primary sexual characteristics.

In other words it is action and not gender which determines their inclusion. One such female attribution is Iris, Greek "goddess of the rainbow". Iris was the personal messenger of Zeus, the founder of the Olympian dynasty, and was responsible for the delivery of his missives to both gods and men. She was winged and carried a caduceus wand, more often associated with Hermes, when about her official business and therefore has an equal claim on the sphere of Hod.

As we know, the Sephiroth were emanated sequentially and not simultaneously, so that each Sephirah contains in embryonic form the pattern of the subsequent emanation. Therefore, although Chokmah is the quintessential masculine sphere, it nevertheless has imprinted upon it the "information" that creates the female potency of Binah.

It should not, therefore, come as a surprise to discover that some mystic sects have regarded Chokmah as the seat of the "starry wisdom" they term "Sophia" which is feminine in essence.

Sophia (or Sophia-Prunikos) herself was the mother of Ialdabaoth who was held by the Gnostics to be the creator of the sensible (and therefore inferior) world. They also claimed that Ialdabaoth could be identified with the God of the Old Testament, IHVH, the name of the One God which corresponds to Chokmah.

The goddess Athene is perhaps the best classical representation of the wisdom aspect of Chokmah. She was born fully armed from the fore-head of her father Zeus, presenting thereby a neat and apt image of the emanation of the second Sephirah from the "White Head" of Kether. Although a goddess skilled in the arts of war, it is as a teacher of men and personification of the spirit of wisdom that she is best known and which most immediately identifies her with Chokmah.

Chokmah's archangel is Ratziel, "The Herald of the Deity", an elevated form of divine messenger. It was Ratziel who befriended Adam on the latter's expulsion from the garden of Eden and who is said to have given him a great book engraved on sheets of sapphire, containing much wisdom and guidance for *the man of dust's* enlightenment during his period of exile. Ratziel is an angel particularly associated with the stars and solar bodies, as befits one whose natural home is in Chokmah, the mundane chakra of which provides the raw material and basic data for the art of astrology.

The order of angels in the sphere of Chokmah are the Auphanim, or "Wheels", a word derived from the root *AVPh* which means "to encircle". Although at this high level of the Tree there is little concept of form, for the first formal intimation that energy may exist other than in its free state does not appear until the establishment of Binah, Chokmah's host seems to pre-figure the processes which occur in the third Supernal.

The containment and interlocking of energy patterns implicit in the idea of "encirclement" is further developed in Binah, albeit on a very abstract level, but the presence of the Auphanim seem to suggest that the concept is already emerging in Chokmah.

The transcendental morality of the sphere is "Devotion", this virtue being less of the Sephirah itself than a requirement for its attainment. There is no vice associated with Chokmah, although the order of Qliphoth, the *Ghagiel* or "Hinderers", might be considered to represent one, which whilst no part of the Sephirah itself, is of a nature antipathetic to the sphere's proper functioning.

As the translation from the Hebrew suggests, the Hinderers obstruct the free-flowing energies of Chokmah from their full expression, although it could be argued that they also provide some necessary "friction" against which the out-rushing forces may gain a useful purchase.

In the system of the three-fold division of man we have seen that the Supernal Triad as a whole is referred to *Neshemah*.

The second of the three subdivisions of *Neshamah, Chiyah*, is assigned to Chokmah. *Chiyah* represents the creative impulse and the will of the individual, and is usually related to the *Ajna* Chakra.

This chakra is situated near the pineal gland, an organ which is extremely active in youth, when it secretes a hormone known as *melatonin* which determines the onset of sexual maturation, but is of less obvious significance in later life. Its traditional association with the "third eye" is given some credence by the fact that it does seem to contain some light-sensitive neurones and in at least one species of lizard the equivalent organ is an obvious evolutionary relic of a fully functional third eye.

78

Galen (AD 129-99), Marcus Aurelius's personal physician, and Herophilus, an influential Greek anatomist of the third century BC, both considered the pineal gland to be responsible for regulating the thoughts, while René Descartes (d.1650) suggested that it was in fact the natural abode of the spirit and the organ through which was expressed the will of the divine, a function which could well be equated with the *Chiyah*.

The chakra may be visualised as a two petalled lotus of a white "lightning like" hue, perhaps indicative of the light of Kether as it first impinges on the Briatic world. Shyam Sundar Goswami says of the *Ajna* centre:...

"It is clear that the seat of mind is in the Ajna system, and that its aspect as sense-mind is in Ajna proper. Other aspects of the mind are above it". (*Laya Yoga*).

Appropriate symbols for Chokmah include all those that represent the erect phallus, and the phallus itself as the supreme symbol of male potency. Single standing stones, towers, and of course, church steeples, are all examples of what might be termed "architectural lingams". The letter *Yod*, is also sometimes used as a symbol for the sphere, for the reasons given earlier; as is the "straight line", which combines the concept of the first movement outwards from Kether with a simple pictorial glyph, again suggesting the phallus.

"The Inner Robe of Glory" is found both as a symbol and a title, occasionally even as a weapon. The inner robe may be taken to signify the "true self" of the magician, in the same manner that the "Outer Robe of Concealment" referred to Binah has as one of its meanings the physical body.

The magickal weapons are two in number, the one being the symbol of the other. The wand which corresponds with Chokmah is the phallic wand, which represents the will of the adept, and therefore symbolises the true weapon of the path which is, as should by now be obvious, the erect phallus.

There are many forms of wand used in magickal ritual work, each one of which symbolises a discreet facet of the creative impulse, but all have their roots in the wand of Chokmah. Whereas it is permissible to list the phallic wand as a weapon of the second Sephirah if one bears in mind that it is but an analogue of the primary weapon, it is also one of the weapons of the fourth Sephirah, Chesed, where as a reflection of the Supernal lingam it is possibly more appropriately placed.

Chokmah's magickal power or spiritual experience, is the "Vision of God Face to Face". Clearly such an experience would prove shattering to the unprepared soul, for as it is written:....

"And he said, Thou canst not see my face: for there shall no man see me and live." *(Ex.33:20)*

The important point to note here is the use of the term "no man", for therein lies a clue to its hidden meaning. "No man", or Nemo, is a title of the Magister Templi, the one who is "Not"; he who has crossed the Abyss and attained to Binah whose magickal grade it is. Such a one, may, in due course, approach the sphere of Chokmah and on assuming its grade look upon the face of God, as did Jacob upon the face of His angel, "with his life yet preserved".

The magickal grade of Chokmah is that of Magus $9° = 2^\Box$.

The Magus both attains to Wisdom (the Sephirah and the state), and utters his creative word. Although there may at any given time, be a number of adepts who rightfully lay claim to this exalted grade only one may utter the Magickal Word which ushers in a new aeon and marks the end of the old. By this action is proclaimed a new formula appropriate for the dawning age, and the planet thereby transformed and re-invigorated.

An "aeon" is a rather vague measurement of time, being (very) approximately two thousand years long. It represents one "month" of what astrologers term a "Great Year"; the time it takes for the Earth's poles to complete a circle around the pole of the ecliptic. It takes around 25,800 Earth years for the process to complete and for Earth's poles to return to a repeat alignment with any given constellation.

The end of an aeon is termed by occultists an "Equinox of the Gods". Thelemites believe that the last such great equinox was heralded in Cairo, in April of 1904, and that we are privileged to be living through the birth-pangs of a new era for man-kind. 1904 is considered to have signalled the end of the aeon of Osiris and the sacrificed gods, and marks the beginning of the aeon of Horus, "The Crowned and Conquering Child". This being accepted, he who received the new "word" and its secret formula, in the form of the *Book of the Law*, must be considered the Prime Magus of this aeon. This adept, called in that same revealed document, "the scribe Ankh-af-na-khonsu" and the "chosen priest &

apostle of infinite space ...the prince-priest the Beast", is known in the world of men as Aleister Crowley.

Those others who attain to the grade of Magus must work within the new current as expressed in the word of the aeon and fully identify themselves with it, for it is not fitting nor indeed is it possible for such as they to be in conflict with the work of the supreme Magus who has uttered that word.

A Magus is master of magick in all its forms, is "entirely free from internal division or external opposition", (*One Star in Sight*) and is necessarily master of the law of change.

It is worth repeating that the magickal grades given under the Sephiroth are not always attained fully or in strict sequence by every adept, nor may the individual magician be necessarily capable of manifesting the nature and function of his grade on every plane.

The usual magickal image of Chokmah is a strong male figure of kingly bearing, with a full well formed beard, suggesting both his royal provenance and his virility. He may be visualised simply as a head seen full face or as a complete male figure, the essence of the image being strength, nobility and male potency.

The colours in the four worlds are: in Atziluth, a pure soft blue which represents the sky and which is deep enough to also suggest the Mazloth itself. In Briah the colour shades to grey, the intermediate stage in the movement from white to black, soft and slightly translucent. The pearl grey of Yetzirah is a fusion of the preceeding two colours; whilst the white flecked with the primary colours of red, blue, and yellow seen in Assiah gives a clear image of the flashing primal creative power of Chokmah as it impacts the material world.

The animal associated with the second emanation, and to a certain extent an additional symbol for it, is, naturally enough, the male of any species, but most especially the human male as only we are the exact microcosms of the Holy Tree. The perfume therefore is musk, or the fragrance of semen.

A possible alternative might be the sexual-attractant, Ruthvah, compounded from equal parts musk, civet, and ambergris, although this might be more appropriate for the Supernal Triad as a whole as it contains the perfumes of all three of the superior Sephiroth.

There are two precious stones assigned to Chokmah. The first, the Star Ruby, is suggestive of the essentially masculine energy of the "creator star" and has given its name to a powerful banishing ritual.

The second, the Turquoise or "Turkish Stone", is sacred to the Pueblo Indians of New Mexico for whom it symbolises courage and strength and serves as a reminder that man has a spiritual dimension as well as a physical form. It also represents the background colour of *Mazloth*, the sphere of the Zodiac, Chokmah's mundane chakra.

The "flowers of immortality", Amaranth and Mistletoe, are assigned to Chokmah for their fabled life sustaining properties.

Crowley also gives the Bo tree, under which the Buddha gained his enlightenment, as its leaves are somewhat suggestive of the phallus.

Chokmah's vegetable drug is traditionally given as Hashish, and is so assigned in 777. However Crowley also suggests, later in the same work, that "cocaine pertains to Chokmah by its direct action on the deepest nervous system".

In the Book of Thoth it is the four twos that correspond to Chokmah. These cards are the "Lords" of the pack and represent the elements in their highest aspect. The titles are as follows: the two of Wands is called the "Lord of Dominion"; the two of Cups is called the "Lord of Love"; the two of Swords is referred to as the "Lord of Peace"; and the two of Disks is known as the "Lord of Change".

7

Binah

UNDERSTANDING   THE SANCTIFYING INTELLIGENCE

"The Third Path is the Sanctifying Intelligence, and is the basis of foundation of Primordial Wisdom, which is called the Former of Faith, and its roots, Amen; and it is the parent of Faith, from whose virtues doth Faith emanate".   *(The Yetziratic Text)*

From the monadic point, dimensionless and unlocated, the second point was extended as a straight line. Now, in the third point of Binah, is found the final co-ordinate necessary to produce the simplest angular figure capable of enclosing space, the triangle.

"Thus this Sephirah completes and makes evident the Supernal Trinity", *(Gematria,* Equinox vol.1 no.5)

Binah is situated at the head of the Pillar of Severity, opposite the sphere of Chokmah, from whence it receives its impetus. As its position might indicate, here is the first of the Sephiroth of form.

The Pillar of Severity is comprised of the three "form Sephiroth", being, in sequential order, Binah, Geburah, and Hod. These are the passive, feminine, potencies that accept and structure the unrestrained energies which emanate from the "force Sephiroth" of the Pillar of Mercy. The "severity" aspect of the negative pillar lies of course in its action as the constraint and discipline of dynamic energies.

The blazing male force of Chokmah is brought to a temporary rest in Binah. It is said that; "the house that was built in Chokmah is established in Binah". As the Old Testament phrases it;

"Through wisdom (Chokmah) is an house builded; and by understanding (Binah), it is established", *(Prov: 24:3)*

As the force of Chokmah, rushing outward, implied the necessity of eventual containment, so does Binah represent that containment and the restriction of uncontrolled power. It accepts the energy of the second Sephirah and envelops it. With the establishment of Binah we now have the two potencies, male and female, positive and negative, active and passive, revealed and at work in the universe, without which no further development would be possible.

As the *Zohar* explains; "Every-Thing, that existeth, every-thing which the Ancient: Blessed be Its Name! has formed, can endure only through the male and female".

Although Binah contains within itself the concept of form, this concept is still of an archetypal nature. It is the root from which form springs but is itself intangible. All forms and all modes of manifestation, be they apparent on the physical plane, or of an emotional, intellectual, or spiritual nature, are found to have their source in Binah. The third Supernal may therefore be considered to be the reservoir of the Platonic "forms" or "ideas". For as Rabbi Abraham of Beacaire, a 12th century commentator on the *Sepher Yetzirah*, says: "Binah, in it are engraven the ways of the letters; in the original image of all details and species etc.. The (imprinted) forms of every herb, etc...and also of the minerals etc...".

Binah is the first feminine Sephirah, and is called by Qabalists the "Great Supernal Mother". As the Great Mother she contains within herself all possible forms or expressions of the feminine principle and is, as it were, the archetypal womb from which all life springs.

"Thou shalt call Binah by the name of Mother" says the *Zohar*, and the Bible adds; "Say unto wisdom (Chokmah), Thou art my sister; and call understanding (Binah) thy kinswoman".

(Proverbs 7:4)

The reference here to "wisdom" as "sister" suggests that aspect of Chokmah, which, in spite of its masculine potency, has been identified with the Sophia\Eternal Eve figure by some mystical traditions.

Binah is also referred to by Qabalists as "The Upper Shekinah". The concept of the Shekinah has been much neglected in the published works of the modern school of Qabalism, although undoubtedly it represents a major element in the more orthodox Judaic tradition.

The "Shekinah" (which may be translated as "brightness", "Bride", or "dwelling"), is essentially a form of the Holy Spirit, but one viewed as specifically feminine in nature. It is the Holy Spirit "above all" and "Stands to the other Lights of Creation like the soul to the body" but, "to the Most High like the body to the soul". *(Zohar).*

She has also, along with Chokmah, been equated with the Greek Sophia, "wisdom" viewed as feminine, hence:

"She is the tree of life to them that lay hold upon her: and happy is every one that retaineth her". *(Prov 3:18)*

In some Hebrew texts the Shekinah is described as the "Mystic Bride" and is considered to represent the Church of Israel, or even an idealised image of Israel itself, viewed as a spiritual rather than a secular state. Some early Christian thinkers developed this idea further; Issac Myer for example quotes the 14th century pseudo-Clement of Rome as stating that:...

"The male is Christ: the female, the Church". *(Qabbalah 1888)*

Other Qabalists have described the Holy Spirit as Mother and the Church (of Israel) as her daughter. She is also the "Sabbath Bride" of Jewish liturgy, to whom are addressed some of the most moving of devotional poems in sacred literature.

The Shekinah is that presence seen as a cloud of fire upon the Mercy Seat, and described in Ezekiel's vision thus:

"And I looked, and, behold, a whirlwind came out of the north, a great cloud, and a fire infolding itself, and a brightness was about it, and out of the midst thereof as the colour of amber, out of the midst of the fire". *(Ezekiel 1:4)*

And again, in verse 28 of the same chapter: "As the appearance of the bow that is in the cloud in the day of rain, so was the appearance of the brightness round about. This was the appearance of the likeness of the glory of the LORD. And when I saw it, I fell upon my face, and I heard a voice of one that spake."

Interestingly, in spite of numerous references to the Shekinah in Jewish literature, most notably in the Talmud and Midrashim, there is no absolutely no suggestion in the early works that it might represent the feminine element of the Deity. Throughout, it is regarded as the "Great Radiance" of God, the *Ruach-ha-Qadesh*, or Holy Spirit, out of which comes the divine word.

The Shekinah was thus considered an aspect of the Deity as He extends Himself to communicate with His creation, the form in which He appears to His prophets.

It is not until we enter the world of Qabalistic literature, in books such as the *Sepher Bahir*, and, particularly, the *Zohar* that we find it described in the overtly female terms of; "Bride", "Queen", "Princess", and "Matrona" or "Mother".

For the orthodox Jew the Qabalistic concept of a feminine Shekinah presents grave difficulties for it seems to undermine the very basis of his faith, which is predicated on the doctrine of the absolute indivisible unity of God.

It is all the more remarkable then that this particular aspect of Qabalah should be the one which has gained the most recognition and acceptance among the devout. It is plain that a deep-seated religious need was being addressed, and met, by this new interpretation of the scriptures, as is demonstrated by the enthusiasm with which the idea was adopted by the Jewish communities of both East and West.

Certainly no other Qabalistic concept has so caught the imagination of the Jewish congregation, unless it be the doctrine of emanation itself.

The tenth Sephirah, Malkuth, may also be found described as the Shekinah, but here the description refers to a "Lower Shekinah".

The manner in which the lower form relates to the upper might best be described as the final concretion of the Holy Spirit of Binah. She is the spirit made into flesh, the executive power of the upper mother, and the presence of the Deity in the material world.

This then is the spirit that walks abroad on the earth, God's ambassador to His people. She is at one and the same time the blissful Bride of God, and the exile in a far land; the joy of His presence, and Rachel weeping for her children.

A possible Christian interpretation of the Supernal Triad is to view Kether as the Father, Chokmah as the Son, and Binah (Shekinah) as the Holy Spirit. This scheme assumes of course that the son proceeds directly from the father without the intervening medium of the mother. In some early Qabalistic writings Binah was placed as the second Sephirah, giving a sequence of Kether, the Father; Binah, the Mother; and Chokmah, as the third Supernal, Son; in which case the Christian concept assumes a more natural form.

The God name of the sphere of Binah is IHVH Elohim, which is said to give the full name of God as if all the Supernal Sephiroth were subsumed in the third Sephirah. The name Elohim supports this view in that it is a feminine noun with an added masculine plural, thus further emphasising the combination of potencies, and incidentally reminding us once again that above the Abyss all ideas contain their own opposites.

Binah's mundane chakra is Shabatai, Saturn, the first of the planets to be so assigned. At first sight this may seem an odd attribution for the archetypal feminine Sephirah. It is however an entirely apt correspondence. Saturn, for all its mythological background, is essentially feminine in its function. Astrologically the planet represents the principle of restriction and limitation. It compresses and contains, giving structure and form where once there was only potential. The processes involved are those of contraction and encapsulation, followed by a focusing and directing of otherwise uncontrolled energies. In the same manner Binah responds to the force of the second Sephirah, accepting and containing its dynamic free-flowing energies, and conditioning them for eventual manifestation. In this sense Binah may be likened to a womb; receptive of the energetic seed, which it then contains, nurtures, and ultimately brings forth into the light of day. The Saturnine principle of restriction is necessary for the expression of the spirit on the physical plane, and is perfectly in accord with what we have already learned of the nature of the third emanation.

Saturn has traditionally been associated with death and was known, as it still is in uninitiated forms of popular astrology, as the "Greater Malefic" (Mars, also placed on the Pillar of Severity, being the lesser).

With the attribution of Saturn we find a link with Binah as the gate-way of birth, for in that capacity she is also the gate-way to death. As it is truly said, "all that liveth hath its term", it is clear that that which chooses to incarnate chooses also to experience death. In Binah the first steps are taken on the road to eventual incarnation in Malkuth, one of whose titles is indeed "The Gate of Death".

Any change of state may be viewed as a form of death, relative to the original condition. Hence, from the point of view of the free energy of Chokmah its absorption in Binah and the restriction that is thereby imposed is seen as a "dying". From the point of view of the spiritual essence of a man, incarceration in a physical vehicle, limiting, as it must, the spirit's perfect freedom of movement, can likewise be seen as a species of death. On the inevitable destruction of the physical vehicle, with its accretion of a lifetime of experience, the essence of which is not only the heritage of the spirit but its sole purpose in choosing to incarnate, that spirit is once more freed from the bonds of earth and is "re-born" on another plane.

The birth\death cycle may be likened to the cycle of the seasons, moving continuously from one condition to another in a natural rhythm. Imagine this cycle as a great revolving wheel which is bisected by a horizontal line. On either side of this line obtain conditions which are so radically different that for the most part the denizens of one half can have no knowledge of the other. As this mighty wheel turns any given point on its circumference will pass repeatedly through the two states divided by the line. The arrival of such a point in, let us say, the lower level, would be greeted as a birth, for what was not resident on that plane now becomes so. Conversely, from the point of view of the upper sector that which was once a feature of its own plane is lost to sight, and therefore would be considered as a death, and so on *ad infinitum.*

Except for a very few individuals, whose natural sensitivity or special training enables them to perceive the totality of this cycle, we can only ever be fully aware of one half of our total experience. Of course our hypothetical point on the circle cannot evolve or benefit from its experience, it is utterly unchanged by its progression from one state to another. The human soul on the other hand not only benefits from this process, it is absolutely essential for its development.

Physiologically, Saturn governs the skeletal structure and the skin, the body's support and its outer boundary. At the time Saturn was first assigned to the sphere of Binah it was literally the outer boundary of the solar system as it was the most distant planet then discovered. Here too we can see the wisdom of Qabalistic correspondences. Binah's function as both container and support of Chokmah's expansive energy precisely mirrors Saturn's role in the planetary hierarchy. The image of skin is especially apt, for Binah initiates the process by which the spirit is "enclothed" by the fleshy body of manifestation.

As all modalities of the female are present within Binah it follows that both the "light" and "dark" aspects of that principle should be suggested by the sphere's multiplicity of titles.

Two of Binah's most common names demonstrate these twin opposites very clearly. The first is AMA, "The Dark Sterile Mother", and is composed of two *Alephs* bracketing the third letter, *Mem*. The *Alephs* may be taken to refer to the primal beginnings of life, both as source and the return to source, as they occur as the first and last letters of the name. The central letter *Mem* means "water", suggesting the waters of life and form, the primal ocean from which life on earth developed and which we still carry in our bodies. As yet, however, the waters indicated here are undisturbed by the impact of the creative will, symbolised by the letter *Yod*, the spermatozoon of Chokmah; they are barren and unfertilised.

AIMA, "The Bright Fertile Mother", with the addition of that *Yod*, now contains the seed that will bring forth its fruitfulness. The waters of creation are now alive with that creation, the amniotic fluid which will sustain, and in full term, allow for the birth of new life.

The vast oceans of the Earth's first nursery are again suggested by the title of "Marah, the Great Sea". The word for sea in many Indo-European tongues is of a similar sound and spelling to "Marah", suggesting a common etymology, and it will not escape notice that personal names such as Mary, which derive from the same roots occur frequently in Binah's correspondences. Indeed one of the titles of the mother of Jesus, is "Maria Stella Maris", Mary, Star of the Sea.

Another of Binah's many titles is that of "Khorsia the Throne". The throne is that seat of power which both supports the royal personage and elevates her above the level of the multitude. It is has been accurately described as a "thrust-block", against which the unrestrained energies of Chokmah may be propelled into eventual manifestation.

Binah is the very throne upon which are raised the negative potencies of the Tree, and is also the support of the Supernal Triad itself, "the basis of foundation of Primordial Wisdom". (*Sepher Yetzirah*).

All goddesses, and especially those associated with motherhood, may, in their highest aspects, be assigned to Binah. However there are specialised versions of the Goddess who, whilst having their roots in the third Sephirah, are more appropriately referred to other Sephiroth. These goddesses are to be viewed as lower analogues of the Supernal Mother, even as she is a lower analogue of Nuit, "Infinite Space, and the Infinite Stars thereof", who may be equated with the Ain.

As might be expected, the complementary opposites of AMA and

AIMA are reflected in the goddesses of the sphere, who represent both the creative and destructive sides of womanhood.

Shakti, the embracing, dynamic, and uniting power of the Goddess in the Hindu pantheon, is often attributed to Binah, although there is a good case for considering her as an Indian equivalent of Nuit, and therefore properly to be assigned to the Ain.

The goddess Kali represents, superficially at least, the awesome and destructive opposite to Shakti. Garlanded about with skulls, dancing on a prone male body, her tongue writhing in obscene ecstasy, she may be thought a perfect example of the "darker" side of Binah. But Kali is more than just a destructive, malevolent force for she is equally the "Ultimate Initiatrix" into the mysteries; liberator, protector of her servants, and goddess of transcendence through the power of sex.

Also from the Hindu pantheon, Parvati, gentle, benevolent consort of Shiva and personification of sensual pleasure might be considered to correspond with the "light" side of the sphere.

It must be repeated that terms such as "light" and "dark" as used in the context of this work carry no moral implication, any more than do the use of such terms as "positive" and "negative", "mercy" and "severity" when applied to the pillars of the Tree.

These descriptions are entirely neutral and merely express differing modes of operation, each essential to the others existence and are used rather in the manner in which an electrical engineer might refer to the polarities within a circuit....

"Let there be no difference made among you between any one thing & any other thing; for thereby there cometh hurt", (*AL.1:22*)

Another goddess very appropriate for the sphere of Binah is Isis, sister-consort to Osiris and mother of Horus, whom the Egyptians called the "Perfection of Motherhood", and whose name not only translates as "Throne", a title of Binah, but is a *notariqon* of the phrase, Infinite Stars - Infinite Space, relating her back to the Egyptian conception of the Ain, symbolised by Nuit.

Isis must be considered as the personification of the light side of Binah whilst her sister Nephythys (again in her highest aspect only) corresponds to its darker aspect.

Nephythys was barren to her brother-husband Set but became pregnant after the seduction of her sister's husband and gave birth to

Anubis, whom it must be said she treated very badly indeed! Although she represents the darker side of womanhood she and her sister Isis are joint protectresses of the dead and are often pictured with their winged arms above the corpse.

In the Christian tradition, the Virgin Mary, as mother of Jesus, could be considered the light aspect of motherhood, but as the Mater Dolorosa, watching her first born being nailed to a cross, she suffers the full burden of motherhood.

The image of the sorrowful mother, the Mater Dolorosa, leads us immediately to the Magickal Power or Spiritual Experience of the sphere, which is the "Vision of Sorrow". As a mother may look upon a newly born infant and grieve for the pain and suffering that she knows must be part of its life experience, so Binah may look upon the first intimations of incarnation as they develop within her and grieve likewise. It is not only to the physical pain of labour that the Lord God refers when he says to Eve;....

"in sorrow thou shalt bring forth children". *(Gen 3:16),*

but also to the mother's fore-knowledge of what may await them, for the road they must travel is often hard and perilous.

However, as the *Sepher Yetzirah* reminds us, Binah is also the "Creator of Faith.....It is the parent of faith, whence faith emanates" and what greater demonstration of faith could there be than that of the mother who would bring into the world another soul? By such individual acts of heroism do we move towards our destiny.

The Archangel of Binah is Tzaphkiel, "The Contemplation of God", occasionally called "The Watcher" or "The Spy of God". It is Tzaphkiel who presides over the Akashic Records, the imprinted memory of all that occurs during periods of manifestation, every action and thought recorded for eternity. He is the very memory of God, and is sometimes referred to as "The Keeper of the Records of Evolution".

Binah's order of angels are called the Aralim, which name also means "thrones" but may also be translated as "The Strong", "The Mighty" or the "Heroic Ones". The implication of these names is that here is limitless strength and courage; a sturdy container for the vigorous energies of Chokmah and a support upon which is raised the whole edifice of the manifest world.

The order of Qliphoth is the *Satariel,* "The Hiding", which given that Binah is the first bringing forth into manifestation, albeit on a very high octave indeed, is an obvious denial of the primary characteristic of the sphere.

The symbols of the third Sephirah are essentially those of the yoni and the womb. The yoni, the female sex organ, is both the joyful receptor of the fertilising seed of the lingam and the gateway into life through birth. In the womb is developed the new life after the impact of the seed, the concealed environment within which flesh is spun round the spirit, and the ultimate symbol of Binah. The womb of every woman is an analogue of the womb of Binah, even as the womb of Binah is an analogue of that of Nuit.Any shape suggestive of the enclosure of the womb or of the receptivity of the yoni may be used as being symbolic of Binah, or to be more accurate, as symbolising the symbols of Binah. Traditional versions are the *Vesica Piscis* and the *Kteis*, both representing the primary female sexual attributes. Versions of the *Vesica Piscis*, or "fish-bladder" are to be found in the fabric and design of temples and churches the world over. The sacred geometry of many a medieval cathedral conceals a multiplicity of ovoid patterns, while Christ and the Saints are regularly seen framed in the *vesicae* of stained-glass windows.

The cup or chalice is often given as a symbol, but for our purposes we will class it as a weapon for later consideration.

For a really concentrated arrangement of Binah symbols one has to look no further than the seal of the *Ordo Templi Orientis* which contains within a *Vesica Piscis* both the descending dove of the Holy Spirit and the chalice of the Grail, the latter with a suggestion of a supine crescent moon.

Images of the sea also correspond to Binah for the reasons given earlier, and for those same reasons those creatures, sounds, smells, and colours thought most typical of the sea, may be useful auxiliary symbols in certain workings.

The "Outer Robe of Concealment", the corollary of the "Inner Robe of Glory" which pertains to Chokmah, is listed as both a symbol and as a weapon. In a sense it is both; it can be thought of as another euphemism for the vagina, or a symbol of the physical body.

The Virtue or Transcendental Morality of Binah is silence, the fourth power of the sphinx, and unfortunately the one with which many modern occultists have the greatest difficulty!

However, the silence of Binah is not only an absence of speech, blessed though such a prospect may at times appear, but also the silence of the stilled mind. Without this mental silence, respite from the chattering *Cacodaimon* - the mental static that so disturbs the tranquillity of the untrained mind - entry into higher states of consciousness becomes impossible.

All magickal systems, after their own fashion, require that as a preliminary to active magickal work the student should first practice some form of mental discipline to still the background chatter in order that the mind is made both responsive and receptive to the forces invoked.

The techniques that may be employed are many and varied, and have been brought to a high state of development in the east. Although some form of Raja yoga, following on from expertise in the asanas of Hatha yoga, is highly desirable not all students in the west are constitutionally able to master the required skills. Paradoxically, techniques from even further east, from China and Japan, have proven to be highly effective for occidental students. T'ai Chi is one such example where the dynamic, flowing rhythms of this martial arts based "dance" form seems to fit in particularly well with modern western life-styles.

The use of ritual in magick has of course as one of its main rationales the aim of suppressing all thought and mental activity that is not directed toward the operation in hand, whilst intensifying willed and directed mental energies in what is in effect a sensory overload. When every item in a temple and every word and gesture of a ritual is directed towards the one end there simply is no time for intrusive thoughts.

Avarice, the vice referred to Binah, is the first to be so assigned, as both Kether and Chokmah are considered to be beyond any such attribution due to their propinquity to the ineffable purity of the unmanifest realm. It is the only vice to have a double attribution for it is also assigned to Malkuth, the sphere in which the processes put in train in Binah are brought to their logical conclusion.

Avarice has been described as the "pathology of form", resulting as it does from an obsession with forms and therefore "things" for their own sake, rather than for their utility, intrinsic beauty, or actual value. Avarice is not only an insatiable desire to acquire, but an inability to let go of things once acquired; a condition that a Freudian psycho-analyst might diagnose as "anal retentive".

In the traditional three-fold division of the perfected man the

Supernal Triad as a whole is referred to the *Neshemah*, with each of the Supernals being equated with one of its three further sub-divisions. In this system Binah is assigned the faculty of the *Neshemah* proper which represents the highest level of the faculty of intuition, the "Understanding" of Binah's title.

It is usual to assign the *Vishuddi* chakra to Binah, although, because it is located within the spinal column at approximately the level of the larynx, a number of occultists favour attributing it to Daath.

The *Vishuddi* is visualised as a sixteen petalled lotus whose colour is of "shining smoke", and is called by yoga practitioners "The Great Purity Centre".

The Magickal Grade of the third emanation is that of Magister Templi, the Master of the Temple $8° = 3^□$. The temple referred to being Binah itself, of which all others are but reflections and necessarily crude analogues.

This grade is the first above the Abyss. Its attainment is the result of a successful crossing of that great gulf and represents a new and radically different state of consciousness.

The Magister Templi is "free from internal contradiction or external obscurity", he is a "Master of Mysticism", "Master of Samadhi", and, possessed of the power of Binah, is also "Master of the Law of Sorrow". He must work towards a perfect understanding of the universe and, as Nemo or "No-Man", tend his "garden" of disciples.

In order to attain to this exalted level, the aspirant must first free himself from the limiting tyranny of thought by balancing each and every idea with its opposite, and in so doing bring himself to the point where he prefers neither; or rather that he comes to recognise that each idea contains its own opposite.

The attainment requires that the adept effects a total destruction of his personality, which hitherto has presented a barrier to the expression of his true self. He must also have, "consecrated himself as a pure vehicle for the influence of the Order to which he aspires". (*One Star in Sight*")

Detailed descriptions of the nature and work of the magickal grades that obtain above the Abyss (insofar as they are known and can be communicated) are somewhat beyond the scope of this work. The student is advised to make a careful study of the following; "*One Star in Sight*", an account of the grades of A∴A∴; *Liber CLXV "A Master of the Temple"*, the account of Fr. Achad's work towards attainment; *Liber CCCCXVIII, "The Vision and the Voice"*; and the Holy Book *"Liber Liberi vel Lapidis Lazuli" sub figura VII.*

The ultimate Magickal Weapon of Binah is the yoni, although a cup or chalice may be also be used. The cup is the symbol of the understanding of the magician, and that which "receives the influence from the highest". Its relation to the wand of Chokmah is as the relation of the yoni to the lingam.

Care is needed that the cup of Binah, which is symbolic of the sphere's true weapon, is not confused with the elemental cup which symbolises the element of water.

Binah's Magickal Image is traditionally that of a mature woman or matron, although as the archetypal fount of the feminine principle almost any female image would suffice. As always it is important to be aware of the possibility of confusion with the magickal images of other Sephiroth, and care should be taken to build up these images in such a way that they are consistent and specific.

The supreme female deity of whichever tradition the aspirant feels most in sympathy with; Mary, Mother of Christ; Isis, Mother of Horus, or many another, would provide a very potent working image. However if using such highly charged figures as the great goddesses it must be made clear at the outset that they are being considered as representative of the sphere of Binah as a means of developing some comprehension of its nature and are not being themselves invoked.

Binah's colour in the Atziluthic world is a rich crimson, suggesting the blood of the goddess, and the blood also of the aspirant to whom it is said; "Thou shalt drain out thy blood that is thy life into the golden cup of her fornication". (*Liber Cheth vel Vallum Abiegni: verse 2*). In Briah the crimson becomes a dense black, as at this level Binah is totally absorbent, receiving all and holding all within herself; while in Yetzirah, as always, we find a combination of the first two colours, producing a dark reddish brown. In the world of actions that is Assiah the colour shades to a grey flecked with the pinkish hue of the sixth Sephirah. As Crowley puts it in his detailed explanation of the tables in *Liber 777:* "As the grey of Chokmah was perfected to the white of Kether, so the Black of Binah is perfected to the grey of Chokmah. The grey is flecked with the pink of Tiphereth. This is the dawn of the child with which she is heavy, for this is the symbol of her perfection".

There can be little doubt about the correct "animal" correspondence for Binah, which is of course, Woman.

Two perfumes are traditionally given; Myrrh which through its long association with sorrow and mourning suggests the vision of the sphere, and Civet "the uncleanly flux of a cat", the female equivalent of the perfume of Chokmah.

Binah's plant correspondences include; Cypress, traditional tree of Saturn, and white poppy flowers, whose extract is said to have the properties of inducing sleep, understanding, and, eventually, one presumes, silence!

Although the opium poppy is assigned to the sphere for the reasons given above, opium itself is the drug of the fourth Sephirah, Chesed, and should not be used in connection with Binah. The correct vegetable drug for Binah is Belladonna, whose name means "Beautiful lady" and is commonly called "Deadly Nightshade". It is slightly narcotic in its action, being used as a sleeping draught and as a means of suppressing glandular secretion. In Homoeopathic usage it is a specific for scarlet rashes which, like the drug, come under the presidency of Saturn.

The mineral drug is Silver, also the corresponding metal of the sphere, which is now almost exclusively used in a homoeopathic preparation for which it is effective against, amongst other things, dyspepsia and colic, and therefore a useful antidote to the poisonous nature of Binah's vegetable drug.

It might also be permissible to include lead here, both as the metal and as a mineral drug as it too is ruled by Saturn, although the student should not need reminding of its potentially lethal nature.

One of the symptoms of lead poisoning is a progressive deterioration of brain function not dissimilar to an early onset of the extreme old-age which Saturn in part represents.

Any plant whose shape is suggestive of the yoni can be considered to pertain to Binah, with the usual proviso that some examples may be specific to another of the thirty two paths.

A good "general purpose" plant correspondent is the Lotus, which has long been a symbol of the feminine in the East.

Binah's precious stones include that most beautiful product of the Great Sea, the pearl, whose ethereal translucence is achieved by the aggregation of a hardening secretion around an irritant seed, the perfect symbolic stone for the sphere. Another appropriate gem is the Star

Sapphire, whose colour, like Chokmah's Turquoise, is suggestive of the deep night sky and the "infinite stars thereof" and which contains three light points, immediately bringing to mind the Supernal Triad itself.

In the Book of Thoth Binah is assigned the four threes, in each of which is expressed a mode of "understanding". Crowley says of them:

"The idea has become fertilised; the triangle has been formulated. In each case, the idea is of a certain stability which can never be upset, but from which a child can issue".   *("Book of Thoth")*

Like the cards of Chokmah the four threes are also termed "Lords", they are: Wands, "The Lord of Virtue"; Cups, "The Lord of Abundance"; Swords, "The Lord of Sorrow"; and Disks, "The Lord of Work".

8

Daath

There is no text in the Sepher Yetzirah which can be referred to the pseudo-Sephirah Daath, as it is a comparatively recent concept.

The early Qabalists recognised only ten emanations of the Holy Tree. If an auxiliary sphere was postulated at all it would perhaps have been close in nature to the astrological concept of "mid-points", i.e. hypothetical sensitive foci which are presumed to be a meaningful product of the angular relationship between two planets. These points are the result of aspecting planetary forces and have no fixed independent existence. Lunar nodes, which are much used in Eastern astrology, and in assessing karmic factors in a natal chart, have a similar role, being simply the point at which the moon's orbit crosses the plane of the ecliptic.

In Hebrew "Daath" means "knowledge", although the sphere may be found in some older Qabalistic documents titled "Science".

Its position, (if indeed it could be said to have one) is conventionally drawn upon the Tree with broken lines, approximately mid-way between the first emanation, Kether, and the sixth, Tiphareth, astride the great gulf of the Abyss.

Crowley has suggested that Daath exists in another dimension to the rest of the Tree, and that it represents an extra-dimensional consciousness, being, as it were, the point of contact between the macrocosm and the microcosm, partaking of both but fixed in neither.

It stands as a bridge between the Supernal Triad and the seven Sephiroth of the "Lesser Countenance"; between the Atziluthic and Briatic worlds above, and the world of Yetzirah below.

Daath seems to operate as a focus of the power of the Supernals, and in particular of Kether; concentrating and distilling their essential energies. It may be likened to a prism (which is one of its many symbols) in that it receives the brilliant light of the Primal Glory (already polarised through Chokmah and Binah) and directs it down through the balance of the Tree. As in a prism the original unity of the input is broken down into its components and then radiated as a spectrum.

In the Practicus ritual of the Golden Dawn this concept of Daath acting as a diffracting and transmitting agent is described thus:

> "And a river, Naher, went forth from out of Eden, namely the Supernal Triad, to water the garden, namely the rest of the Sephiroth, and from thence it was divided into four heads in Daath, whence it is said "In Daath depths are broken up and the clouds drop down dew"." (see also *Proverbs 3-20*).

Daath represents both birth and death, the principles of generation and regeneration, situated as it is at the interface between two dramatically different states of being. It is the first product of the union of opposites and the conduit of Supernal power, functioning as a gateway as well as a bridge.

It may well be that, whilst it is generally true that the ten Sephiroth have an objective reality, and the twenty-two interconnecting paths represent subjective experiences, Daath is the exception to this rule, and that which is sometimes termed "Daath consciousness" is necessarily subjective.

From Daath the realm of form begins to develop below the Abyss. Up to this point the concept of form has been of an archetypal nature, emanating from Binah. As this concept impinges upon the world of formation, focused through Daath, it becomes progressively less abstract and more tangible in each of the succeeding spheres, although form, as a recognisable structure, only begins to manifest in Yesod, the ninth Sephirah, and then primarily in terms of psychic forces, before eventually in Malkuth, the tenth and final sphere, it becomes fully material and accessible to our physical senses.

A number of Qabalists, notably Issac Luria and Moses de Cordovero, write of Daath as the "Son", the product of the union of Chokmah and Binah. In this case Daath may be regarded as the letter *Vau* in the Tetragrammaton. In the MacGregor-Mathers translation

of the Zoharic *Book of Concealed Mystery* we find the following....
"Daath is the conjunction of the second and third Sephiroth, Wisdom
and Understanding, (they being) the *Yod* and the *Heh* of IHVH."

And further, from the same translator, in the book called *The
Lesser Holy Assembly*; "And when all things are comprehended they
are comprehended therein and are called by the name of Father,
Mother, and Son. And they are Chokmah, Wisdom, Father; Binah,
Understanding, Mother; and Daath, Knowledge. Since the Son as-
sumeth the symbols of his Father and of his Mother and is called
Daath, Knowledge, since he is the testament of them both".

This variant on the attribution of the letters of the ineffable name,
Tetragrammaton, differs from the more orthodox view that the *Vau*
should properly be assigned to Tiphareth as the Son.

It is unproductive to be too dogmatic about such attributions, or
indeed any other aspect of the Qabalah, as the system, within the
inherent constraints of its own logical structure, is designed for
flexibility with each possible interpretation throwing additional light
on the nature of the Tree and the relationship of its components.

Much useful insight can be gained from the various permutations
of attribution, however bizarre and unlikely some may at first appear.
The varied applications of the four-lettered name offers an excellent
example with each possibility subtly modifying and changing the
emphasis of the formula of IHVH and thereby serving to expose and
illustrate some of the less obvious dynamics within the glyph.

The Prime Deviation or "Fall" of Christian theology is said to have
taken place at the level of Daath, the transition point between the
perfected world of the Supernals (in other words, "Eden") and the
realm below the Abyss. At the point of Daath grew the Tree of the
Knowledge of Good and Evil, of which IHVH said

"Ye shall not eat of it: for in the day that thou eatest thereof thou
shalt surely die". *(Gen 2-17)*

It was here too that the Abyss formed, the dislocation of the
Neshemah, man's highest, most god-like attribute, from the rest of
his being. As the powers of the intellect, or *Ruach*, increased so also
did his knowledge, often at the expense of understanding (Binah) and
wisdom (Chokmah); but:.."Doth not wisdom cry? and understanding
put forth her voice?" *(Prov. 8:1)*

It is a function of Magick to reforge and vivify the link between spirit and matter. Man alone of all creation is "the living soul" a microcosm, complete in every detail, of the Holy Tree. In each individual the Abyss must be essayed and crossed in order that he might reclaim his birth-right "the remnant of his heritage".

Having once more attained to his original "state of grace" by his own will, he is now able to offer up the accumulated experience of countless incarnations on the lower planes, which would have been denied him had not that "fall" occurred.

In a very real sense the seductive serpent of the Garden of Eden was perfectly correct when he said unto Eve, tempted by that forbidden fruit,

"Ye shall not surely die... For God doth know that in the day you eat thereof then your eyes shall be opened and ye shall be as gods knowing good and evil." *(Gen. 3:4/5)*

And God did indeed know that such would be inevitable result of man experiencing the Tree of the Knowledge of Good and Evil, for He says

"Behold, the man is become as one of us, to know good and evil: and now, lest he put forth his hand, and take also of the tree of life, and eat, and live for ever:" *(Gen. 3:22)*.

He then expels the errant couple from the garden and sets it about with,

"Cherubims, and a flaming sword which turned every way, to keep the way of the tree of life". *(Gen. 3:24)*

Unfortunately, in the best traditions of the successful salesman, the "subtil" serpent had conveniently forgotten to mention that it was likely to be a very long day indeed before we actually became "as gods", but it nevertheless behoves us to keep trying.

It is also worth reflecting on the intriguing fact that the Hebrew words for Serpent and Messiah, *Nahash* and *Mashiah*, share a common numerological value, and therefore by the rules of Gematria are considered to have a close affinity. This shows the action of Eden's serpent in an entirely different light, and also suggests the need for a reappraisal of the mediating role of Jesus Christ in our relationship with God.

Exoteric Christianity has chosen to view the serpent as the very personification of evil, identifying it with the Devil itself and as one of the means by which God chastises his errant children.

This has not been the case in all religions however and even in the Bible there are examples of serpent symbolism which are at the very least ambivalent, as for instance when John has Jesus say;

"And as Moses lifted up the serpent in the wilderness, even so must the Son of man be lifted up".   (*John 3:14*)

In many cultures serpent symbolism suggests, not evil or subtle cunning, but enlightenment and supreme adeptship, and as such is often used to describe the powerful spiritual energies believed to dwell at the base of the spine.

This coiled force, called in the east "Kundalini", may through various techniques be aroused from its lower refuge and directed up through the channel of the spine, thus uniting the chakras and making of the adept a "god-in-becoming".

The Uraeus crown of Egypt, shaped as a rearing Cobra with an inflated hood, was a potent symbol of kingship, which in Egyptian terms also implied godship. The poised serpent worn as a headress suggests a fully opened and active *Sahasrara*, or "Thousand Petal Lotus", chakra, the most important of all the subtle plexus.

The myth of the Garden is less a simple tale of temptation and fall than an illustration of man's struggle to regain his own divinity.

It is worth noting also that Adam, the "Man of Dust", received the forbidden fruit from the hand of his espoused, Eve, first amongst women. In much the same manner the archetypal feminine sphere of Binah passes its essence on to Daath, an essence comprised of the combined Supernal energies, Inspiration, Wisdom and Understanding.

The mundane chakra of Daath is now accepted by many, although by no means all, occultists as the first magnitude binary star known to us as Sothis or Sirius, to the ancient Egyptians as Sept, and to farmers and mariners alike as the "Dog Star" - whose rising in the northern hemisphere marks the start of the "dog days".

Sirius is situated in the mouth of the "Greater Dog" (Canis Major). Its name is said to derive from "serios" which means scorching or sparkling. The Chinese sages knew it under the name of *Tseen Lang*, or the "Heavenly Wolf".

Astrologers consider Sirius to be a star of exceedingly good omen betokening fortune and beneficence. Traditionally it is described as being of the nature of a conjunction between Jupiter and Mars, (Ptolemy), or alternatively a triple conjunction between Jupiter, Mars, and the Moon (Alvidas).

The Egyptians considered Sirius to be the celestial home of the goddess Isis. It has been described in some esoteric traditions as the "secret sun", the "sun behind the sun". In a like manner Daath can be thought a similar "secret sun", the hidden sun (or "son") behind the visible orb of Tiphareth.

The god name of Daath is not given specifically, as the sphere is outside of the original conception of the Tree, but it is now generally accepted to be a conjunction of IHVH and IHVH Elohim, the god names of Chokmah and Binah respectively.

It is the four Archangels of the Cardinal Points who preside over this enigmatic sphere. These beings must be viewed in their highest aspects, and are; Raphael, "The Healing of God", who is of the element of air; Michael, "The Likeness of God", of the element of fire; Gabriel, "Man God", who is of water; and Uriel, "The Light of God" representing the element of earth.

These are the angels who are visualised in the directional quarters when performing the Lesser Banishing Ritual of the Pentagram: Raphael in the east, Michael in the south, Gabriel in the west, and Uriel in the north.

They are also the bearers of the Ark of the covenant, in which role their directions are altered somewhat, with Gabriel and Uriel exchanging places.

The order of angels is the "Shining Serpents" which are closely related to the *Seraphim*, or "Fiery Serpents" of Geburah, but operate on a much higher level both within the emanating worlds and the aspiring human consciousness.

As might be expected Daath's subsidiary titles tend to emphasise its uniqueness and intangibility. Two common ones are "The Invisible Sephirah", which is self-explanatory, and "The Mystical Sephirah", the reason for which will become clearer as we discuss the path which bisects it. Another secondary title is that of the "Upper Room" which represents the highest point of achievement prior to crossing the Abyss. In Christian symbolism the "Upper Room" can be taken to signify the room in which was held the last supper. The Upper Room is also a cube shaped figure which contains six sides, relating to the Qabalistic concept of the six dimensions of matter; above, below and the four sides.

Daath is termed "The Unrevealed Cosmic Mind", by some Qabalists, although, strictly speaking the sphere is one in which the process of revelation is already well under way.

There is no path leading directly to Daath, and in this it is unique. It does however straddle that which connects Tiphareth to Kether, and which is referred to the Hebrew letter *Gimel*. In the Tarot this path corresponds with the third trump, "The High Priestess", or to give it its full title, "The Priestess of the Silver Star".

As this is the only one of the twenty-two paths proper to have such a relationship with a Sephirah we must presume that here path and emanation function together in a particular and unique manner.

It is because of this close and unusual relationship that we are justified in not only considering Daath as a discreet Sephirah in its own right, but also as the focus of the typical energies of the *Gimel* path.

This approach has the additional advantage that any investigation of the bisecting path can only enhance our understanding of the sphere.

However it is extremely difficult to discuss the *Gimel* path in isolation for it is also the final section of a vertical triad of paths that are known as "the way of the mystic", or sometimes, rather confusingly, "the path of the mystic".

This extended "path", from Malkuth to Kether, is a direct journey up the column of equilibrium. Unlike the more circuitous travels of the magician, the mystic rises through the planes of consciousness on a vertical axis, deviating neither to one side or the other, from the material world to eventual union with his God.

The first stage of this journey is the path that links Malkuth with Yesod, referred to the letter *Tau* and corresponding with the "Universe" card. The second, designated by the letter *Samekh*, runs from Yesod to Tiphareth and corresponds with the fourteenth trump, "Art", usually titled "Temperance" in older packs.

The letter *Gimel*, applied to the third and final stage of ascent, signifies a camel, the "ship of the desert", bringing to mind an image of a long, dry, and hazardous journey across lifeless inhospitable terrain. It will be recalled that one of the "spiritual conditions" reported by St.John of the Cross, amongst those others who have recorded their travels on this path, is that of "dryness", which fits in well with *Gimel's* desert symbolism.

It is in the sphere of Daath, just prior to the great adventure of crossing the Abyss, that the full impact of that state or spiritual condition traditionally called "The Dark Night of the Soul" occurs most forcefully. It is not of course peculiar to the *Gimel* path nor indeed to Daath; similar, though less intense, conditions are to be met with on every level of the Tree, most noticeably upon those paths that lead to and from Tiphareth. The experience of the *Gimel* path is however on a much higher octave, a devastating journey for which its lower analogues can be only preparatory.

There must needs be perfect balance and perfect integration on the part of the individuals who would travel this path. They must be prepared to sacrifice all their worldly riches, their previous attainments and powers, their preferences and their prejudices if they wish to complete successfully their mission. Not for nothing is it said that it is easier for a camel (*Gimel*) to go through the eye of a needle (Daath), than for a rich man (i.e. one who is in any way encumbered) to enter the kingdom of heaven (the Supernal realm). This triple path, the way of the mystic, is also the way of the ascetic, the one whose sight is ever upwards and unfaltering regardless of the penalties that may be exacted on the material plane. Should they ever succumb to the seductive attraction of magickal power for its own sake and become thereby so enamoured that they cannot bear to lose it, then in that moment they lose all.

On this path the accumulation of magickal power is a distraction, as it is to the eastern yogi.

For magicians of course the opposite is the case. Using a different methodology to attain the common goal, magicians consider these same powers as weapons to be developed, honed, and perfected as a means to achieve what is willed. But even magicians, mighty in all the skills of their art, must abandon their hard-won powers, even as they must abandon their own self, and are in turn abandoned by their angel on venturing to cross the Abyss.

As Kether is seen to crown the Tree and all the subsequent Sephiroth that proceed from its primal root, so might Daath be seen to "crown" the microprosopos of the seven Sephiroth below the Abyss. Daath may appear as Kether itself from the limited viewpoint of the lower planes, for it is the focus of the Supernals and partakes, in part, of their nature. It is the highest level possible of strictly human consciousness, the fleeting achievement of which may leave an unprepared mind stunned and shattered.

Certainly there are many recorded cases where temporary "Daath consciousness" has resulted in the mistaken belief that the mystic or magician concerned has in fact succeeded in their ultimate aim of union with God. In such cases Daath may be elevated as a false crown to Kether's rightful place, with knowledge then becoming the final goal. A knowledge however that lacks the Understanding of Binah; the Wisdom of Chokmah; and the Inspiration of Kether, and therefore a knowledge that is both sterile and ultimately destructive.

As Daath is the product of the union of Chokmah and Binah, the positive polarity with the negative, it is the initial balance point of the Tree, in which the differentiated potencies are held in a state of equilibrium. With this balance comes the necessity that a mechanism be developed to allow for the adjustment of all that might impinge upon it, in order that such balance is maintained.

This then is the first sphere of karmic adjustment, which is as exact as it is impersonal. The individual who contacts this area of activity without first developing within themselves an equivalent degree of equilibrium and harmony will face the severest consequences. An unbalanced personality may be badly damaged by a premature Daath experience; in extreme cases it may even have the effect of destroying the physical vehicle. Less dramatically, but equally damaging in the long run, those so effected may survive physically but evince such a fanatical and obsessive attitude as to be considered functionally insane.

Of the gods and goddesses that correspond to Daath perhaps Horus in his aspect of Hoor-Paar-Kraat (Harpocrates), "Lord of Silence", "Hidden Child", and "Babe in the Egg of Blue", may be deemed the most appropriate.

Hoor-Paar-Kraat represents both the "higher-self" and the Holy Guardian Angel (not necessarily the same thing) and as such accords well with Daath as the point of contact with the god-head, a hidden and mysterious sphere.

Gods associated with the concept of justice may also be included under Daath; for instance, Maat, as the personification of truth and justice of the Egyptians. Other gods and goddesses with similar virtues may be assigned to the sphere, although as with both Maat and Hoor-Paar-Kraat they may be equally applicable to other Sephiroth. This is especially true of those deities who combine the martial and judgmental functions and who are perhaps more appropriately placed in Geburah.

The Roman, Janus, whose twin faces look both upwards to the Supernals and downwards to the microprosopos presents a good image for Daath, although one must be careful not to confuse this attribution with that of Chokmah where he is assigned in his aspect of "Janus Pater", the creator and "beginning of things".

Januarius, "The Door Keeper", is another aspect of the god appropriate for a sphere which, as it straddles the Abyss, is an interface or doorway between the Supernal Triad and the lower Sephiroth.

There is no specific magical weapon associated with Daath, unless it be knowledge itself. It is permissible however to "borrow" the weapon of the Gimel path which is the bow and arrow, for as we have seen Daath represent a concentration of that path's characteristic energies. The weapon further emphasises the vertical ascent of the mystic, the path of the arrow, and suggests a projection of the human will to the most rarefied heights.

Among the symbols appropriate to Daath is the prism, which breaks down white light into its coloured components in the same manner that Daath breaks down and transmits the light of the Supernals. The sacred mountains of any religion are also apt symbols for the sphere, being the tallest of natural structures and therefore at their peak the nearest one can physically approach a god who is assumed to dwell on high.

In many mythologies the summit of a mountain was the site of the revelation of some form of divine knowledge, the most notable example being that of Moses reception of the Decalogue on Mount Sinai. Interestingly, Sinai translates as "moon", which is both the astrological correspondence of the *Gimel* path and the Mundane Chakra of Yesod, a sphere whose position midway between Malkuth and Tiphareth mirrors Daath's location between Kether and Tiphareth.

An empty room is an excellent symbol for Daath as is, paradoxically, a complete absence of symbol! Likewise the condemned cell or the antechamber of a temple where the hood-winked candidate waits prior to entrance to the temple proper and initiation (anyone who has undergone ritual initiation will appreciate that the comparison between condemned cell and temple antechamber is far from fanciful!).

The Virtues of Daath are detachment, confidence in the future and justice. In fact, as is so often the case with the higher Sephiroth, these "virtues" are less of the sphere itself than representative of the state of preparedness necessary to achieve Daath consciousness in the first place. The Vices are, in effect, the opposite of the virtues, but here again it is unlikely that one who is "cowardly" or suffers from "apathy and inertia", and is "unjust" would come within the orbit of Daath's influence at all, for to do so would require that these vices were first annihilated.

Daath's colour in the world of Atziluth is lavender, while in Briah it becomes a silvery grey. In Yetzirah we encounter the usual admixture of colour, which in this case produces violet, and in Assiah is found a more solid form of the Briatic grey but now flecked with the yellow of Tiphareth, reflected up from below.

9

Chesed

MERCY   GEDULAH

The Fourth Path is named Measuring, Cohesive or Receptacular; and is so called because it contains all the holy powers, and from it emanate all the spiritual virtues with the most exalted essences: they emanate one from the other by the power of the primordial emanation The Highest Crown.   *(The Yetziratic Text)*

Chesed is the first Sephirah below the Abyss, the fourth in order of emanation and the central sphere of the Pillar of Mercy. From the Supernal Triad of the Macroprosopos we now move into the lower Tree, the Microprosopos or Lesser Countenance, which comprises the Sephiroth below the Abyss, excluding the pendant sphere of Malkuth.

After the stabilisation and structuring of Chokmah's free-flowing force in the sphere of Binah and its equalisation in Daath, the creative impulse is once again released into a dynamic mode. In Chesed the energies expand and move outwards on their journey down through Zeir Anpin.

In the traditional division of the Tree into triads of Sephiroth, the first or Supernal Triad is *Olam-ha-Mevshekal*, the "World of the Intellect". The second triad, which comprises Chesed, Geburah, and Tiphareth, is called *Olam-ha-Morgash*, the "Moral" or "Sensuous" world. The second triplicity, like the others, is composed of male (positive or Yang energies), female (negative or Yin energies) and a point of balance or harmony between the two.

Chesed represents the dynamic male aspect of the second triad, as might be expected from its position in the very centre of the pillar of Mercy, the active, masculine column of the Tree. It is negative to Chokmah which precedes it on the pillar of Mercy but is positive to Netzach and Geburah.

Looking at the Holy Tree we can see that the second triad is a direct reflection of the first. This being so, Chesed must be considered to be a particular reflection of the sphere of Chokmah, a lower arc of the divine wisdom expressed therein, and partaking, to a considerable degree of its paternal authority.

The fourth Sephirah functions after the manner of Chokmah, but now with an added stability introduced by the feminine influence of Binah. Although Chesed, like Chokmah, is a positive, dynamic sphere, it can be said to be more "balanced" than the second Supernal, being in receipt of the combined energies and potencies of the entire Supernal Triad, refracted through Daath.

From the worlds of Archetype and Creation, which jointly represent two stages of "potential manifestation", the progression is now definitely towards "actual manifestation".

Although Chesed is the first Sephirah of the world of Yetzirah, or "Formation", we are still at a considerable remove from anything remotely discernible by our untrained senses; and many stages of concretion away from the reality of material existence.

According to the *Zohar* there have emanated six principles, or Sephiroth, called the *Sephiroth-ha-Benyin*, or "Sephiroth of Construction", which symbolise the dimensions of matter.

"The universe consists of six dimensions, above, below, and the four sides, in the mystery of Zeir Anpin which contains six sides. Therefore there are six working days.....but the Sabbath is Malkuth the Wife (rest or passivity)."

(R.Chayim Vital Calabrese {1543-1620} *Tree of Life*)

The book of Genesis records:

"Thus the heavens and the earth were finished, and all the host of them. And on the seventh day God ended his work which he had made; and he rested on the seventh day from all his work which he had made."   *(Gen.2:1/2)*

Each of these Sephiroth of Construction, the "six days of the creation", represents a stage in the sequential development of the "dimensions of matter". It is in the final sphere of Malkuth (i.e. the seventh day), which is both pendent to, and independent of the Microprosopos or Zeir Anpin, that we finally encounter the phenomenon of materialisation.

110

"Chesed" is most commonly translated as Mercy, although it will also be found rendered as Love, or Majesty. In some older Qabalistic works the translation may appear as Grace, and occasionally as Compassion.

Its secondary title, and that by which it is called when performing the ritual of the Qabalistic Cross, is Gedulah, which translates as Glory or Magnificence.

One of the principle attributes of Chesed's "opposite number", the fifth Sephirah of Geburah, is Power. When the Tree is applied to the human body these two Sephiroth lie at the level of the shoulder, and form the horizontal arms of a cross, thus establishing the familiar "Power and the Glory" axis. The vertical component is then formed by Kether/Ain, visualised as slightly above the crown of the head, and Malkuth at the feet.

It hardly needs stressing that the common form of the Christian gesture of crossing oneself is rooted in a far older tradition; predating the crucifixion of Christ in whose memory the rite is performed.

The God name attributed to Chesed is often given as EL but is more correctly transliterated as AL. It is derived from two Hebrew letters, *Aleph*, which as we have seen in the chapter dealing with Kether, is held to signify the "roots or the beginnings of things", and *Lamed*, the twelfth letter of the Hebrew alphabet.

Aleph is said to represent an Ox, because in its primitive form the letter was shaped rather like a stylised bull's head, similar in design to the astrological glyph for the sign of Taurus. Its present shape is also somewhat suggestive of a yoke.

Lamed, again by reference to its shape, traditionally symbolises an "Ox-Goad". The image that immediately springs to mind when these two letters are conjoined in the order, *Aleph Lamed*, is of the Ox being hard driven by the Goad, which suggests very strongly that the outrushing primal force of Chokmah, first harnessed in Binah, is now being set to productive work in Chesed.

AL in Hebrew has the literal meaning of God, but also carries the alternative translation of "The". The numerological value of *Aleph* is, of course, one, whilst the value of *Lamed* is thirty. The resulting total of thirty-one is of particular significance for Thelemites, as indeed is the name, AL, that being the title of the *Book of the Law*, *Liber AL vel Legis*, the central document of the Thelemic canon. AL, and its reflection LA, which means "Not", a term which takes on special significance above the Abyss, provides an important key to understanding the *Book of the Law*.

In his commentaries on AL, Crowley explains that;

> "AL is the true name of the Book (initially titled "L"), for these letters, and their number 31, form the Master Key to its Mysteries".
> *(AL. frontis)*

The interested student can do no better then to read his analysis of the names AL & LA, and the formula of LAShTAL, which follows *Liber V vel Reguli*, "The Ritual of the Mark of the Beast", to be found in *"Magick in Theory and Practice"*.

The mundane chakra of the fourth path is *Tzedek*, the sphere of Jupiter. Astrologically, Jupiter represents the principal of expansion and growth, and is both the complementary opposite and the balance to Binah's Saturn. In the same manner that the Saturn of Binah is a necessary response to the unchecked enthusiasm of Chokmah, Jupiter is an equally necessary response to the constriction and structure of Saturn.

The qualities of Jupiter, considered by astrologers to be the "great benefic", are precisely those suggested by Chesed's secondary title of Gedulah, "Glory" or "Magnificence"; but according to some early astrological correspondences, most notably those of the Chaldean system, Venus, "the lesser benefic", is the correct attribution.

There is a some justification for this arrangement in that one of the fourth sphere's secondary titles is "Love", by tradition a Venusian quality, and its elemental correspondent is water, which again, astrologically if not Qabalistically, could suggest Venus.

On balance, however, the judgement must fall to Jupiter, whose effervescent expansiveness and robust masculine nature combined with its colour correspondence with Chesed would seem to make it the natural choice.

Venus is now generally accepted as the mundane chakra of Netzach, the Sephirah directly below Chesed on the pillar of Mercy.

Regardless of the fact that Venus is not the natural planet of Chesed the fourth Sephirah is one in which the quality of love is strongly emphasised. Indeed its spiritual experience is that of the "Vision of Love".

The oft abused and misunderstood phrase "Do what thou wilt shall be the whole of the law. Love is the law, love under will" - the sublime distillation of the message and formula of the *Book of the Law* - is especially applicable to Chesed, balanced as it is with Geburah, the Sephirothic exemplar of Will.

In the gematria of the Greek Qabalah, *Thelema* (Will), and *Agape* (Love), both add to 93; clearly demonstrating thereby the closeness of the relationship between the two concepts. So important is this relationship that the magickal energies which express the conditions of the aeon of Horus are termed the 93 current, and the number is often found used as convenient short-hand for the full formula of "Do what thou wilt".

"The Vision of Love", which is the Magickal Power of Chesed, is the realisation that the prime dynamic of the universe is change, and that love is of its essence. For, to quote from Crowley's commentaries on the *Book of the Law*;...."Change being the life of all matter soever in the universe,..we have accepted love as a mode of motion of the will to change. To us every act, as implying change, is an act of love", and further, from the same source; "Remember that Magick is the Art of Life, therefore of causing change in accordance with Will; therefore its law is "love under will", and its every movement is an act of love". *(New Comment AL 1:52)*

The Archangel of Chesed is Tzadkiel, the "Righteousness" or "Justice" of God, who works closely with the "avenging angel" Khamael, resident in Geburah; while the order of angels are the Chasmalim, "Brilliant Ones" or "Scintillating Flames", the "shining angels of divine love".

The Thebean god Amun, husband of the sky-goddess Mut, and father of Khons, god of the moon, is jointly assigned to Chokmah and Chesed. In the second Supernal we met him in his early ithyphallic form, as Amun-Ra, and "he who abides in all things". It is his paternal aspect and his rulership over the "Great Ennead", the family of nine superior deities of ancient Egypt, which qualifies him for inclusion in Chesed.

Both Isis and Hathoor, although female, can in certain of their aspects be assigned to the sphere. Isis as water, the element of Chesed and Jupiter; and Hathoor, in her aspect as goddess of the Nile, the fertilising medium and indeed the very source of life for the Kingdoms of Egypt.

From the Greek pantheon both Poseidon, ruler of the seas and lord of water, and Zeus as the all-father (although not as the Supreme Unity, which relates to Kether) are assigned to Chesed.

The Roman god, Jupiter, an obvious correspondent in the light of Chesed's mundane chakra, is assigned in his earlier form as a god of storms and of thunder, although once again not in his later aspect of "Supreme Creator".

The Norse equivalent here would be Thor, in a more benevolent guise than the warrior form we will meet in Geburah.

Another of the Scandinavian gods who, by virtue of his association with water in its "masculine" aspect, is appropriate to this watery sphere is Aegir, who personified the strength of the sea. Aegir was also mightily fond of feasting and drinking, both characteristic pleasures of the sphere of Jupiter, and was blessed with the nickname "Alebrewer". It is therefore not too surprising to discover that Aegir was a most popular god, whose worship was enthusiastically pursued by his happy devotees.

The Hindu deity who best corresponds with Chesed is Indra, and again, as with Thor, the appropriate aspect here is Indra as a god of fertility rather than as a god of battle.

It will be noted that a number of the gods attributed to Chesed have both a martial and a paternal aspect. This is perfectly logical for we have only to look to the world of nature to see that an animal's right to fatherhood is often determined by its prowess in battle. Those who have proved their superiority by vanquishing all other rivals for a female's attention are those whose hereditary characteristics are passed on to subsequent generations.

What is true of the lower animals is largely true of humankind, and therefore of the "gods" who are after all developed in our own idealised image.

Here is a good example of the manner in which opposed Sephiroth function together as a complementary unit. On the one hand we have Chesed, sphere of generative power and fatherhood, while on the other, in Geburah, are found the dynamism and martial abilities which make fatherhood a possibility in the natural world.

In the three-fold division of man, the Sephiroth from Chesed to Hod, (the fourth to the eighth spheres) correspond to the faculty of the *Ruach*, or Intellect, which may be loosely defined as a mechanism developed by the Self for the purpose of investigating and relating to the perceived universe.

The *Ruach* is itself comprised of five components. In sequential order these are; Memory, Will, Imagination, Desire, and Reason.

The faculty of memory, which is allocated to Chesed, corresponds well with the sphere, given that its elemental attribution is water, which has a traditional association with the memory; due no doubt to the sea's unplumbable depth, its almost inexhaustible capacity, and its ability to take the shape of any container.

Certainly homoeopaths would claim that water is in itself capable of retaining a "memory", at least as a template of a material that after repeated dilution can no longer be detected as a physical presence and yet can still reproduce the effect of the original mixture.

Chesed's position on the Tree would also seem to emphasis the importance of the faculty of memory. Chesed is the first Sephirah below the Abyss in the descent from the Supernals, and therefore contains the impressed (although not necessarily accessible) memory of a mode of existence radically different in nature to that which obtains in the lower Tree. On the journey of return the sphere is then the final Sephiroth before the great gulf, and becomes the repository of the accumulated experience of multiple incarnations on the physical plane.

The chakra appropriate to this level of the Tree is the *Anahata*, the twelve petalled lotus, which is subtly located at approximately the position of the heart in the physical body. This location relates to the heart-centre of Tiphareth which is both central to the middle pillar and the pivotal point of the arrangement of the five Sephiroth comprising the *Ruach*. Tiphareth is also the focus of the triad of *Olam-ha-Morgash*, which includes Chesed and Geburah.

In the system adopted throughout this work the *Anahata* chakra is assigned jointly to the three spheres of *Morgash*.

As we discovered in Chapter 4 there are a number of ways in which the chakras may be disposed around the Tree. In the case of Chesed there is only one major objector to this triple attribution, namely Dion Fortune, who allows no chakra correspondence for the sphere, and assigns the *Anahata* centre to Tiphareth alone.

Tiphareth is undoubtedly the focus of the *Anahata* energies, but it should be remembered that Chesed is a sphere of love, which is traditionally seated in the heart, and Geburah expresses the quality of courage, which again is by tradition located in the heart.

Chesed's symbols include the tetrahedron as having three sides and a base making the total number of planes four, the natural number of the sphere. (It is important to note that while the position of a Sephirah, resulting from the order of emanation, gives it its natural number, this is a different matter from that of the "mystical number" which is sometimes given. The mystical number of any sphere is derived from the addition of the natural numbers of the preceding Sephiroth with the one in question, i.e. the mystical number of Chesed is 10, that is $1 + 2 + 3 + 4$.)

With the figure of the tetrahedron we have continued the progression from the dimensionless and unlocated point of Kether, to the extension of that point as a line in Chokmah, on to the enclosure of an area by the triangle of Binah, until now in Chesed we have arrived at the first geometric structure that is capable of enclosing a volume.

All solid figures, as defined by geometry, are ultimately related to Chesed, as is the equal-armed cross, which is symbolic of the four elements in a state of equilibrium.

Other symbols, such as the Orb, Sceptre, and the Crook, relate to the "kingly" qualities of the sphere, demonstrating, along with the wand, the magickal weapon of Chesed, different aspects of sovereign power.

The wand as a magickal weapon is a reflection of the weapon of Chokmah, the lingam; male creative potential brought into concrete actuality. It is specifically a phallic instrument and should not be confused with other forms, such as the Fire or Lotus wands.

The magickal image of Chesed is that of an enthroned king, mature though not elderly, magnificent and mighty. robed and crowned in his splendour.

Chesed's Virtue or Transcendental Morality is traditionally given as obedience, but this may be somewhat misleading for the obedience referred to here is not the blind unquestioning obedience of an "inferior" to a "superior", nor the abject fearful obedience of the powerless to the powerful, but is rather obedience to the dictates of one's own true will:...

"So with thy all; thou hast no right but to do thy will." ..."Do that, and no other shall say nay". *(AL 1.42/43)*

When a person is living entirely in accordance with his or her true will then and only then are they in harmony with themselves and with the universe. Indeed, they will find that they have the "inertia of the universe to assist them".

Therefore it should be clearly understood that the king of Chesed's magickal image, to whom is due the obedience which is the virtue of the sphere, is a king internal and not a king external!

The Magickal Grade of Chesed is that of Adeptus Exemptus 7°=4°, one who has perfected all the magickal skills of the previous Sephiroth and has "attained the supreme summit of meditation".

As it is not possible for an individual to remain as an Adeptus Exemptus for ever he is confronted with two possibilities as he is propelled inexorably towards the Abyss. He may there develop as a "Babe of the Abyss", to emerge in the fullness of time as a Master of the Temple, or, through reasons of ego or weakness, in other words incomplete or inadequate preparation for the ordeal, to remain in the Abyss as a "Black Brother" there to perish through lack of sustenance and nourishment.

Part of the work of an exempt adept during the time the grade is held is to prepare and make available a thesis in which is set out his understanding of the nature of the universe. Such work may take many forms, and by no means all would be classed as obviously magickal in content. The fields of poetry, visual art, music, and that border-line area of human speculation where science and mathematics merges with philosophy and metaphysics, each have examples to show to those who have eyes to see, and ears to hear.

Perhaps the most difficult step the adept must take at this critical juncture is the absolute relinquishment of all his previously gained achievements and powers. This abandonment applies even to the consolation of the Knowledge and Conversation of his Holy Guardian Angel, as he strips himself naked in preparation for the "great adventure". Self annihilation to the absolute degree is the prerequisite for the adept's eventual metamorphosis into a Magister Templi; anything less is certain destruction.

An adept who has attained to Chesed in all respects will be freed from the necessity of incarnation having abrogated the accumulated karma of his previous life-times. He may, however, choose to undergo future incarnation for the benefit of the whole of mankind.

Chesed is also known as the "sphere of the masters"; a rather loose term which encompasses a great number of often contradictory theories as to who or what these beings actually are, their origin and their function.

117

Certainly Chesed is a sphere where the teachings of highly evolved beings, whose natural realm is within the Supernal Triad, might be expected to first manifest below the Abyss; although a valid claim could also be made for Daath in this respect.

On one level the "masters" of Chesed could be considered to be the exempt adepts who have attained to its magickal grade; but equally, the sphere may play host to a variety of entities whose places of origin are far from the world of man.

The typical vices of the sphere; Bigotry, Hypocrisy, Gluttony, and Tyranny are all in a sense perversions or abuses of the authority of Chesed. Bigotry, which might conveniently be defined as an inability or refusal to accept that "Every man and every woman is a star", and Hypocrisy, the paying of lip service to an ideal whilst refusing to "give the last drop of ones blood" are the especial dangers that confront the Exempt Adept.

Gluttony of course, is very much a vice of Jupiter, an overemphasis of its pleasure principle to the extent of reversing the positive qualities of the planet into negative ones.

Historically, tyranny has marred the rulership of many lords of the Earth, both temporal and spiritual, and is the dark side of the principle of kingship.

The order of Qliphoth associated with the fourth Sephirah is the *Gha'agsheblah*, the "Smiters", suggesting the bloodthirsty, tyrannical aspect of power untempered by love and compassion, again suggesting the negative aspect of sovereignty.

The colours in the four worlds are; in Atziluth, deep violet, the combination of the Atziluthic colours of Chokmah and Binah. In Briah, the blue of water, elemental correspondent of Chesed. In Yetzirah, deep purple, which as with all the Yetziratic colours, is a combination of the colours of Atziluth and Briah; and in Assiah deep azure flecked yellow, the azure again recalling water, with the yellow flecks suggestive of meditative ecstasy and the pervasive influence of Tiphareth.

The Unicorn is the animal most sacred to Chesed, both because of the phallic nature of its single horn, and because of the traditional association of Jupiter as ruler of the sign of Sagittarius whose glyph is a Centaur or a mounted archer.

The Olive, because of its richness and softness, as well as its watery colouring, is attributed here, as is Opium, both as a plant and as a vegetable drug. The drug extracted from the opium poppy is also, it will be remembered, attributed to Binah. This shared correspondence may be accounted for by the stages of intoxication produced by the drug. Whereas the later stages of usage are said to confer the sleep and "understanding" appropriate to Binah, the earlier stages of its consumption are reported to be characterised by Jovian good humour!

The Shamrock or four-leaved clover which is sometimes given for Chesed obviously suggests the "good-luck" of its mundane chakra and also the natural number of the Sephirah itself.

Lapis-Lazuli and Amethyst are the two gems most in sympathy with the fourth Sephirah. Lapis-Lazuli, a hybrid name taken from both Latin and Arabic and meaning simply "blue-stone", is attributed for two reasons, the most obvious being because its colours, blue and violet, are those not only of Atziluth and Briah but also Jupiter in its most exalted aspect. It is also a stone through which it is believed positive psychic energies are easily transmitted and has the power to develop in the user the inner strength and self-confidence which characterise both Chesed and its mundane chakra.

Amethyst, again because of its violet colour, has associations with the "great benefic" of Jupiter and historically has been a stone closely identified with religious authority. Its name is derived from the Greek, *amethystos*, meaning sober or "not drunk" as it was believed that the crystal protected its wearer from the more deleterious effects of alcohol. It is therefore an excellent remedy for over-enthusiastic worship of Aegir "The Alebrewer", and the tendency to excess in all things which is the negative side of Jupiter.

It is also a stone which has remarkable healing properties and which is believed to assist the process of spiritual awakening in a number of ways, not least being its ability to calm the troubled mind and create a "still centre" by reducing the effect of strong emotions.

The Tarot cards attributed to Chesed are the four "fours" of which Crowley says:

"The important characteristic is that Four is "below the Abyss"; therefore, in practice, it means solidification, materialisation. Things have become manifest. The essential point is that it expresses the Rule of Law". (*The Book of Thoth*).

In the light of the above it is interesting to consider the titles of the four cards, which are; The four of Wands, "Completion"; The four of Cups, "Luxury"; The four of Swords, "Truce", and the four of Disks, which is titled "Power".

10

Geburah

> The Fifth Path is called the Radical Intelligence, because it is itself the essence equal to the Unity, uniting itself to the Binah, or Intelligence which emanates from the Primordial depths of Wisdom or Chokmah.   *(The Yetziratic Text)*

Geburah is the fifth emanation of the creative sequence and is positioned centrally on the negative column, the Pillar of Severity. It is the second Sephirah of the triad of *Olam-ha-Morgash*, (the "Moral" or "Sensuous" world), and represents the negative, Yin, or feminine principle; the complementary opposite to Chesed.

The Sephirah of Chesed is now destabilised and pours its expansive energies into Geburah. The primary function of the fifth Sephirah is to strengthen and direct the creative impulse, adding the element of discipline necessary for its eventual manifestation.

We have already seen that Chesed and Geburah function in harmony, as indeed do all the pairs of opposites on the Tree. According to early Qabalists the duad of Chesed and Geburah is like unto "the two arms of God" a linked pair for "Judgement is not without Mercy". (*Zohar*) Geburah is often described as the "left arm" of the Microprosopos, with Chesed as its right.

This sphere may be viewed as the organising aspect of the principle of rulership first expressed in Chesed, and one in which the martial qualities are emphasised, for the king of the fourth Sephirah no longer sits benignly on his throne - in Geburah we find him driving his chariot at the head of a mighty host, going forth to do battle with his enemies.

As Chesed is a reflection of Chokmah, so Geburah is a reflection of Binah. Although Geburah's attributes are of strength and power,

121

qualities more often associated with the masculine potency, it is nevertheless a feminine sphere and is in a sense the focus of the Pillar of Severity. All the Sephiroth of this pillar are negative or female in essence, as all the spheres of the Pillar of Mercy are male or positive, but each, within its own column, is negative in relation to its predecessor and positive in respect of the subsequent sphere. Geburah then is negative to Binah and Chesed, but positive to Hod and Tiphareth.

We have seen that in the order of emanation, the Jovian qualities of Chesed were developed as a necessary response to the Saturnine aspect of Binah, and that the Martial nature of Geburah is likewise a response to the unchecked effervescence of the fourth Sephirah.

Geburah is also highly responsive to the influence of Binah, its superior at the head of the Pillar of Severity. The supplementary text from the *Sepher Yetzirah* states that Geburah unites "itself to the Binah", so we may expect to find that the bond between the two spheres is particularly strong.

An indication of the closeness of this bond lies in the fact that the mundane chakras of both emanations are astrological "infortunes"; that is to say they are traditionally considered to be malevolent in their influence, Binah's Saturn being termed the "greater malefic", and Geburah's Mars being considered the "lesser".

As they are placed on the negative pillar both Geburah and Binah could be said to represent "latent" energy, whilst Chesed and Chokmah are of the nature of "kinetic" or dynamic energies. Geburah and Binah are likewise Sephiroth of form, where Chesed and Chokmah are primarily spheres of force.

Geburah's function is, however, somewhat different in kind to that of Binah. Instead of the relatively passive process of incorporating free energies that we witnessed in Binah, Geburah is altogether more energetic in its activity. It accepts the influence from Chesed and initiates a catabolic process that breaks down any inappropriate pre-existing patterns, conditioning and restructuring Chesed's energies to a form suitable for the next stage of emanation.

It is not too fanciful to think of Geburah as a vast critical testing ground, whose function is to carefully examine all that it comes within its orbit and, if it be found wanting, to exercise its ruthless powers to either correct or destroy.

Where Binah begins to develop manifest life by weaving a web of form, so Geburah modifies and adapts that form to the conditions found in the lower Tree.

Geburah functions to break up the structural constraints of Binah. Where Binah would envelop the newly polarised primal force and impose restriction upon it, Geburah, by destructive force and directed energy, opposes and attacks that restriction.

As Binah's Saturn strives to bind ever tighter, the Mars of Geburah seeks to shatter the restraining bonds. As Chesed's Jupiter, expansive, confident, and beneficent spreads outwards, Geburah's Mars, with its powerful initiatory force further energises the creative impulse, giving it renewed vigour and a more positive sense of direction.

This activity is not "good" nor "bad" in itself, such subjective judgements are hardly appropriate; rather it is a necessary part of the mechanism of the Tree striving for equilibrium in an intricate system of checks and balances. Such a process is necessary at this stage to act as a safe-guard against the undirected over-enthusiasm of Chesed, and the tendency towards excessive restriction found in Binah.

Analysis of the various titles and names of Geburah helps us to understand its surprisingly complex nature, for it is by no means the simple destructive or "evil" sphere that one may at first suppose. After all, the ten Sephiroth of the Tree are equally holy, and whilst it is perfectly true that the unchecked power of Geburah can be damaging in the extreme, to a certain extent the same could be said to be true of the unbalanced energies of any other sphere, regardless of how benign it might at first appear.

The Yetziratic text goes so far as to declare that Geburah resembles the "Unity", i.e. Kether, by which is meant that its energetic action is analogous to the upwelling of primal force expressed by the first Supernal, although on a much lower arc. But, as the text reminds us, this is the "Radical Intelligence", and it must be expected that such a sphere will present certain dangers to the unwary.

"Geburah" means Strength; both martial and moral. From strength grows power, and with power comes choice. Those who are truly strong are able to choose their way of life, and are able to defend that choice; the weak are at the mercy of fate. The strong have the capacity and the resources to benefit the world, should they so choose; whilst the weak can benefit not even themselves.

It should hardly need stressing however that not all strength is necessarily of a physical nature, nor need it always be apparent for:

"A king may choose his garment as he will: there is no certain test: but a beggar cannot hide his poverty"   *(AL.2:58)*

With strength, however it might be manifest, must come justice if that strength is not to degenerate into oppression, of others or of the self. It is worth noting that the nine and ten of wands, the suite which best corresponds to Geburah in the Thoth deck, are in fact titled respectively "Strength" and "Oppression". In the first instance the power and dynamism of Geburah is stabilised and balanced whereas in the second it is dissociated from its spiritual roots and is out of control. This final card of the wand suite can be seen as the five of Geburah redoubled, an over-concentrated form of the sphere's fire showing the element in its most destructive form.

A major secondary title of Geburah is "Din", which means Justice or Judgement, for the more dynamic aspects of these principles develop from this emanation.

Geburah is a sphere of Karma (Fate or Nemesis if you prefer) a cold impersonal cosmic law, whose sole function is to maintain equilibrium by constant adjustment and re-adjustment, ensuring that every action does indeed have an equal and opposite reaction.

In Qabalistic terms Judgement, and therefore Justice, is not something which is imposed from outside, it is a quality inherent in all things and is a principle in which limitation and restriction are necessarily concomitant with its action. Choosing one thing or one course of action over another can only be done at the expense of other options. It is therefore a wilful act of self-limitation to choose between alternative courses, and yet clearly it is an act which is essential if the self is to maintain a coherent identity and continuity of being.

We have said that the judgmental function is inherent in all things, and indeed it would be surprising if this were not so, for the principle arises within God Himself.

It is possible to argue as some Qabalists, notably of the Luria school, have done that the first crystallisation of the Ain to Ain Soph, from Nothingness to Limitlessness, was itself a conscious act of Din, or Judgement, and therefore an act of severe self-limitation on the part of the manifesting Deity. And further, that each succeeding level of concretion represents another judgmental action as the creative force increases in specialisation.

As the title *Pachad*, translates as Fear, Geburah is sometimes referred to as the "Lord of Fear", in the same way that Chesed is occasionally called the "Lord of Love". It is perhaps this element of Geburah, along with certain misunderstandings of the nature of its mundane chakra, that has given rise to the idea that the sphere itself may be closely identified with the scriptural Adversary, a figure that is presented as the embodiment of all evil.

It should be clear by now that such simplistic attributions are highly misleading and demonstrate a lack of understanding of the nature of the Holy Tree for the principle at work here is one of opposition, which may just as easily imply balance as enmity.

However some Qabalists hold that the principle of evil (however one chooses to define it) is inherent in the original creative act, and that it was the introduction of the power of stern judgement in that initiating process which corrupted the system and allowed for the presence of discord in the Tree.

One rationale behind this belief is that such acts of judgement proceed from the dark, negative, and destructive side of God; an aspect of the Deity which is little understood and consequently greatly feared.

As long as the rigorous, wrathful, and fiery aspect of God, concentrated in the sphere of Geburah, is tempered and balanced by the qualities of Love and Mercy shown forth in Chesed, all is well. The one aspect cannot properly operate without the other. As the traditional title, "The twin arms of God", suggests, they are two sides to the one coin. It is when one of these complementary forces is allowed to function alone that trouble arises.

Any energy, principle, or force that acts outside of its own proper sphere, or in a manner inappropriate to its nature may be described as being in some sense "evil", the term for our present purposes being considered contingent rather than absolute. So it is only when one of the two linked forces which represent these "hands of God" is activated independently that the possibility of evil arises.

In the case of Geburah its typical forces are so constituted as to have a natural tendency to break away from their partnership with those of Chesed. In other words, where the forces of Chesed incline towards union, those of its complementary opposite incline towards fission. It is the "free", and therefore unbalanced, Geburah energies that in aggregation form much of the material from which the Satanic realm is constructed, but the fifth Sephirah, being one the glories of the Holy Tree, is not itself a part of that dark realm.

Nevertheless it is easy to see why Geburah has traditionally been viewed with some trepidation. Its violent internal function and the disconcerting tendency of its energies to escape from their proper place make it a restless and dangerous presence on the Tree, and one which needs particular care in its exploration. But, as we have seen, it is not the Geburah energies themselves that are at fault; in their rightful place, balanced and ameliorated by Chesed, they are essential elements in the proper functioning of the Tree, and therefore in the creative process. It is only when they are exaggerated by lack of restraint, or intrude into inappropriate areas of activity, that we have any justification in identifying them with the Biblical Adversary as envisaged by the Christians.

It is also well to remember that even the utter-most evil will be redeemed and re-absorbed into the body of God at the Ending of Days, and that it too has a role to play in the continuing drama of creation, even if, for some people, that role is an uncomfortable one.

In Christian terms the sphere of Geburah might be considered to be appropriate to the concept of the "Fear of God", or terror in the face of God's might. An overemphasis on the aspect of fear, rather than a quite understandable awe in the face of God's creation, is an unfortunate element in many Judeo-Christian sects, which have historically had great difficulty in accepting that God has a fourth, and most important aspect, namely that of Destroyer.

The name of God in the sphere of Geburah is Elohim Gibor, the God of Battles, which has the correct meaning of "God in his Strength", and not the frequently found but erroneous "God Almighty".

Of all the Holy Sephiroth it is perhaps Geburah that is most easily identified with its mundane chakra. *Madim*, or Mars, has the reputation as being one of the astrological malefics, a planet of evil repute second only to Saturn in its degree of malevolence.

Essentially the principle of Mars is that of initiatory force and male sexual energy. Its glyph is that of the circle of the spirit surmounted with an arrow, signifying its energetic character.

The arrow may also be seen as a phallus, and in this sense the glyph is still used as a universal sign for the masculine in nature.

The earliest form of the Martian glyph pictured the the circle of spirit topped by the cross of matter,the exact reverse of the symbol for Venus, showing that material considerations were here placed above spiritual values. The Chaldeans, anticipating the glyph's future developments simply used an arrow-head as a symbol.

Mars rules the signs of Aries, appropriately the first sign of the zodiac, the initial month of the solar year. The planet also has traditional rulership over the sign of Scorpio, exoterically the sign of death, but also the sign of rebirth, for Scorpio has two emblems; the scorpion of self-death, and the eagle of self-transcendence.

As Mars rules both Aries and Scorpio it also rules the first and the eighth house. The first house in a natal chart is intensely personal and refers to the physical characteristics and self-orientated interests of the native. It is the point where the incarnating soul first experiences independent existence.

The eighth house is concerned with transmutation and transcendence. It is also the point at which the native confronts the inevitability of death. As with so much connected with Mars, and therefore by extension with Geburah, both extremes are present; the point of arrival on the physical plane and the point of departure. It should be clear by now that these events are not in anyway contradictory but are merely the more obvious episodes of a continually repeating cyclic process.

There is an esoteric teaching regarding the nature and function of Mars that, far from viewing the planet as the simple malefic of tradition, assigns to it a quite different role. For some, Mars represents the "secret saviour", the "sun behind the Sun", the dynamic creativity that both initiates and redeems the universe. In this the fifth sphere's mundane chakra forges a link with Daath, which also has a secret redeeming function and which is sometimes described in very similar terms.

The Archangel of the sphere of Geburah is Khamael, "God's Burner" who is both an avenging angel and the protector of the weak. Khamael's fiery powers may be used either to vaporise or to cauterise the imperfect proto-forms which come under his sway. In accordance with the nature and function of the fifth sphere what cannot be repaired or adapted for further development is mercilessly destroyed.

The order of angels in Geburah is the *Seraphim*, the Fiery Serpents, "the exalted angels of wrath".

The Order of Qliphoth is the *Golachab*, "the Flaming Ones", a name very similar to that of the order of angels. In a sense the action of both the angelic and Qliphothic orders in Geburah are similar. Both are dynamic, energetic and powerful. The difference lies in the fact that, whereas the angels of Geburah work according to the totality of the sphere's potential, in Justice as well as in Strength, the Qliphoth are unrestrained and unbalanced in their activity. The power and strength of Geburah is then perverted into wanton destruction and vicious tyranny.

As might be expected the gods associated with Geburah are, for the most part, an unlovely and aggressive collection.

Ares, originally Thracian but adopted (after a fashion) by the Greeks, personifies the warrior aspect of Geburah but never really developed sufficient complexity of character to be truly typical of the sphere in any comprehensive way. In a sense Ares is more akin to the Qliphothic Geburah than to the Sephirah as a whole. He was a figure noted for his violent anger, vicious bloodletting and general wickedness, who wasn't much liked it seems even by his own worshippers. Not surprisingly (he was after all a far from ideal parental role model) he was the father of Deimos (terror) and Phobos (hate) after whom the moons of Mars are named.

Another Greek god, Hades, is sometimes attributed to Geburah, although this assignation is strictly in respect of his aspect as a god of fire, rather than in his better known role of Lord of the Underworld. Interestingly, as Lord of the Underworld, Hades assumes the mantle of Pluto, the namesake of the planet which is considered by modern astrologers to be the correct ruler of the sign of Scorpio, previously thought to be under the rulership of Mars.

This attribution is not universally accepted even now however, with some astrologers preferring to assign a joint rulership.

Thor (originally called Donar), is the Norse correspondence. He was a massive red-bearded direct sort of deity, who revelled in physical activity, especially of the fighting /drinking /eating /copulating variety, but is an altogether better rounded character then Ares and much more popular with his adherents.

The Roman, Mars, a god of war towards the latter part of his career, is also a more comprehensive figure for the fifth sphere than the simple warrior god of Greece. To begin with, and most appropriately for the initiatory sphere of Geburah, he was a god of the spring. The month of March, first point of Aries (the vernal equinox), and the beginning of the solar year, takes its name from Mars.

He was also reputed to be father of Romulus and Remus, mythological founders of the city and culture that epitomises both the best and the worst of Geburic values.

For Thelemites the most important god to be associated with Geburah, and the one in which its qualities are best exemplified, is Horus, particularly when viewed as the "Lord of Force and Fire". Horus is a dual god having two distinct aspects. One is that of the "Concealed Child", Hoor-paar-kraat or Harpocrates, the Lord of Silence who contains within himself all possibilities that have yet to manifest.

This aspect of Horus, the "Babe in the Egg of Blue", is both the Fool of the Tarot, and a representation of the Holy Guardian Angel. Hoor-paar-kraat may be considered the god's negative potency, while the positive element in his make-up is that of Ra-Hoor-Khuit, the activated dynamic twin. He is a "God of war and of vengeance", the aspect of the duad that best typifies the Geburic principle; both initiating and cleansing through the fires of destruction, and establishing his rule with a harsh uncompromising justice.

Even though it is the fiery aspect of Horus that most obviously relates to Geburah, and that which is of particular concern to us here, it must not be forgotten that he is indeed a dual god, and one with a complex set of attributes. He blends the dynamism of the fifth Sephirah with the quiet containment of the third Supernal, linking Geburah with Binah; as he proclaims in *Liber AL vel Legis*":

"I am the Hawk-Headed Lord of Silence & of Strength; my nemyss shrouds the night-blue sky". *(AL 3:70)*

In the classical three-fold division of man, Geburah is the second Sephirah of the *Ruach*, the intellect. The particular element of the *Ruach's* own fivefold division assigned to the sphere is, naturally enough, that of the faculty or function of Will.

The human will is a real and powerful force which recognises no limit to what it may achieve. The will of the magician, trained and directed, is therefore a most valuable weapon in his armoury. The two major requirements for successful magickal work are will and imagination, the latter being a faculty associated with the sixth Sephirah, Tiphareth, next in order of emanation.

The will can be likened to a current or carrier wave which can be projected into any sphere or situation but which has to be modulated by the function of imagination in order to configure itself to the particular requirements of the work in hand. It is a force that is available to every individual on the planet to use as they might, the tragedy is that it is more often the uncontrolled will that uses them.

Will, in the sense that a magician might use the term, is above and beyond mere desire, indeed there is often a painful conflict between them. One example of this conflict might be found in the case of that growing band of people who are trying to lose weight or to stop smoking. It is undoubtedly the will of these individuals to improve their physical condition and hopefully thereby to enhance the length and quality of their lives but this involves an often desperate struggle against the desire for one more cream bun or another cigarette. If the will is strong enough to overcome the want then all is well and the successful individual achieves the goal of a healthier life. But, as the frequency with which one encounters overweight magicians with permanent smokers-cough testifies, will is not always the victor in the battle against desire, even amongst those who have devoted a good part of their lives to its study and development.

One might say that will arises out of the life-condition and spiritual/biological destiny of the individual, whereas want is a transient distraction arising primarily from cultural conditioning, over-attachment to sensual pleasures and material possessions, and not infrequently, from feelings of insecurity and personal inadequacy.

Of course there is no reason at all why we should not enjoy the manifold pleasures of our material world. After all we would hardly have put ourselves to the considerable bother of incarnation just to eschew the very things that make this earthly plane such fun. For as Nuit herself says:...

> "But there are means and means. Be goodly therefore: dress ye all in fine apparel; eat rich foods and drink sweet wines and wines that foam! Also, take your fill and will of love as ye will, when, where and with whom ye will! But always unto me." *(AL 1:51)*

As long as one is able to identify will and want, and learns to discriminate between them, and further, does not allow the latter to flourish at the expense of the former, a whole world of sensual pleasure is opened up for our use and enjoyment (although the would-be adept might be well advised to meditate on the meaning

130

of the last sentence of Nuit's proclamation before embarking on a life-long debauch, for she lays a heavy responsibility on her followers).

Lacking any clear understanding of the nature and function of will the individual is often at the mercy of powerful but barely recognised internal forces. A will that is disregarded or actively suppressed will exact its vengeance in no uncertain terms. The appropriate image here is that of a fire, will's ancient symbol, which if not contained and directed towards a positive purpose will rapidly spread out of control and consume everything in its path.

If an undirected will is a danger then much more so is one which is suppressed, for unlike our analogy of the fire the will cannot be conveniently controlled by smothering and depriving it of its equivalent of oxygen, for there is always plenty for it to feed upon in the murkier corners of the human unconscious.

For a more extended, but still brief, discussion on the nature of will the student is recommended to read Crowley's *Liber II*, "The Message of the Master Therion", which may be found in the "Blue" Equinox (vol.3 no.1) and elsewhere.

As this is the the fifth Sephirah the symbols of Geburah include all five sided objects and figures; for instance the pentagon, a figure that seems to have a particular affinity with matters martial, particularly when used as a building plan!

The five-petalled rose so beloved of Tudor England is another symbol of Geburah, once again due mainly to its numerical correspondence. The generic rose is the flower of Netzach, the seventh Sephirah, an intimation of the relationship between these diagonal opposites which parallels that between the mythological figures of Mars and Venus.

Other symbols, such as the sword and the spear, are of a more overtly war-like nature, and may in fact have a dual function as weapons. The sword can be used in a number of ways, as a simple weapon of destruction or as the means of cutting the Gordian Knot.

As a symbol of the intellect it may also be taken to represent the five Sephiroth of the Ruach combined, but is more often simply used to represent the analytical faculty of the ritualist.

Swords are used in Geburic ritual work as an appropriate weapon of Mars; for instance in the "Supreme Ritual", an invocation of Horus.

The spear also symbolises more than its obviously destructive

131

character might at first suggest, and may be considered another phallic representation as well as an image of directness and concentration of effort.

The Scourge is sometimes given as a symbol of Geburah, presumably because of its punitive character, but strictly speaking this is the Magickal Weapon of the sphere. The Chain likewise, though often given as a symbol, is properly a weapon.

The Scourge is made from iron, the metal of Mars/Geburah which represents severity; copper, the metal of Venus/Netzach which represents love, though on a lower arc than that found in Chesed; and lead, the metal of Saturn/Binah which suggests austerity and the passage of time. It is essentially a weapon of severity, the use of which encourages the adept in his aspirations. In ritual use it has less to do with actual mortification of the flesh than as a means of reminding the magician to keep his mind on the task.

The classic images of Osiris risen show the god holding two weapons crossed against his chest, the Scourge of Geburah and the Crook of Chesed - Severity and Mercy conjoined and brought to the sphere of Tiphareth, the realm of the sacrificed gods.

The Chain restricts any tendency to mental wandering or woolgathering on the part of the magician, and serves to bind his thoughts to the work. It is made from iron, the martial metal, and has 333 links, that being the number of Choronzon, the Demon of Dispersion, and is itself a "restriction unto Choronzon" by not allowing such dispersion to occur in respect of the magician's power of concentration.

The Magickal Image is that of a powerful bearded warrior, armed and armoured standing ready to smite the unjust. Alternatively he may be visualised driving in his chariot at the head of an army.

The Virtue or Transcendental Morality of the sphere is energy, which in view of the nature of Geburah hardly needs further explanation. Likewise the alternative virtue of courage is self-explanatory, except perhaps to say that courage, like true strength, is not necessarily overt and may be cloaked in an outer garment of apparent mildness. Courage and Fear are both features of Geburah and are closely linked, the former being impressive only to the degree that the latter is overcome.

The Magickal Grade is Adeptus Major $6° = 5^{□}$ whose task is to obtain a general mastery of the forms of practical magick of the second rank "although without comprehension", and also to develop "absolute self-reliance".

The Magickal Power or Spiritual Experience of Geburah is the "Vision of Power". In this Sephirah the adept must learn to master the use of power without himself being mastered by it. He will, through his initiation into the sphere, be possessed of a great potential to influence and control others on the lower levels of the path by the force of his will and the magnetism of his enhanced personality. The adept must be aware of this and exercise his influence with care and discrimination, and always in the knowledge that *"every man and every woman is a star"*. *(AL 1:3)*

The vices inherent in Geburah have been touched on above and are obvious inversions or exaggerations of the sphere's principle characteristics. A tendency towards cruelty and destruction, the two traditional vices, may seem to be implicit in the nature of the forces that flow from Geburah, but, as we have seen, these are completely neutral in themselves. It is the expression of them in inappropriate ways that deems them "good" or evil".

The colours in the four worlds are: in Atziluth, an orange, suggestive of the sphere's blazing energy, and in Briah, the scarlet red of fire, traditional colour of Mars. In Yetzirah we find the admixture of the previous colours to be a bright scarlet, while in Assiah we again encounter a red but one now flecked with black which indicates the influence of the Supernal Sephiroth of Binah immediately above and also the gravitational pull of Malkuth below.

The mythical Basilisk, is considered to be the animal that best represents Geburah, as it was able to slay its victim by the power of the "flame of its glance". *(777)*

"What shield of Ajax could avoid their death
By the Basilisk whose pestilential breath
Doth pearce firm Marble, and whose banefull eye
Wounds with a glance, so that the wounded dye".
(Du Bartas, *"Divine Weeks & Works"* 1606)

Oak and Hickory are attributed to the sphere on account of their extreme hardness, and Nettle because of its burning sting. The Nettle also has a pronounced astringent effect with excellent blood-purifying properties, its energetic action being highly appropriate to Geburah. Nux Vomica is another plant that is applicable to Geburah when prepared as a drug. Other drugs that are compatible include Atropine, because of its stimulating nature and its use as an antidote to overdoses of opiates, and Cocaine, again because of its stimulating action, although by this logic amphetamines would also qualify.

Tobacco has been given as Geburah's aromatic, but Crowley and others have not found this to be an entirely satisfactory attribution.

However tobacco is often consumed in large quantities when enervated and creatively active, as a brief inspection of the over-flowing ashtrays of many writers and artists would confirm. In this way there might be found a connection, albeit tentative, between Geburah's mundane chakra, Mars, a planet of energy and striving, and the pernicious weed.

The ruby is the gem associated with Geburah for the most obvious of reasons, its colour, which is suggestive of blood and of fire. The ancients believed that the stone contained an inner heat, powerful enough to boil water once the secret of releasing it was known.

Interestingly, in the light of Geburah's relationship with Chesed, the ruby crystal has for centuries been a symbol of undying love. It is also claimed to aid regeneration of the subtle heart-centre, the chakra of which is jointly attributed by Crowley to Chesed, Geburah and Tiphareth.

To Geburah is assigned the four fives of Tarot, a doleful collection as may be guessed from their titles: The five of Wands - "Strife"; The five of Cups - "Disappointment"; The five of Swords - "Defeat"; and the five of Disks - "Worry".

As Crowley says in his *Book of Thoth*;

"....the introduction of the number Five shows the idea of motion coming to the aid of that matter. This is quite a revolutionary conception; the result is a complete upset of the statically stabilised system. Now appear storm and stress".

11

Tiphareth

BEAUTY   HARMONY

The Sixth Path is called the Intelligence of the Mediating Influence, because in it are multiplied the influxes of the emanations, for it causes that influence to flow into all the reservoirs of the Blessings, with which these themselves are united.   *(The Yetziratic Text)*

Tiphareth is the sixth Sephirah of the Holy Tree and the third sphere of the triad of *Olam-ha-Morgash*. It occupies the central position of the glyph, equidistant between Kether and Malkuth on the Middle Pillar, the Pillar of Equilibrium. It is in effect the Sephirothic equivalent of the Sun in our solar system in that the rest of the Tree appears to revolve about it. As the ancients viewed the Sun as the very heart of the universe, so too can Tiphareth be viewed as the heart of the Tree of Life.

Tiphareth is held in balance between the physically manifest world of Malkuth and the unmanifest primal energies of Kether.

Likewise it is suspended between the polarities of the pillars of Mercy and Severity, the negative and positive currents of the Tree. The sixth sphere might be considered as being Kether on a lower arc, and Yesod on a higher. It is both Son and King; being the son of the Supernals, a particular reflection of Kether and the "apparent king" of Malkuth.

Tiphareth functions as a bridge between the upper and lower Tree. It is the sphere in which God is made manifest and accessible to human consciousness; the unbearable brilliance of the Supernals reflected and veiled in such a manner that it becomes approachable by incarnate life.

From the limited point of view of many belief-systems, in which there is little conception of a sequence of emanation, Tiphareth represents the summit of spiritual ambition. It may appear to those whose only experience of such matters is within the rather narrow frame of reference of exoteric religion that Tiphareth is indeed the "King", the pinnacle of achievement, usurping the place of Kether.

Rather as Daath may on occasion be confused with the Supernal Glory, Tiphareth offers a similar subtle but seductive trap which may discourage the unwary aspirant from further labours on the Tree, believing that his work is done.

Tiphareth brings about a reconciliation and equilibrium of the energies expressed in Chesed and Geburah; the two polarities are now balanced and brought into harmony. By this union of the spheres of Mercy and Justice we now approach Beauty, which is the generally accepted meaning of "Tiphareth".

The sixth Sephirah harmonises and synthesises the energies of the other emanations. It has an integrating function which follows from its strategic position at the mid-point of the Tree's central column.

It lies at the centre of a complex web of inter-relationships with no fewer than eight paths leading to and from it - nearly twice the number of any other sphere. With the sole exception of Malkuth these paths link Tiphareth with every other Sephirah of the Tree.

To quote the *Sepher Yetzirah* ... "in it are multiplied the influxes of the emanations, for it causes that influence to flow into all the reservoirs of the Blessings, with which these themselves are united." Tiphareth is also central to the pentad of the *Ruach* where it serves as the nexus of the five component spheres, and to the *Sephiroth-ha-Benyin*, or "Sephiroth of Construction".

Describing the net of relationships formed by the eight paths which link Tiphareth with the other Sephiroth as a "web" is especially apt as the spider is one of its magickal animals.

Like the arthropod, Tiphareth sits in the very centre of its web, if not exactly controlling the space around it at least highly responsive to every twitch and vibration travelling through its widely spread net. In this way the sixth sphere functions as the nerve and communication centre of the entire Tree as well as its heart.

"Tiphareth" is usually translated as "Beauty", and it is by this English title that the Sephirah is most often called in medieval representations of the glyph. It might also be found with the names "Harmony", "Reconciliation" or "Clemency" in some older Qabalistic documents, and even on occasion be described as "Heaven".

136

An alternative name, Rahamin, meaning "Compassion", is often used in the *Zohar*, with "Tiphareth" appearing only occasionally but this version is unlikely to be encountered outside of the Zoharic texts themselves.

The name of God in Tiphareth is IHVH Eloah ve-Daath, which means "The Lord God of Knowledge" or "God manifest in the sphere of the mind". It is composed of two previously encountered names. The first, IHVH, or Jehovah, commonly referred to as the Tetragrammaton, is the given name of Chokmah, the second Supernal, and means "To Be", signifying the God of elemental forces, while the second, again one with which we are already familiar, is "Daath", or "Knowledge".

It will be seen later that the word "knowledge" has a very specific technical meaning in the context of Tiphareth.

In this one name we have a direct connection with the God name of Chokmah, the first positive Sephirah and with Binah, the first negative Sephirah, both of whom contain the Tetragrammaton.

There is also a reference to the sphere that is placed above Tiphareth on the middle pillar. "Daath", of course, is not itself a name of God but that of the "pseudo-Sephirah" which stands between the sixth emanation and the first and which seems to operate as a bridge between one mode of existence and another.

By the repetition of this name Tiphareth and Daath are shown to have a close relationship, perhaps even a commonalty of function, with Daath perhaps acting as Tiphareth's "Dark Twin".

Tiphareth's mundane chakra is, naturally enough, the sphere of *Shemesh*, the Sun.

The Sun is by far the largest body in our planetary system, weighing over 500 times the total of all other local bodies, and accounting for 99.8% of the system's matter. Around it revolve the ten known planets and countless lesser bodies, held to their course by the gravitational pull of the central star.

The Sun is the ultimate energy source for all life on Earth. Everything we consume, all that enables our continued existence, is derived, directly or indirectly, from the power of the Sun.

The very foods we eat, regardless of origin, whether they be animal or vegetable, are little more than mechanisms for converting and storing solar energy. In a very real sense it can be said that we live by eating the Sun. An acknowledgement of this central fact of our material existence may be seen in the solar disc of the Eucharist wafer which mysteriously becomes the body and flesh of the Son after which transubstantiation it is ceremonially consumed.

Without the Sun's beneficent influence it is doubtful if life could ever have developed on this planet, and certainly not in any form that we would now recognise. And without the continued benefit of the Sun's warming presence, life would abruptly cease to be.

We need adequate exposure to solar rays to facilitate the production of essential vitamin complexes within our bodies and for the general healing and tonic effects that the Sun has upon our systems. Just how important the Sun is to us psychologically may be seen by the high incidence of depression and anxiety during a prolonged winter period which in especially sensitive individuals may even lead to suicide.

Recent studies have shown that an effective way of relieving this by no means uncommon suffering is to ensure a regular exposure to artificial light sources that approximate the rays of the Sun.

It is impossible to over-emphasise the importance of the sphere of Shemesh to every area of life, for it is both the giver and the sustainer of that life. It is hardly surprising then that the Sun has played such a central role in the mythologies of people from all quarters of the globe and has been firmly identified with the supreme creator in so many religions.

> *Shemesh* is indeed the: "Lord visible and sensible of whom this earth is but a frozen spark turning about.... with annual and diurnal motion, source of light, source of life"....
>
> *(Collect no.1, The Gnostic Mass, Liber XV)*

Astrologically, the Sun is taken to represent the creative principle. In a personal birth chart it is usual to consider it as corresponding with the "true underlying self-hood" of the native and the power to express that sense of self-hood in the world. Actually the matter is a little more complicated than this as it is most important not to confuse the principle expressed by the Sun with the native's essential individuality. It is rather to be thought of as the mechanism by which the fractured psyche is integrated to form a cohesive and coherent whole. Individuality as such is the product of the totality of planetary influences, and not the exclusive domain of any one sphere. The integrating function of the Sun in the human psyche is a precise mirror of Tiphareth's role on the Tree, harmonising and mediating the diverse elements which make the whole.

On a more personal level the Sun in a natal chart is taken to signify the subject's father figure, either the natural father, or the dominant male influence in early life.

In astrology the usual symbol for the sun is a circle with a dot in its centre, In terms of Thelemic imagery the circle is that of Nuit, infinite and eternal, whilst the dot is Hadit, spirit of primal motion. This symbol immediately relates the Sun of Tiphareth to the sphere of Kether, as the dot within the circle is also one of the first Sephirah's own symbols.

Another common glyph used to symbolise the Sun is the solar cross or swastika which is, like the dot within the circle, also a symbol of Kether, suggesting a swirling outward of primal creative energy.

Among the several additional titles of Tiphareth is Zeir Anpin or the "Lesser Countenance". This title is also on occasion applied collectively to the Sephiroth below the Abyss. Once again we find a reference to the close relationship existing between Tiphareth and Kether for the first Supernal has as one of its subsidiary titles Arik Anpin, or "Vast Countenance".

Another common title is "The Son", suggesting that Tiphareth is not only the sum of the preceding Sephiroth, but is a particular product of the Supernal Triad. In this way, according to one Christian interpretation, it is possible to view Kether as "God the Father", and Tiphareth as "God the Son."

It may also be titled Melekh, "The King", husband of Malkah, "The Bride", a subsidiary title of Malkuth.

Thus Tiphareth again shows itself to be the "mediating intelligence" of the Yetziratic Text, for as it lies balanced between the Primal Glory and the World of Actions it demonstrates its intimate relationship to both by the evocative imagery of its titles.

In many modern works the Archangel of the sphere of Tiphareth is given as Raphael, "The Healing of God"; the being who stands in the eastern quarter of the element of air, first point of the risen Sun.

However It will be found in a number of the earlier Qabalistic treatises that a quite different correspondence is given, for the Archangel Michael is also, with considerable justification, attributed to Tiphareth.

Michael is known as "The Likeness of God", or "The Perfect of God" and stands guard in the southern quarter, relating to the element of fire.

Whereas Raphael's function as a healer is is undoubtedly apt for Tiphareth, his elemental attribution of air would tend to place him in the sphere of Hod which also has elements of the healing arts contained within its Hermetic mysteries.

Michael, whose Kerub rules the sign of Leo (itself under the rulership of the Sun), is an excellent substitute for the commonly assigned figure of Raphael; given his elemental correspondence and the fact that his name, "The Likeness of God", recalls the close relationship of Tiphareth with Kether.

Note too that Michael is a healer, but one who heals deep seated disease and not surface wounds which are the province of Raphael.

Michael heals in the only true and lasting manner, holistically from within, by restoring balance and harmony to the diseased system, whereas Raphael concentrates his energies on binding together ruined flesh and protecting it from infection by outside agencies, a mode which is more appropriate to the sphere of Hod.

Qabalah is, however, an eminently flexible tool, the traditional dogma of which, though valuable, can in no way replace personal experience. As the student develops his own appreciation and understanding of the Tree he will find that the researches and speculations of others, be they ever so revered, are nevertheless not always easily reconciled with his own experiences and understanding. Working with the Tree of Life requires both science and art if it is to be fruitful; the methodical, critical experimentation of the scientist, mixed with the intuitive genius of the artist.

Essentially the message is; if it feels right it probably is right; and if it's not, you can be quite sure that you will soon be brought to recognise your error.

Tiphareth has two orders of associated angels; *Malakim*, "Kings", "Royal angels of the middle place"; and the *Shinanim*, whose name in Hebrew is suggestive of fire and spirit and who seem to be a more balanced development of the *Seraphim* found in the preceding sphere of Geburah. It is however the *Malakim* who are most often to be found assigned to Tiphareth in modern Qabalistic studies.

The associated order of Qliphoth is the *Thagirion*, or "Litigators" who bring disruption and discord where once was harmony; enmity and schism, where before existed only unity and balance. The *Thagirion* may be described as a grosser form of the Thaumiel or "Contending Heads" of Kether.

The sixth Sephirah not only has two orders of angels it also has the unique distinction of having two Magickal Powers or Spiritual Experiences.

The first is the "Vision of the Harmony of Things", a descriptive title that is largely self-explanatory. The sphere of Tiphareth is quintessentially a place of harmony and reconciliation, the achievement of which confers the ability to perceive the essential "interconnectedness" of all creation and an instinctive awareness of the rhythm of the universe. The first power of Tiphareth shows its adept the "spiritual musculature" of the natural world; the very sinews of creation which are both its support and motivation.

The initiate is brought to recognise the spiritual principles behind manifest forms and to understand that those forms are but specific expressions of the God-head. In this way does the vision of harmony slowly become the experience of harmony.

The second of Tiphareth's Magickal Powers is the "Vision of the Mysteries of the Crucifixion", which may be approached on a personal level or on the level of the cosmic Redeemer figure common to many mythologies, who takes on himself the sins of the world and then absolves its people of guilt by a magickal act of sacrifice.

Tiphareth is known as "the sphere of the sacrificed gods", and as we shall see many such are assigned to it.

However, times change, aeons progress and our understanding grows as, hopefully, does the ability of mankind to accept its faults along with its virtues. A society that is able to recognise its essential divinity and is prepared to accept responsibility for its own actions has little need for a god to sacrifice.

There are today a growing number who would echo the words of the "Mass of the Pheonix" and say:... "There is no grace: there is no guilt: this is the Law; DO WHAT THOU WILT!"

Nevertheless, the image of the sacrificed god and of the crucifixion in particular is a potent and seductive one, and even if the magickal formula that is expressed therein is considered abrogate by many in this our newly-born aeon, still the subject deserves both serious study and the respect due to a once entirely appropriate expression of the

141

relationship between man and his God. After all, the mystery of the crucifixion was central to the life and work of many of the finest minds of the last two-thousand years, and it still contains much of significance and value if we can but free ourselves of the accumulated detritus of twenty centuries of cultural conditioning and superstition.

On a personal level Tiphareth requires that we engage in an act of dedication that has many of the hallmarks of sacrifice, for the virtue of the sphere is "Devotion to the Great Work".

And yet the concept of sacrifice is perhaps rather inappropriate here for the term suggests the voluntary abandonment of something held to be of value or importance, or more often, something that gives pleasure and satisfaction to the aspirant but which is felt, in some way, to hinder his development. Commonly it is the very difficulty of the act of renunciation that is thought to confer some special state of grace. The efficaciousness of a sacrifice is then held to be directly related to the worth to the individual of the thing sacrificed. But as there can be nothing of greater importance to the individual or the race than the furtherance and eventual accomplishment of the Great Work all other considerations pale into insignificance.

This is not to say that the work is always easy, or that the aspirant will not be beset with distraction and temptation, but with such a goal in view how can ignoring the snares and distractions of the path be considered sacrifice?

The Great Work to which the virtue of Tiphareth binds its initiate, begins with the consciousness of the adept's innermost divinity. The adept through his devotion to the work seeks to rediscover his own heritage, to function to his full potential on all planes of existence and to reintegrate the fragmented components of his extended being into a harmonious whole, becoming in the process nothing less than a god.

Before we leave the subject of sacrifice it might be worth returning to its prime exemplar and ask ourselves what degree of personal sacrifice was demonstrated by Christ's Crucifixion.

Although without doubt an unimaginable degree of pain must have been suffered on that awful cross it is nevertheless the case that (according to scripture) the end result of the crucifixion process was that Jesus was reunited with his Father in Heaven; resuming his former disincarnate condition, his work on earth being largely completed for this phase of revelation.

It could well be argued that the true sacrifice of Christ occurred at the beginning of his life and not at the end, and that therefore the real sacrifice was the trauma of incarnation and not the release of crucifixion.

It should now come as no surprise to anyone having read thus far that the classic Vice of Tiphareth is Pride.

The Gods of Tiphareth include many of those most closely associated with its mundane chakra *Shemesh*.

The great Egyptian sun god, Ra, is an obvious correspondent of the sphere, as are the solar deities of numerous other mythologies from the Pacific rim to the ice-bound fjords of northern Europe.

Hoor-paar-Kraat, or Harpocrates, the "Babe in the Egg of Blue", is placed in Tiphareth as he is the Child and the Centre, even as Tiphareth is the Child and Centre of the Holy Tree. Harpocrates is also considered to represent the Holy Guardian Angel, whose area of activity this is. Similarly the figure of Iacchus in his aspect as Holy Guardian Angel, is also assigned here.

Apollo, one of the twelve Olympians of ancient Greece, represents a number of Tiphareth attributes. He was the god of the Sun's light, in which capacity he was called Phoebus "the shining one"; a god of reason and youthful masculinity, and later of healing and scholarship.

The slain and risen gods of this sphere include, as well as the figure of Christ; Osiris; Adonis (whose name is a corruption of the Hebrew for "Lord"); Dionysus, equivalent to the Roman, Bacchus; the Phrygian spring god, Attis, self-castrating consort of the goddess Cybele; and another Phrygian deity, the flute playing spirit of nature Marsyas, who was tied to a tree and flayed alive by Apollo, and who therefore has a double connection with the solar sphere having also been exposed to the Sun's negative aspect.

The painful history of this last god gives us a timely reminder that the Sun may burn as well as warm; blind as well as illuminate.Its rays bring forth life from the fertile soil but may also so corrupt that life that it becomes a travesty and an abomination.

With a rapidly depleting ozone layer we are already seeing the damage which the unshielded might of the Sun can cause on the unprotected earth. Mutations and carcinomas in both plant and animal alike are on the increase while drought and famine, although always with us, seem to increase in severity with each passing year.

Like any source of power, and there are few greater, the Sun must be approached with some caution and in a proper state of preparedness.

As with its mundane chakra the sphere of Tiphareth also has a potentially damaging aspect which is disregarded at peril. As one would not gaze with unprotected eyes at the Sun in its glory so the would be adept must ensure that he or she is properly equipped in knowledge and purity to face the searing light of the sixth Sephirah and partake in the rites thereof.

In the traditional division of man into his three parts we have seen that the five Sephiroth from Chesed to Hod comprise the *Ruach* or intellectual function. Tiphareth stands at the centre of the *Ruach* and represents the faculty of the imagination, which we have already touched on in connection with Geburah.

Of all the many aspects of this exceedingly complex and underestimated faculty it is the ability to use creative visualisation that is of most importance to the practical Qabalist.

Visualisation techniques of one sort or another are required in virtually all magickal workings. A magician must be able to construct and sustain complicated mental images for long periods of time. These images may vary from classical god-forms, angelic and archangelic beings, environments specific to individual paths, and other more or less complex ideas, through to pure symbol and colour. Time spent in developing a controlled creative imagination will be repaid many times over when it comes to practical work on the Tree. Along with a trained will, a trained imagination is an absolute prerequisite for successful magickal work.

However, the student should not make the mistake of believing that, because imagination plays such an important part in Qabalistic and general occult work, the subject itself is built on illusion. This is emphatically not the case. The imaginative faculty allows us access to planes, realms, worlds, call them what you will, that are every bit as real (or as unreal!) as the material world with which we are so familiar. It is perhaps more accurate to think of imagination as being a personal key to these realms rather than as the sole creator and sustainer of them.

Increasingly, orthodox disciplines are coming to recognise the power locked in the human imagination. Exercises are prescribed for cancer sufferers, amongst others, which utilise this power and which are capable of producing astonishing results. Visualisation techniques in particular have proven effective in stress-reduction and relaxation exercises, many of which are in fact variations on the Qabalistic Middle Pillar Exercise popularised by Israel Regardie.

Some modern psycho-therapies use guided imagination as a means of exploring and exposing deep seated drives and complexes, and also as a way of safely approaching the more painful areas of a patient's life, which they might otherwise be unable to confront.

Such methods are especially effective in overcoming phobic conditions in which the individual may be utterly unable to face their fears in the "real" world. By imagining detailed scenarios in which patients, in the safety of the therapist's consulting room, progressively approach the object of their phobias, they are able to familiarise themselves with all aspects of that phobia and hopefully so "defuse" the fear on an imaginative level that it becomes possible to cope with it in the world at large.

There is an obvious parallel between these techniques and traditional magickal working where the main emphasis is on manipulation and modification of natural forces in their more subtle aspects, leading to an analogous effect occurring in the material world.

The symbols of Tiphareth include all six-sided figures such as the cube and the truncated pyramid. The various forms of hexagram may also be included, but it should be noted that these are assigned to Tiphareth because of their quality of "sixness" and not for the significance of any individual figure. For example, the hexagram of water may be assigned to the sixth sphere only because it is composed of six discreet lines and not for its elemental symbolism.

Various forms of the cross are found in Tiphareth, mirroring the multifaceted nature of the emanation. The solar cross, also known as the Fylfot Cross and Swastika, is shared with Kether as a symbol.

The equal-armed "nature cross" can also be attributed to Tiphareth representing as it does the equilibrium of natural forces, the elements in balance and harmony.

The Calvary Cross or "Cross of Suffering" must be considered an especially apt symbol for the sphere for reasons which hardly need explaining. It is undoubtedly the cruciform most readily brought to mind by the average occidental, to whom it has acted as a beacon and a promise for the last two thousand years.

The figure of the Rose-cross, which is less familiar than the Calvary Cross to the non-initiate, is also assigned to Tiphareth, and the achievement of the sphere's magickal grade marks the entry of the adept into the inner order of that name.

The Magickal Image may take the form of either a majestic king, youthful in appearance; a young child, perhaps as the image of the young Horus; or a sacrificed god, of which there are a goodly number from which to choose.

Tiphareth's Magickal Weapon is the Lamen, the symbol worn upon the breast of the magician representing the nature of the forces with which he is working. The breast, and the heart in particular, is the area of the physical body which corresponds with the sixth Sephirah.

The *Anahata* or Heart Chakra, which on the subtle body is located in this central region, is not assigned to Tiphareth alone but to all the Sephiroth of the Triad of *Olam-ha-Morgash*, although the sixth Sephirah is undoubtedly the prime focus of its function.

The Magickal Grade is that of Adeptus Minor $5° = 6^{\square}$. Its achievement requires that the aspirant has attained to the first of the two critical stages of his magickal progress, this being the "Knowledge and Conversation of the Holy Guardian Angel".

As Crowley writes in *Book Four Part II*; "The task of attaining to this Knowledge and Conversation is the sole task of him who would be called Adept".

What then is a "Holy Guardian Angel" (abbreviated as HGA for the remainder of this essay)? There are two schools of thought on this matter; one which claims that it is a superior aspect of the individual, and which it variously describes as; the "true self", the "higher genius", or the "Augoeides"; the other, which insists that it is a separate entity altogether, having no current or historical relationship to the adept except in so far as it has taken on the responsibility for a certain stage of his or her magickal career.

The concept of an HGA as being a manifestation of the self, a creature within, a sort of "super-me" or "myself-raised-to-the-nth power", is perhaps the view most acceptable to modern occultists, but it also has a long historical pedigree.

Exponents of Abulafia's methods of prophetic Qabalism, using Yogic breathing and rigorous meditation exercises, have written of their confrontations with prophesying entities in terms which strongly suggest what might be termed "HGA experiences", and which seem to identify such beings with their own higher selves. For instance in Rabbi Abraham Ibn Ezra's commentary on Daniel 10:21 he says that, "In prophecy the one who hears is a human being and the one who speaks is a human being". This is in accordance with the words of another of Abulafia's contemporaries who wrote that we should;

> "Know that the complete secret of prophecy consists for the prophet in that he suddenly sees the shape of his self standing before him and he forgets his self and it is disengaged from him and he sees the shape of his self before him talking to him and predicting the future".

While a fellow commentator of the same period records the following experience:

> "....I call heaven and earth to witness that one day I sat and wrote down a Qabalistic secret; suddenly I saw the shape of myself standing before me and myself disengaged from me and I was forced to stop writing".   (*Major Trends in Jewish Mysticism*)

In the context of the full passage it is clear that the last writer is describing a genuine confrontation with an aspect of himself that is beyond any known to him previously, and not, for instance, an experience of what might be called involuntary bi-location.

Self-confrontation of this sort was considered by these early Qabalists to be an experience greater even than apprehension of the divine light which was a notable product of their religious ecstasy.

It is probable that most members of the Golden Dawn considered the HGA to be just this sort of higher-self, and Crowley himself, at the beginning of his magickal career, saw no reason to dispute this interpretation, although in the latter part of his life he took the opposite view. In the letter entitled "Self Introversion" published in *Magick Without Tears* Crowley describes Aiwass, his own angel (and in a sense the HGA of the current aeon) as being "quite certainly both more than human, and other than human", and goes on to say that "the Angel is an actual Individual with his own Universe, exactly as a man is: or for the matter of that, a bluebottle".

Those who hold the belief that the HGA is a separate entity, and some would go so far as to say that any assertion to the contrary is not far short of blasphemy, claim that the angel is a highly evolved soul, a master who has elected to selflessly assist the younger brethren along that path which ultimately we all must tread. The HGA is therefore not an elevated abstraction of the individual, nor a wish fulfilment of that individual's longing for perfection and omnipotence, but an external and objective being in its own right.

Proponents of the separate entity theory claim that the validity of their position is demonstrated by the fact that HGA's frequently evince knowledge and understanding of an order far above any that could be possessed by an incarnate individual; and that associated angels do not in general share the personal characteristics and mannerisms of their "clients", although they of necessity share the same class or type of will. Also, certain of these angels may be identified as historical figures; teachers and initiators whose history and appearance is verifiable, and who therefore cannot be dismissed as projections of the aspirant's unconscious mind.

Whatever view is taken of the nature and origins of the HGA there can be no doubt that the achievement of Knowledge and Conversation is the crowning glory of the early magickal career.

The relationship between an adept (for such may he now be termed) and his angel is intense and intimate. At one and the same time he (or she) may be a; father/mother, brother/sister, critic, lover, friend, taskmaster and guru.

The phrase "knowledge and conversation" should not be taken to mean simply that one is aware of the presence of, and able to communicate with, the angel; such would be closer to the power of Malkuth, the "Vision of the Holy Guardian Angel". The knowledge referred to in the title is more complete than mere recognition of an entity's existence, it is closer in essence to the biblical usage of the term, up to and including full sexual experience.

Once having attained to the full power of Tiphareth, the adept is armed with his most formidable weapon, which will not desert him until that second great crisis of his magickal career when he is at last to confront the Abyss.

The colours of the four worlds in Tiphareth are; in Atziluth a clear rose pink suggesting the dawning of a new age, deepening and thickening in Briah to yellow. In Yetzirah the combination of the previous two colours produces a rich salmon pink, while in Assiah is seen a golden amber colour which combines the gold of the harvest field with the dawn of the day.

The animals assigned to this sphere are the Lion, which is the natural animal of the Sun; the Spider, on account of the symmetry of its web, and the Phoenix, an especially apt symbol for the work of the Adeptus Minor.

Another creature which is appropriate to the aspect of "redeemer" in Tiphareth is the Pelican, who was thought to feed its young by the self-sacrificial act of stabbing its own breast and making available its life-blood as a food for its offspring.

The Acacia is assigned to Tiphareth as it is the traditional plant symbol of the resurrection. The Oak, considered a solar tree by the Druids, is another traditional correspondence, but one which is also sacred to Jove or Jupiter as its distinctive forked branching in somewhat reminiscent of a thunderbolt.

Many other plants have found their way into Tiphareth's extensive table of correspondences including Bay and Laurel, both sacred to Apollo; and the Vine which is sacred to Dionysus.

Another strongly solar plant that is very much of this sphere is Ash, a wood used in the manufacture of certain types of wand.

The final plant of note is Gorse, the "burning bush" of Moses, which in full flower suggests the very Sun by its multitude of bright yellow flowers. Gorse is also the plant symbol of the Great Work, adopted as the heraldic emblem of the A∴A∴ .

The typical drugs of the sixth emanation tend to be cardiac stimulants of one sort or another, either actually or apparently. These include Digitalis, Stramonium and Caffeine. Alcohol is also included as being appropriate for Dionysus, although strictly speaking only grape wine is entirely accurate.

Tiphareth's precious stones include the Golden Topaz, because of its solar colour; and the Yellow Diamond for the same reason and also its suggestion of being a reflection of Kether in the lower sphere, as the diamond is the natural stone of the Primal Glory. Topaz means "fire" in Hindu and has the property of stimulating dreams and relieving stress. In medical usage they have a generally revitalising function and are considered particularly beneficial for pulmonary complaints. The lungs of course are part of the cardiac plexus ruled by Tiphareth and provide the air principle to the fiery furnace of the heart.

The four sixes of the Book of Thoth are assigned to Tiphareth and in each the sixth Sephirah's first principle of harmony is found. The titles of these cards are as follows; The six of Wands, "Victory", the six of Cups, "Pleasure", the six of Swords, "Science", and the six of Disks, "Success".

"The four sixes are thus representative of their respective elements at their practical best."   (Crowley, *Book of Thoth*)

12

Netzach

VICTORY   FIRMNESS

The Seventh Path is the Occult Intelligence, because it is the Refulgent Splendour of all the Intellectual virtues which are perceived by
the eyes of the intellect, and by the contemplation of faith.

(The Yetziratic Text)

Netzach is the last of the three Sephiroth on the positive pillar, the pillar
of Mercy. It is the seventh emanation and the first sphere of the third and
final triad of the Tree. This triad is known as *Olam-ha-Mevethau* which
means the "Material World".

We know from our investigation of the patterns on the Tree that
the traditional names of triads are far from satisfactory, and in the
case of this last arrangement, actually misleading.

A title such as "The Material World" immediately conjures up the
idea of physical reality, a condition that does not occur until the final
Sephirah of Malkuth. In *Olam-ha-Mevethau* we find the preliminary
stages which prepare the way for the emanation of a true material
world. Here the emphasis is on the subtle forces that underpin and
animate the manifest universe, but which are themselves, at least to
the untrained eye, rarely evident in that universe.

The third triad represents power and stability. However the stability
referred to here is the stability of change, and not the false stability of
stagnation, reflecting a fundamental principle of Chokmah, at the
opposite extreme of the pillar, that "Change is Stability".

As in the two preceding triads the male or positive potency is
manifested first, followed by the feminine or negative principle, both
finding their balance in a third sphere.

The typical energies expressed by the two opposite elements in any
given triad may be described as "centrifugal", i.e. tending to move

away from the centre and "centripetal" tending to move towards the centre. In the third sphere these two opposed energies are cancelled out and a state of equilibrium is reached.

The state of equilibrium that existed in Tiphareth, the pause and consolidation of the lighting flash in the descent of power, is now overthrown for in Netzach we once again find ourselves in an active, dynamic sphere full of enthusiasm and energetic assertiveness.

Netzach is negative to both Chesed and Tiphareth but is positive to Hod and Yesod. This is in keeping with the principle that the Sephiroth, regardless of the fact that each may be either positive or negative in themselves by virtue of their position on one of the pillars of manifestation, are always negative to the Sephiroth that precede them and positive to those that succeed them.

It will be found in Netzach that the sphere functions with pronounced "feminine" characteristics at times, but this should not be taken to mean that the polarity designation is in any way suspect.

In the same way that Hod, an essentially feminine sphere, externalises as male, Netzach, although placed on the Pillar of Mercy, presents its typical energies as female. It is in fact the last Sephiroth in which the creative energy issuing ultimately from the Ain is in a fully fluid state for as it impacts Hod, the bounds of form, although tenuous and largely intellectual in nature at this early stage, begin to severely limit its perfect freedom of expression.

It is true that this process of limitation and fixation of free-flowing energies commences in Binah and is continued in Geburah but its full effect is felt in Hod which, being the last of the negative emanations, is subject not only to the combined coercive influence of its sister spheres on the negative column but also to the increasingly powerful gravitational pull of Malkuth below.

The previous Sephiroth have been characterised by increasingly concrete and specialised functions. In Netzach we are still at a remove from ultimate concretion, but nevertheless we are now entering realms where the degree of abstraction becomes noticeably less and less.

Netzach is often characterised as the realm of the "natural world" and as the sphere of the "group mind", in contrast to the individual consciousness which begins to develop in the eighth Sephirah.

However the *Sepher Yetzirah* also describes Netzach as the "Occult

Intelligence" by which is meant "that which is hidden from plain view", and so we should expect to find that the immediately apparent or more obvious characteristics of the sphere conceal deeper mysteries. As we have seen, the concept of the "natural world" does not refer to the world made manifest in any tangible manner but rather to the "spirit of nature" that animates it; the creative principle that underlies the drive to growth and union.

Here we find a reflection of the expansive quality of Chesed, which is Netzach's immediate superior on the Pillar of Mercy. The principle of expansion found in the seventh Sephirah differs from that found in the fourth due to the mediating influence of Tiphareth and the forceful, disciplining presence of Geburah which allows for a more controlled and balanced expression of these energies.

Balanced and controlled though the forces of Netzach may be in comparison with Chesed's mode of action, they are nevertheless imbued with an irrepressible exuberance and sheer lust for life.

One has only to look at the attribution of mundane chakras to these two spheres to see why this should be for between them they encompass both of the astrological benefics; in the case of Chesed, Jupiter, "the greater benefic" and with Netzach, Venus, the "lesser".

"Netzach" means "Victory" or "Triumph". There are also a number of subsidiary names or titles which may throw further light on its nature, the most commonly encountered being "Firmness" and "Eternity". On occasion the last title may be found rendered as "Endurance", or even in an extended form as "The Lasting Endurance of God".

The name of God in this sphere is IHVH Tzabaoth, usually, if somewhat confusingly, rendered as "The Lord of Hosts", or "Lord of Armies". Hod, Netzach's opposite number on the pillar of Severity, has as its God name, Elohim Tzabaoth, "God of Armies" or of "Hosts". The *Zohar* describes these two spheres thus:....

"Therefore these two Sephiroth are called: the armies of IHVH"

and again;

"By Triumph (Netzach) and Glory (Hod), we comprehend extension, multiplication and force; because all the forces which were born into the universe went out of their bosom, and it is for this reason, that these two Sephiroth are called; the armies (hosts) of IHVH".

153

Issac Myer says:..

"These Sephiroth are called, Netzach, i.e. Triumph, the male or positive, sometimes termed Victory; and the female or negative, called, Hod, i.e. Glory or Splendour; by which two, sometimes termed by the Qabalists, the arms (sic) of God; the *Zohar* intends the centripetal and centrifugal energies and potentialities, in the entire universe". *(Qabbalah)*

It is clear from this, and from the duplication of the second element of the name, that these two Sephiroth, like Chesed and Geburah before them, are designed to act in concert.

Ancient Qabalistic doctrine stated that all "emanated and existing Things" are sourced from the ninth Sephirah, Yesod, the "Foundation", which is the focal point of the third triad, and which receives and harmonises the polarised essence of both Netzach and Hod.

The input of energies from these two spheres results in the eventual emanation of these "existing Things" as they come into manifestation in Malkuth through the agency of the Foundation, for the *Zohar* declares that; "All the energies, forces and increase in the universe, proceed through them".

Although Netzach is pre-eminently a sphere of nature, in all its savage beauty, the sphere cannot really be said to be creative in its own right. It is only in the latter stages of Yesod that there is any possibility of fertility and production.

Netzach and Hod together so condition the descending energies that they provoke in Yesod an automatic creative response which comes to final fruition in Malkuth.

Netzach is a realm of fire and emotion, qualities which of themselves signify nothing, while Hod is able to cool and temper those roaring flames and provide an intellectual framework, adding shape and direction before passing on the modified impulse to Yesod in a form suitable for incorporation in "The Treasure House of Images" that is the ninth Sephirah.

The ancient Qabalists were quite right to consider Netzach and Hod to be inseparable in their function as the "armies of God" for without the compensating action of its opposed sphere each of these Sephiroth is dangerously unstable. Like the combination of "The Twin Arms of God", Chesed and Geburah, whose principles of Mercy and Judgement are inextricably linked, the powers represented by the

154

seventh and eighth Sephiroth need to be balanced against each other if they are to fulfil their intended function.

Although the ultimate integration of the energies expressed by any pair of opposed spheres is always to be found in the third point of their triad, in this case in Yesod, Netzach and Hod demand to be viewed as a working unit; two poles of a creative dynamo which discharges into the ninth Sephirah.

Emotional energy alone can never develop into anything substantial or productive without the organising function of the intellect to direct its unfocused force. Equally, intellect without feeling, devoid of all emotion, is a souless and sterile condition from which little of lasting benefit may be expected. In other words, Netzach's emotional responses humanise Hod's cold analytical approach to life, while Hod confers a welcome degree of order on the chaotic maelstrom of Netzach's emotive outpourings.

Where Netzach is very much a place of relationship and union, Hod is something of an island unto itself. This is clear when we recall that Netzach is the Sephirah of the "group mind", the collective consciousness in which all created beings partake to a greater or lesser extent, while Hod is very much the sphere of the "individual mind" and is indeed the first point where such a concept appears on the Tree.

Netzach's mundane chakra is the "morning star" Venus, called *Nogah*, "The Shiner" and *Hele Ben Shahar* or "Son of Dawn" by the ancient Jews. At one time it was held that the proper attribution was Mars, presumably because the element of Netzach is fire, but this suggestion, though interesting, can be discounted entirely in favour of the planet Venus which more accurately reflects the nature and condition of the seventh sphere.

Astrologically, Venus represents the the principles of Unison and Harmony. In a natal chart the relative position of the planet and its aspects to the angles and other bodies indicates the native's power of establishing relationships.

The characteristics of Venus may best be understood by a brief look at the two signs of the zodiac of which it is ruler.

The first, Taurus, is a fixed earth sign and suggests an earthy practicality with a particular fondness for the natural world, an intense love of beauty in all its forms, and a deep appreciation of the bounty of the planet. Taurus is also a sign that confers great strength of character on its subject, who is apt to be somewhat stubborn and well prepared to defend what are considered to be its rightful possessions. The second sign is that of Libra, the sphere of balance, which is the cardinal air sign in the great wheel of the zodiac. Libra, like Taurus, is a sign much concerned with the ideals of beauty, and as the most dynamic of air signs one would expect its native to be highly communicative and companionable. The natural propensity of Libra is to promote harmony and reduce friction in all its areas of influence but whilst Taurus may be characterised as essentially introverted, Libra is decidedly extroverted, and so goes about its mission in an outgoing and self-expressive manner which the more dour Bull sign may on occasion find rather irksome.

We may summarise the main qualities of Venus as having great inner strength and tenacity, which is often underestimated or altogether disregarded; a powerful drive to establish harmony and to relate closely to others; and a keen appreciation of beauty in all its forms. The planet also has a close affinity with growing things, and the world of nature in general.

This small selection of Venusian characteristics, along with its many others, may be reduced to the one word which seems to sum up the essence of the planet, Love.

We have already discussed in the chapter dealing with Chesed the nature of love as it pertains to the principle of change, and we have also seen that the triad of the "Material World" is the triad of change *"par excellence"*. Of the component spheres that make up this third triad, Netzach, the first and most active element, best represents that principle.

Love is also the drive to union, the need to become one with another or with all creation for as *Liber AL vel Legis* says;....

"...There is no bond that can unite the divided but love: all else is a curse. Accurséd ! Accurséd be it to the aeons ! Hell".

(AL 1:41)

The love that radiates from Venus includes in its expression sexual love, as this is implicit in the impulsion towards union.

It is in the nature of the universe that opposite polarities are drawn together in a desire to be reconciled and made whole, completed as it were, in a third. The third element resulting from such union may be some tangible and independent product, such as a child; or it may be the act of union itself, creating during its brief span something that is assuredly greater than the sum of its parts. This process is repeated throughout nature and may be seen clearly represented in the glyph of the *Otz Chiim*, where the outer polarised columns "....divided for love's sake, for the chance of union", find the resolution of their differences in the middle pillar.

In order for any circuit to be completed it is necessary that there should exist two polarities, one of high potential and one of low. It is not necessary, however, that these polarities be expressed in obviously physical terms. As we have seen during our study of the glyph positive spheres are capable of functioning in a negative manner under certain conditions and are able to relate to neighbouring Sephiroth in quite different ways simultaneously, as indeed the negative spheres are able to function in a positive mode.

The same might be said to be true of any area of human activity. In the venerable "T'ai Chi" ("Supreme Ultimate") symbol of ancient China, which shows the Yin and Yang principles in an entwined black and white design, the two elements each contain a portion of the others colour, showing that even at the most fundamental level there is no "pure" expression of these energies.

As individuals we too are composed primarily, but not exclusively, of one polarity, which may present itself as male or female.

However, the most aggressively masculine of men has some feminine component even as the most female of women contains an element of the masculine. This intrinsic bi-sexuality may not always be apparent, in some the primary polarity may be exaggerated whilst the secondary element is repressed, in others the reverse may be the case.

It should not be too surprising then to discover that Netzach is the sphere to which the Jungian contra-sexual figure is attributed.

These archetypal images represent the female in man and the male in woman. C.G Jung described the anima figure thus:....

"The anima is an archetypal form, expressing the fact that a man has a minority of feminine or female genes. That is something that doesn't appear or disappear in him, that is constantly present, and works as a female in a man".

(Richard I.Evans *"Jung on Elementary Psychology 1964"*)

As the anima figure represents the female component in a man, so the animus figure represents the male component in a woman.

Although it is perfectly true that Netzach embraces a great number of magickal archetypes it is particularly a sphere of the anima, which first emerges as a fully developed image in the seventh Sephirah, but has its roots in Malkuth, the world of actions.

The animal figure is again brought to mind by Netzach's magickal image which is that of a beautiful naked woman. It is usual to visualise this image as one of the classical representations of Venus-Aphrodite, perhaps as in Botticelli's "Birth of Venus", or the antique "Venus of Milo"; although here the student will need to exercise his or her imagination somewhat!

The Spiritual Experience or Magickal Power of Netzach is the "Vision of Beauty Triumphant", which includes in its description two of the sphere's major attributes, Beauty and Triumph.

These two qualities combined emphasis the importance of aesthetic considerations in our lives and hint of a world in which such considerations are paramount. Beauty here is not just an optional extra but is integral and also inevitable in a sphere which is the natural home of the artist and the root of human creativity.

The Vision of Beauty Triumphant could also be taken to refer to the successful acceptance and integration of the contra-sexual figure into the psyche, a process which was begun in Malkuth and further developed in Yesod and Hod, before coming to fruition in Netzach.

The Virtue of the seventh Sephirah is Unselfishness, a necessary ingredient of love, whilst the vices, lust and unchastity, are both considered perversions of the ideal of love.

Just how venial (an appropriate term in the context of Netzach) these particular vices are thought to be is a matter best left to the judgement of the individual. However, we should not forget that Lust has the proper meaning of "passionate enjoyment of life"; whilst Unchastity is subject to any number of definitions, depending on who is doing the defining and why.

Chastity does not depend on sexual abstinence any more that its opposite requires an actively promiscuous life-style. It is rather a state of mind than of body. As a definition of celibacy it may be a truly holy state, or a wretched pathological condition.

Likewise the generally accepted meaning of Unchastity, i.e. sexual incontinence, may be a celebration of life and an offering to the gods, as in the case of the temple prostitutes which correspond to one aspect of Netzach; or it may be, like the negative side of Chastity itself, indicative of serious emotional disturbance.

The archangel of the sphere of Netzach is Hanael whose name means "I, the God". He is also known as Hamiel the "Grace of God"; Anael, "The Ship of God", and Phanael "The Face (or appearance) of God". Some authorities have identified him with Auriel "God's Light" who rules the northern quadrant and the element of earth.

The order of angels are the Elohim, "Gods" or "Principalities", "angelic gods and goddesses who formed the world".

These Elohim are the nature gods, the rulers of the natural realm and builders of the worlds. As both Netzach and Hod are Sephiroth where God is apparent in His diversity, the designation here of the Elohim is quite apt, for in the seventh Sephirah we now have an abundance of gods.

The Qliphoth of the sphere is the *A'arab Zaraq*, the "Raven of Dispersion", who undermines the constructive powers of Netzach and attempts to further scatter the already diversified energies of the Elohim.

Chief amongst the god-forms assigned to Netzach are the various regional varieties of the goddess Venus. Netzach is a sphere where all the designated Gods are in fact Goddesses, with the notable exception of the Christian Messiah and the Lord of Hosts.

Christianity, along with Judaism, is of course at somewhat of a disadvantage when it comes to goddesses, although some branches of the Christian communion have elevated the mother of God and certain of the female saints to divine or semi-divine status.

The Lord of Hosts is an obvious attribution in view of the God name of the sphere, IHVH Tzabaoth, which has that literal translation.

The Messiah figure is also appropriately assigned here as a visible symbol of the love of God, and as nurturer of the spiritual life of the world.

The Grecian Aphrodite, a version of the Middle Eastern Astarte/Ishtar figure was originally worshipped in her Hellenic form on the island of Cyprus. She was said to have been born from the white foam that collected around the discarded genitals of Uranus after they had been thrown into the sea by his emasculating son, Cronus.

She was a goddesses of two distinct aspects and many names.

The "light" aspect is a one of love and of beauty as might be expected in Netzach. In this form she was called variously, Dione (the bright sky), Pandemos (common love), Ouranos (heavenly love) Pelagia (of the sea) Anadyomene (born of salt waves) and many another name besides.

Each region seemingly had a different version but most names refer to her unusual conception, or to her function as the supreme embodiment of love, both "common" and "heavenly".

She was also the deity most favoured by prostitutes who worshipped her as Aphrodite Hetaira, or Aphrodite Porne. It was the prostitutes that gave her the delightful, if somewhat over-familiar, epithet, Kallipyge, or "Beautiful Buttocks".

She was a goddesses who not only embodied the principle of love, but was happy to bestow it on all and sundry. Aphrodite was a whore, a mistress, a lover, and a priestess of the mysteries. In the temples dedicated to her were found the sacred prostitutes whose skill in the arts of love transcended the physical and brought ritual sex to the level of divine worship.

She also had her dark side and could be the cause of much suffering, as Adonis amongst others could testify. In this destructive mode she had more than a passing resemblance to the Indian goddess Kali and was thought to preside over graveyards and to lead men to their ruin. In her negative aspect she was called Androphonos, the "killer of men", or Melainia, the "black one" and can be clearly seen as part of a long tradition of seductive but deadly initiatrixes, whose ultimate mysteries require a painful and often terminal sacrifice on the part of the initiate.

Venus, her Roman equivalent, was originally a local spring goddess who became fully identified with Aphrodite when a temple of the Greek goddess was established on Mount Eryx in Sicily. Her career parallels that of Aphrodite in most particulars, demonstrating both dark and light sides to her nature. She was at one and the same time Venus Genetrix, the universal mother; and an irresistible siren who lured young men to their doom.

The Egyptian goddess Hathoor, in certain of her aspects can also be identified with the Venus Aphrodite figure. Hathoor, whose name means "house of Horus", was a protective sky goddess with a cow-like visage. She was also a goddess of love, dance and music, all of which are especially appropriate to Netzach. Like the other goddesses of Netzach she too had her dark side, being worshipped as a mortuary deity in Thebes. As the "female soul with two faces", she gives a very clear indication of her dual nature.

Nike, the goddess of Victory, represents another aspect of Netzach. The daughter of a river nymph and a Titan, she had three sisters, named; Kratos (force), Bia (violence), and Zelos (jealousy), and was plainly the best of a bad bunch.

Nike is usually depicted as a powerful winged figure holding aloft a victory wreath and was in fact called Victoria by the Romans.

Although in the terms of reference used in this system of classification Netzach is often equated with Freud's concept of the "Id", a complex of unconscious animal drives, it is more accurate to assign this shadowy region to the final triad as a whole.

The traditional attribution of the powerful but unpredictable faculty of emotion is entirely appropriate however for this is a sphere in which emotion is not only generated but also happens to be the most effective mode by which to gain access to its mysteries.

Netzach is a sphere of worship (particularly of nature) and one of the most effective ways of approaching its heart is by "inflaming oneself with prayer". It is responsive to passion and devotion in a way that no other Sephirah can ever be. In the Yoga system the work that leads to Netzach would be termed Bhakti Yoga, or "union by love", as opposed to Hod's Jnana Yoga or "union by the Intellect".

The corresponding chakra is the *Manipura* whose subtle location is in the lower region of the epigastric, or solar, plexus around the level of the navel. It may be visualised as having ten petals, black or otherwise dark in colour, in the centre of which is found a red triangle signifying fire, this being the element of Netzach.

Although Shyam Sundar Goswami says of the *Manipura* that it functions as "the centre for thought-concentration and mental worship", a description which reinforces the *Sepher Yetzirah's* statement that Netzach "is the Refulgent Splendour of all the intellectual virtues", the accent here is on the mental-worship aspect while "thought-concentration" is perhaps better left to Hod.

Netzach's symbols have as their chief the Rose, which has always been the favoured symbol of Venus, and even in our own unromantic age the traditional gift of the lover to the loved.

The convoluted symbolism of the rose is a subject that could itself fill a book. As well as an occasional symbol for elemental air the flower is often used to represent the female sexual organs, as for instance in the ritual of *Liber XXXVI* "The Star Sapphire", in which the Adept is expected to be armed both with his "Magick Rood", and with his "Mystic Rose".

Of the magickal weapons of Netzach the first and perhaps most important is the lamp. This should not be confused with the lamp of Kether, which is a symbol of the divine light that both illuminates and inspires the adept. The lamp of Netzach is carried in the hand and represents the love of the magician which he must constantly nurture and protect.

The second major weapon is the girdle. This is also a traditional weapon of Venus and represents womanly eroticism combined with the power to fascinate and blind through love, and is often used to hoodwink or restrain a candidate during initiation.

Paradoxically (or not, to those who have made a study of the psychology of sexual arousal) the girdle may also be used as a symbol of chastity and continence, making it a particularly apt attribution.

Hidden within the girdle of Netzach/Venus, and often overlooked, is another weapon - the knot by which it is fastened. This knot is of a special and secret design whose pattern must be understood before it can be unravelled. Once mastered, full control over the wiles of Venus is gained for it may then be loosened or tightened at will, freeing the aspirant from the distracting glamour of "Kallipyge" whilst allowing free access to her subtle, or not so subtle, charms.

In other words the function of emotional love is made subject to the needs and intentions of the individual who is therefore no longer at the mercy of uncontrolled desires, for while love is undeniably the law, it must always be "love under will".

The Magickal Grade of the sphere of Netzach is Philosophus $4°=7°$, the last grade of the outer order known as the Golden Dawn.

Beyond the grade of Philosophus the aspirant passes via the linking grade of Dominus Liminis, into the Order of the Rose Cross, which has its first achievement in Tiphareth.

As a Philosophus the aspirant is expected to complete his moral training and to demonstrate his devotion to the Order, in accordance with the principles expressed by Netzach.

The colours in the four worlds are: in Atziluth an amber which Crowley describes as representing the "electric voluptousness of Aphrodite" (777). In Briah, emerald, the traditional colour of Venus, and of the colours of Chesed and Tiphareth combined.

In Yetzirah, the usual combination of the preceding colours; while in Atziluth is found an olive flecked with gold, suggesting the influence of the preceding sphere of Tiphareth.

The seventh Sephirah's animal correspondences include the Lynx and the Cat. Both are traditional correspondences and perhaps owe their inclusion to a commonly held belief in their sexual promiscuity and to their "luxurious voluptousness".

The Raven is included here, as the order of Qliphoth of Netzach is *A'arab Zaraq*, the Raven of Dispersion. As any student of Icelandic sagas will know, ravens are a common sight on fields of battle, and especially in the aftermath of a really bloody conflict. This would seem to relate the raven to the Victory aspect of Netzach, but in a particularly negative way.

The Rose, of course, is the special flower of Netzach, whilst the Laurel, from which is made the victory wreath, is the appropriate plant to represent the triumphant aspect of the sphere. Rose is also assigned as a perfume; as is red sandal.

The vegetable drug of Netzach is Damiana, a tonic and aphrodisiac found in South America and parts of Africa. The use of Damiana as an aphrodisiac is very ancient and is said to be most efficacious when consumed with large quantities of beet juice!

Cannabis Indica is assigned to both the seventh and the eighth Sephiroth, in the case of Netzach because the sensual nature of the induced visions is said to pertain to Venus; whilst in Hod, it is the increased power of self-analysis that commends its use.

The mineral drug is arsenic, which is a specific against many complaints of the nervous system and has been used for centuries as a means of beautifying the complexion.

The precious stone of Netzach is, unsurprisingly in view of the sphere's Briatic colour, the emerald, the traditional stone of the planet Venus. Emeralds have long been held to aid fertility, growth and self-fulfilment and are associated with Taurus, one of the signs ruled by Venus. They also have the useful property of functioning as an antiseptic and may be used to cleanse wounds and clear up disfiguring skin conditions. There is also a link here with Netzach's opposite sphere, for Hermes Trismegistus, one of Hod's most important semi-divine figures, chose emerald as the material on which he engraved the great hermetic axioms.

The corresponding Tarot cards are the four sevens; the seven of Wands, "Valour"; the seven of Cups, "Debauch"; the seven of Swords, "Futility"; and the seven of Disks which is titled "Failure".

Of this rather depressing quartet Crowley says:....

"These cards are attributed to Netzach. The position is doubly unbalanced; off the middle pillar, and very low down on the Tree. It is taking a very great risk to descend so far into illusion, and, above all, to do it by frantic struggle. Netzach pertains to Venus; Netzach pertains to Earth; and the greatest catastrophe that can befall Venus is to lose her Heavenly origin.

The four Sevens are not capable of bringing any comfort; each one represents the degeneration of the element. Its utmost weakness is exposed in every case".   *(Book of Thoth)*

13

Hod

GLORY   SPLENDOUR

The Eighth Path is called the Absolute or Perfect, because it is the means of the primordial, which has no root by which it can cleave, nor rest, except in the hidden places of Gedulah, Magnificence, which emanate from its own proper essence. *(The Yetziratic Text)*

Hod is the basal Sephirah of the Pillar of Severity, the negative or "Yin" column of the Holy Tree. It is the second, and feminine, potency in the triad of *Olam-ha-Mevethau*, the "Material World". Hod is negative to Netzach and Tiphareth but is positive to Yesod and Malkuth.

The eighth Sephirah is diagonally opposite the fourth, the sphere of Chesed, this important angular relationship being modified by Tiphareth, which is equidistant to both. The supplementary text of the *Sepher Yetzirah* suggests, albeit obliquely, that Hod has a special association with Chesed, which it refers to by its secondary title of Gedulah. The use of this particular title, which means "Glory" or "Magnificence", rather than the fourth Sephirah's more common name is important for it establishes an immediate link with Hod, which is on occasion also called "Glory".

Although Hod contains its own due portion of magnificence and glory it seems to have a special affinity with Chesed, responding most positively to the "kingly" aspect of the sphere suggested by its alternative title.

Immediately above Hod lies the turbulent sphere of Geburah which, as we have seen, functions at its positive best when acting in concert, rather than conflict with Chesed, while above Geburah is the massive presence of Binah, the root of form.

Chesed itself is the diagonal opposite of the third Supernal and is

165

therefore at the apex of a triangle which has Binah and Hod delineating its base-line on the Pillar of Severity. This is an important if often overlooked triadic arrangement which illustrates the interaction of energies between these three Sephiroth. (It is mirrored of course by an identical triad based on the positive pillar, formed from Netzach, Chokmah and Geburah).

In this arrangement the sublime understanding of Binah mitigates Hod's tendency towards cold intellectualism, while Chesed plays a mediating role in accordance with its function as the Tree's Justice and Mercy centre. Alternatively one can refer to the mundane chakras of the three spheres and see that Binah's Saturn, leavened by the Jupiter of Chesed, adds a neccesary degree of structure and control to the Mercurial activity which characterises Hod.

The powerful presence of Geburah/Mars, centrally located on the triad's base line and in opposition to its apex, energises the whole figure; providing the motive force and drive which keeps the Sephirothic energies circulating.

A clear indication that the refining and blending of potencies, which has been occurring throughout the descent of power is now nearing completion is to be found in Hod's Magickal Image, which is a Hermaphrodite, the perfect symbol of integration and balanced polarity.

The eighth Sephirah is a sphere of form, with particular reference to mental concepts and to the function of the intellect; mentation and communication being its primary mode of operation.

In Netzach, the first of the two "armies of God", is found the seat of emotion and the group mind. In Hod we now enter the sphere of the individual mind. To Netzach belong the forces of the gods, to Hod their forms. Although Netzach is the sphere in which the "Deity in His diversity" is first apparent by His actions, it is in Hod that the mental images of those "gods and goddesses who formed the world" are first developed.

Hod is a sphere of Magick and occult philosophy; intellectual appreciation rather than practical aptitude. One might say that for most purposes it is Yesod which is the domain of magickal activity, and Tiphareth which is the sphere of mystical activity, but that Hod encompasses the intellectual faculty and the very human trait of curiosity which are prerequisites for the Great Work.

166

Magick has been defined by Crowley in *Magick in Theory and Practice* as "The Science and Art of causing Change to occur in conformity with Will", and it is perhaps the "science" aspect of magick that particularly belongs to Hod.

It is obvious that in order to effect any kind of change the adept needs technique and specialised knowledge, as well as will and imagination. To quote Crowley again:

"The first requisite for causing any change is thorough qualitative and quantitative understanding of the conditions".

(Magick in Theory and Practice)

It should be understood however that as with any skill the true master eventually moves beyond mere technique, indeed reaches a point where technique becomes a barrier to further development.

So it is with the science and art of magick. The intellect must be exercised and strengthened, for it is the first great weapon of the work, but eventually there comes a point when it ceases to serve and begins to hinder the free flight of the soul. The intellect is the servant of the will, it must not be allowed to become its master.

The development of the *Ruach* is finally completed in Hod, which is referred to the faculty of Reason, considered by traditional Qabalists to be the least and the lowest of its five component elements. From the human standpoint of course, looking up at the Tree from Malkuth, Reason is the first element of the Ruach and is therefore commonly considered to be its superior aspect.

The practising magician needs to see the *Ruach's* five-fold division in its proper perspective. Each of the components is of equal importance, indeed they cannot properly function unless in tandem and in harmony, one with another. To raise one faculty above the others, or to down-grade one aspect in relation to the rest creates an imbalance which, especially in the case of the magician who is after all sworn to strive for inner equilibrium, is extremely unhealthy. Each aspect of the *Ruach* has its place and its time as "for everything there is a season". Imagination or emotion has no place in the keeping of a magickal record which ought to be a model of scientific observation and clarity. Equally, reason is of little value in our more profound meditations on the Tree, which are emotional and spiritual experiences whose full richness may only be expressible in symbol.

It should not be thought from this that the magickal tradition is in any way anti-intellectual, far from it, but it does recognise the dangers and limitations of an excessively cerebral approach to matters which are by their nature incapable of resolution and understanding by the mind alone.

The Hebrew name "Hod" carries the meaning "Glory" or "Splendour", which, as Dion Fortune puts it in her masterly work *"The Mystical Qabalah"*, suggests "....the radiance of the Primordial... shown forth to human consciousness."

In Hod are developed the forms of the gods, the invisible rendered visible, the inconceivable made conceivable.

Through the formation of the images of the gods are the gods known. By the use of a technique known as the "assumption of god forms" and by prolonged meditation on divine attributes and mythologies the adept can come, not only to understand the nature of a particular god, but to the point where he can begin to channel the typical energies of that god into his own being.

In the individual mind which develops in Hod the primordial emanation is afforded the possibility of a new "root by which it can cleave", and from whence it can show itself to its creation, in all its Glory and Splendour.

The god-name of the sphere of Hod is Elohim Tzabaoth, "God of Armies" or of "Hosts". It will be remembered that Netzach has the similar god-name of IHVH Tzabaoth or "Lord of Hosts" and that the two spheres are said to function as the "armies of the Lord". Whereas Netzach's part-name, IHVH, referred back to the second Sephirah, Chokmah, which contains the Tetragrammaton, Hod's name refers us upwards to Binah to which the name IHVH Elohim is given.

Unlike those of the positive column the Sephiroth of the negative pillar all partake of one name, for Geburah is also called Elohim, in this case Elohim Gibor, "God in His strength". This suggests both a commonalty of function greater than that found in the spheres of the positive pillar, and also, by the very nature of the shared name, a certain ambivalence of gender.

As might be expected by their god-names both Netzach and Hod relate very strongly to their respective superiors, the Supernal at the head of each pillar. We have already seen that Netzach reflects certain fundamental principles of Chokmah, such as the concept of change equalling stability, and that its mode of operation resembles that of the

168

second emanation, although in a manner appropriate to its position at the base of the column of mercy. In Hod we find a similar relationship to Binah, the Sephirah in which the concept of form is first established, for where Binah contains and holds the outrushing energies of Chokmah, Hod contains and gives substance to the amorphous creative denizens of Netzach. Both Binah and Hod are "form" Sephiroth, as Chokmah and Netzach are Sephiroth of "force" and as such could be said to represent respectively the opposed though complementary processes of catabolism and anabolism, at least in so far as these processes are deemed to function according to esoteric tradition.

The mundane chakra of Hod is *Kokab*, the planet Mercury.

Mercury is the planet closest to the Sun, and, along with Venus, with which it has a close relationship, is one of only two bodies standing between the Sun and Earth. It could be said then that in order for us to penetrate to the centre of the solar system and the ineffable light of the Sun, we must first accept and come to terms with Mercury and Venus; or, alternatively, that in order to reach the sphere of Tiphareth we must first experience and then master both Hod and Netzach.

Astrologically, Mercury represents the power to think and the principle of communication, in all its myriad forms. Its position in a natal chart, modified as always by its relative strength, indicates the manner in which the native uses his mind and his powers of communication.

Mercury rules the signs of Gemini and Virgo, and therefore has a particular affinity with the third and sixth houses, the houses of mentation/communication and of work.The glyphs which represent these two signs confirm the changeable nature of Mercury, and therefore of Hod, as Virgo is always pictured as female, while Gemini is symbolised by the young male twins Castor and Pollux. There is obviously scope for a great deal of confusion here, a confusion which is mirrored in Hod's somewhat ambivalent gender. At the highest level of integration, symbolised by the figure of the hermaphrodite, both the male and the female potencies work together in harmony to produce a functioning whole. When the process of integration is incomplete however dangerous stresses may be created in the psyche which can lead to an inability to relate in a meaningful way to persons of the opposite sex or, at worse, to a full-blown gender-identity disorder.

Mercury is a versatile sign that is in itself somewhat colourless, taking on the hue of whatever happens to impinge upon it.

It is coldly logical and not prone to express its inner self, even though an important part of its natural function is to facilitate the expression of others and is perhaps better thought of as the messenger rather than the message. This contrasts strongly with what we have learned of the mundane chakra of Netzach, the harmonious and emotional sphere of Venus.

The symbol of Mercury is a half-circle or prone crescent moon surmounting the circle of spirit below which is appended the cross of matter. This glyph differs from that applied to Venus by virtue of the crowning half-circle, which could be taken to refer to the sphere of the Moon, as illusion, or if seen as a broken circle, suggesting a certain incompleteness. The upper segment of the Mercury symbol may also represent a pair of horns, which again suggests a certain ambiguity of gender, for although the horns might seem to refer to the masculine potency they are supported by the universal symbol for the feminine in nature.

The Spiritual Experience or Magickal Power of Hod is termed the "Vision of Splendour", a profound, if primarily intellectual, appreciation of the glory of the gods as they manifest themselves in the world. Through the power of Hod may be discerned another dimension of the spiritual forces that create, sustain, and animate the manifest universe.

Hod's Archangel is often given as Michael, the fiery being who stands in the southern quarter, and who is called the "Likeness of God".

As we have already seen in the chapter dealing with Tiphareth there is some debate as to the correct designation of the Archangels to these two Sephiroth.

It may be thought, for the reasons given previously, that Raphael, "The Healing of Wounds" and ruler of the element of air, is a more fitting correspondence for Hod than Michael who is essentially a solar angel and therefore better placed in Tiphareth.

Amongst the many attributes that commend Raphael to the eighth Sephirah is the fact that he has long been associated with travelling, healing and teaching, all appropriate activities of the sphere of Hod.

He is not only a patron of travellers on the highways of the material plane; in common with the Roman god Mercury, who is also assigned to Hod, he functions as Psychopompos, the guide of the dead.

Although fire is sometimes found jointly assigned to Hod and Netzach Raphael's element of air is far more appropriate for a sphere of occult philosophy and communication.

Netzach's fiery nature heats the air of Hod and energises it, adding passion and enthusiasm where cold analysis and detachment would otherwise reign unchallenged. Equally, the intellectual ideas and concepts developed in Hod are fuel to Netzach's emotional furnace encouraging it to burn ever brighter, just as air will intensify the power of fire. In fact if one were to assign any single principle to the spheres of Hod and Netzach that principle would not be a traditional element but the process of combustion itself.

The order of angels are the Beni Elohim, the "Sons of the Gods" "the angelic sons of the gods and goddesses who followed after the children of Adam". These are the angels who went abroad on the earth before the Deluge when "the sons of the Elohim beheld the daughters of Adam." (*Zohar*) and who:

> "saw the daughters of men that they were fair; and they took them wives of all which they chose";

wives who eventually bore them children; children who became the

> "mighty men which were of old, men of renown".   (*Gen 6:2-4*)

The Beni Elohim, as might be gathered from the above, represent the form aspect of the creative process, in the same way that the Elohim of Netzach represent its force aspect.

These two orders of angelic beings may be considered as another level of the "armies of IHVH", working in co-operation to establish the Foundation of the Kingdom.

Of the gods associated with Hod, the one that comes most readily to mind must be the namesake of the sphere's mundane chakra, Mercury himself. Mercury was the Roman equivalent of the Greek, Hermes, who was the great messenger of the gods, father of Pan, and a mighty athlete. He was also the god of traders and merchants, who easily identified with his gift of eloquence and his penchant for travel. Quite apart from his patronage of matters mercantile (and incidentally, perhaps inevitably, with gambling and theft) he was thought to accompany the dead on their journey to Hades, in which capacity he was known as Psychopompos (conductor of souls).

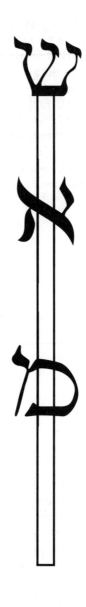

THE WAND OF HERMES

Hermes carried the Caduceus, a great and intricate wand which has become an important Qabalistic symbol representing the creative force of the Hermes/Mercury figure.

The Caduceus itself is a rod surmounted by the winged solar disk of the Egyptian mysteries. Around the stem are entwined two snakes whose bodies cross at Yesod, Tiphareth, and Daath, when the wand is applied to the Holy Tree. The heads face each other from the position of the second and third Supernals, whilst Kether is described by the solar centre of the winged disk. (see illustration).

The three "mother letters" of the Hebrew alphabet, can also be applied to the wand, as the patterns of the snake bodies are strongly suggestive of them. From the disk, these letters are *Shin*, the fire and the spirit; *Aleph*, the primordial motion; and *Mem*, the great waters which together describe an abbreviated formula of the descent of power from spirit to manifestation. (see illustration "Wand of Hermes")

Developing from Hermes is the semi-mythical figure of Hermes Trismegistus, "Hermes the Thrice Greatest". If there were such a beast as a patron saint of magick and magicians, Hermes Trismegistus would be the leading contender. It is from him that the western magickal tradition has taken the term "Hermetic" to describe its arts and sciences. Some commentators, particularly those of the neo-Platonist schools, have claimed that he was none other than the Egyptian God, Thoth; and others that he was the grandson of Adam, the first created man. It was Hermes Trismegistus who composed the famous "Emerald Tablet" upon which was engraved the prime Hermetic axiom, "As above, so below". He is also held to have written some forty-two books of Egyptian magick!

Other gods of the sphere include the Egyptian Mercury figure, Thoth, (although Crowley, in 777, gives Anubis as the lower form of Thoth here). Thoth, also called Tahuti, was originally a moon deity who, moving from Yesod to Hod, became the scribe of the gods and eventually "Lord of Magick" and "Lord of Speech" as well as "God of Truth and of Wisdom". From these titles alone it is clear that it is not by chance that the Tarot, the encoded distillation of centuries of occult knowledge, has become known as the "Book of Thoth".

Almost any god who shares the general characteristics of these Mercurial entities can be assigned to Hod; for example, Odin, god of battles and of wisdom; Loki, "wizard of lies" also from the Norse pantheon, and Hanuman, the cunning monkey god of Hindu mythology.

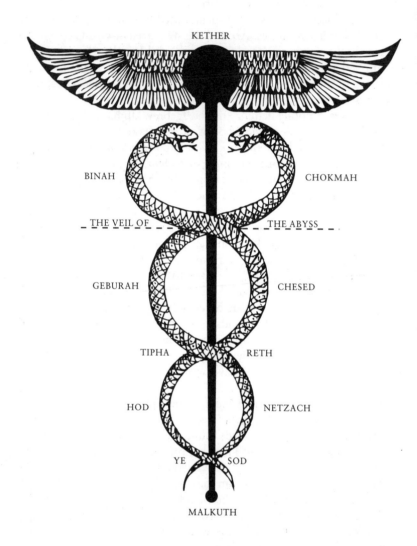

KETHER

BINAH

CHOKMAH

THE VEIL OF _ _ _ _ _ _ _ _ _ _ THE ABYSS _ _

GEBURAH

CHESED

TIPHA

RETH

HOD

NETZACH

YE

SOD

MALKUTH

THE CADUCEUS

The Virtue of Hod is Truthfulness and naturally enough its vice is the precise opposite, Untruthfulness or Dishonesty. Both the virtue and the vices of the sphere are typical of the deities who have been assigned to it. The mercurial gods all have truthfulness as a characteristic, even when such is painful to the recipient, but equally they are somewhat prone to the vice as well.

The Qliphoth of Hod continues this theme, being Samael "The False Accuser" otherwise known as "The Falsehood". Samael is the husband of the Qliphoth of Malkuth, Lilith, the "Woman of the Night", traditionally the first wife of Adam and said to be the mother of a demonic race which predated the coming of the Beni-Elohim.

Crowley is almost alone in assigning the *Svadisthana* chakra to Hod, both J.F.C.Fuller and Dion Fortune preferring Yesod and indeed refusing to give a chakra correspondence of any sort to the eighth sphere.

The *Svadisthana* chakra located just above the genital region in the area of the Hypogastric Plexus. In the Chinese system it equates with the *"Tan T'ien"* or "Cinnabar Field", and is associated with the male prostate gland. It may be visualised with six petals of a vermilion colour, and is known to the practitioners of yoga as the "Support of the Life Breath Centre".

In Hod the borderline between what constitutes a magickal weapon and what a symbol becomes more than usually confused.

Because of the nature of the sphere the primary weapon is the use of words, which of course are themselves symbols.

The first form of Hod's magickal weapon is the "versicle", which might be described as a mantra-like phrase or incantation used by the ritualist to promote, through constant and sonorous repetition, a particular state of mind. The versicles may also be inscribed as talismans describing the nature of the energies with which the ritualist is currently working.

"Names" are another version of the sphere's weapon, a category which includes both the multitudinous names of the gods and spirits, and the mighty barbarous "names of power" to be found in many older magickal tomes. (A particularly impressive collection of "barbarous names" may be found in the Preliminary Invocation of the Bornless One).

Proper pronunciation and intonation of these words is of paramount importance to the effective operation of many rituals, from the simplest of banishings to complex group workings.

The usual description of the proper manner of delivering such names and phrases is "vibration", with that vibration pitched at a level deemed appropriate to the force being addressed. The use of this peculiar vocal style has a long historical pedigree; the term "goetic magick" for instance, as applied to numerous medieval rituals, actually means "howling magick", and can be traced as far back as ancient Greece.

A faint remnant of this tradition may be heard in the sing-song delivery affected by some Anglican priests. A much more vigorous version of the same, rather more satisfying to the ear and to the soul, is to be found in the Eastern Orthodox Churches.

As far as the written word is concerned it should not be forgotten that in ages past the very fact of literacy was somewhat suspect and, outside of clerical orders, was quite liable to taint its practitioner as a black magician; and also that the word "Gramarye" along with its variants, was once used as a synonym for those very "black arts".

Another weapon of this path is the Apron, which covers the loins of the magician. As Crowley puts it:

"The Apron conceals the Splendour (Hod) of the magician, It also explains that splendour by virtue of its symbolic design." (777).

The apron is the traditional garment of the craftsman, one who works with form, for in Hod the magician also works with form, although at this level the magician is actually dealing with thought-forms rather than with anything remotely material.

The relationship of the apron to the lamen is also of interest here. Whereas the lamen covers the magician's body at the point of the Sun-centre, the apron covers it at the point of the Moon-centre but both carry emblazoned upon them a symbolic design appropriate to the nature or level of the work. The fact that it is the moon-centre which is covered in Hod reminds us that the equilibrium of the final triad is found in Yesod, whose mundane chakra is Luna, and that this condition of balance is fore-shadowed in the lower reaches of the eighth sphere.

The Magickal Grade of Hod is that of Practicus 3° = 8□.

The Practicus is expected to continue and complete his intellectual training. He should be skilled in the use of some system of divination, such as Geomancy, Astrology, or the Tarot, and have a profound knowledge of the Qabalah. As he comes to the end of his period as Practicus he should also have reached an understanding of the limitations of the intellect and be prepared to immerse himself in the font of emotion which awaits in Netzach.

The colours in the four worlds are as follows: in Atziluth; a violet purple merging with the brilliance of Kether to produce lavender, which in Briah becomes orange, an intermingling of the colours of Tiphareth and Geburah. In Yetzirah the colour is a red russet, being the combination of the previous two colours; and in Assiah, a yellowish black flecked with white which indicates "activity on many levels", although Crowley suggests that this colour represents a mystery of Mercury which is "improper to indicate clearly". It may or may not have been improper for Crowley to "indicate clearly" this mystery of Mercury, but it would certainly have been most incautious as he is here referring to homosexual love, which at the time of his writing was illegal in England.

The animals assigned to the eighth Sephirah includes many of those notable for their swiftness or cunning. The Jackal is given as being sacred to Anubis, and twin serpents as representing the double-current of Mercury, integral to the design of the Caduceus.

The "animal" most typical of the energies of Hod however is that also given as the sphere's Magickal Image, the Hermaphrodite, which again represents the dual nature of Mercury and is also suggestive of the sacred name Elohim in which that duality is embedded.

Hod's plant correspondences are Moly, given to Ulysses as an antidote to the spells of Circe; and the hallucinogen Anhalonium Lewinii, a South American cactus better known as Mescal, used by the Aztecs in religious ceremonies and said to produce colourful and varied visions.

The perfume is usually given as being Storax, due to its rather anonymous nature. As with the planet Mercury, Storax is itself somewhat colourless but when used as a base allows other perfumes to express themselves to their full potential.

The Opal is the precious stone attributed to Hod because of its multitude of colours, although the planet Mercury is traditionally said to rule amethyst, and the god Mercury to correspond with Chalcedony.

Precious opals are a form of quartz which are extremely porous, being able to absorb up to a third of their own weight in water.This has led them to be considered as essentially feminine stones with an particularly active inner life.

The absorbent and easily influenced nature of Hod is well mirrored by this stone which is affected by acids, alkalis, heat and of course, water. Of the spheres which surround Hod we can equate water with Yesod, heat with Netzach, acid with Geburah and because of its ability to neutralise and equilibrate its received energies, Tiphareth with alkalis.

The corresponding mineral drug is Mercury. Also known as Quicksilver for reasons that would not need explaining to anyone who has ever tried to recapture a wayward globule, this semi-liquid metal burns with a violet hue which recalls the sphere's Atziluthic colour. It has one well known medical use, in the treatment of venereal disease; a not altogether inappropriate remedy for an infection resulting from amorous encounters between the principles of Mercury and Venus.

The appropriate Tarot cards are of course the four eights; The eight of Wands, "Swiftness"; the eight of Cups, "Indolence"; the eight of Swords, "Interference"; and the eight of Disks, "Prudence". Crowley says of these:

> "Being in the same plane as the Sevens on the Tree of Life, but on the other side, the same inherent defects as are found in the Sevens will apply. Yet one may perhaps urge this alleviation, that the Eights come as (in a sense) a remedy for the error of the Sevens. The mischief has been done; and there is now a reaction against it. One may, therefore, expect to find that, while there is no possibility of perfection in the cards of this number,they are free from such essential and original errors as in the Lower case."
>
> (*Book of Thoth*)

14

The Foundation

THE PURE INTELLIGENCE

The Ninth Path is the Pure Intelligence, so called because it purifies the Numerations, it proves and corrects the designing of their representation, and disposes their unity with which they are combined without diminution or division.   *(The Yetziratic Text)*

Yesod is the ninth Sephirah of the Holy Tree and the focal point of the triad of *Olam-ha-Mevethau*. It is the third sphere on the middle pillar (disregarding Daath) and is situated midway between Tiphareth above, and Malkuth below.

Yesod is negative to all the preceding Sephiroth and positive to Malkuth alone. It is the final sphere of the *Sephiroth-Ha-Benyin*, and the sixth "side" of the dimension of matter, completing the universal cube.

In Yesod is found the resolution and integration of the spheres of Netzach and Hod; the ultimate equilibrium of the basal emanations of the outer pillars. The principles of form and force, represented by the left and right columns respectively, return to unity here, as do the negative and positive potencies.

The essences of the combined preceding Sephiroth devolve upon it, all material, energy, and impulse necessary for the ultimate act of manifestation is now gathered, for in Malkuth no new element is added.

Yesod is both the recipient of the qualities and principles of the preceding spheres and the bridge between the worlds of potentiality and actuality.

Here then is the completion of the creative process, awaiting only the development of a place of manifestation, but it is also the first stage of return, for the *Zohar* says:

"Everything shall return to its Foundation, from which it has proceeded. All marrow, seed and energy are gathered in this place. Hence all the potentialities which exist go out through this".

"Yesod" is usually rendered in English as "Foundation" or "Basis", for the material world is constructed on the etheric patterns developed in the ninth Sephirah.

The *Sepher Yetzirah* states that Yesod is the "Pure Intelligence, (and is) so called because it purifies the Numerations (Sephiroth)", by which is meant that the successively evolving forces and forms of the previous Sephiroth are perfected and corrected in the ninth emanation prior to their emergence in Malkuth. The "designings" of the spheres are thus rendered into forms appropriate for the physical world.

Yesod and Malkuth have an intimate relationship with each other, for what is concentrated in Yesod, through the agencies of the combined Sephiroth, and held in the "Treasure House of Images" (a subsidiary title of the sphere) comes to eventual functional form in the tenth Sephirah.

One aspect of the close relationship of the ninth and the tenth emanations is demonstrated by another of the multitudinous methods of dividing the Holy Tree, its organisation into "seven palaces".

This is an ancient and arcane doctrine which throws additional light on the complex relationships which exist between the Sephiroth. The three Supernal Sephiroth combined are considered to represent one palace of the seven, whilst the Sephiroth from Chesed to Hod represent one each. Yesod and Malkuth are jointly assigned to the seventh and last.

As the three Supernals are combined together to form one palace, suggesting thereby a commonalty of nature and purpose, so the same could be said to be true of the conjunction of Yesod and Malkuth, which together include both the world as it manifests to our senses and the astral foundation upon which it is raised.

Through this seven-fold division of the Holy Tree into palaces numerous additional correspondences with other systems become apparent.

In many mystical systems the number seven has been thought to be particularly significant. The Pythagoreans called it "the vehicle of human life", for it "comprehends soul and body"; and, because it may be divided into a three and a four, the three pertaining to the human soul and the four to matter, said of it;

"Therefore. the septenary Number, which consists of three and four joins the soul to the body".

(*A Treatise on Angel Magic {Harley 6482}* Ed. Adam McLean)

Some of the more obvious examples of seven-fold classification include; the seven days of the week; the branches of the sacred candlestick; the lamps of fire before the thrones; the angels which stand before the face of God; the seven traditionally known planets, and the number of Apocalyptic Churches in Asia. The seven-fold scale of the Theosophists may also be more easily integrated with the teachings of the Qabalah when the Tree is divided in this manner.

At least one of these septenary example, the Menorah, or seven-branched candlestick, is an important, if sadly neglected, Qabalistic symbol. It is a representation of the entire Tree, showing not only the ten Holy Sephiroth, but Daath and the four worlds. (see illustration) The exact (and extremely detailed) specifications for the manufacture of the first Menorah were given to Moses on Mount Sinai, "The Mountain of the Moon", which immediately relates it to Yesod whose mundane chakra is the sphere of Luna.

It is possible to assign the seven planets of traditional astrology to the palaces of the Tree, thereby allowing each a mundane chakra of one planet, but dispensing with the Primum Mobile of Kether, and the Zodiac of Chokmah. The resultant permutations are extremely interesting and well worth investigating but are omitted here in order to avoid confusion with the more common planetary correspondences used to illustrate the individual Sephiroth.

It should be clear by now that such manipulation of the Tree does no violence to the principles that underlie its structure but rather demonstrates what an extraordinary and flexible tool we have in our possession.

Yesod has been described as the "engine room" and "powerhouse" of the material world. It is pre-eminently the sphere of Ether which partakes of both mind and matter, as might be guessed from its position in the order of emanation, between Hod and Malkuth, the spheres in which those principles are most clearly expressed.

It is here we encounter the Astral plane, the background, as it were, of the material world and the Foundation upon which it rests.

It could be argued that the whole of the formative world of Yetzirah partakes of the astral plane to a greater or lesser degree, but it is Yesod,

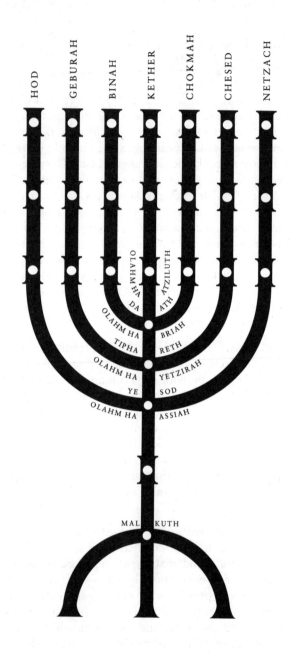

HOD · GEBURAH · BINAH · KETHER · CHOKMAH · CHESED · NETZACH

OLAHM HA · ATZILUTH · DA · ATH

OLAHM HA · BRIAH · TIPHA · RETH

OLAHM HA · YETZIRAH · YE · SOD

OLAHM HA · ASSIAH

MAL KUTH

THE MENORAH

as the culmination and focus of Yetzirah, which best typifies it and which, due to its close proximity to Malkuth, has the most practical consequence for the occultist.

The Astral world both overlays and inter-penetrates the physical realm. By manipulation and modification of astral images magicians are able to effect changes in dense matter which would otherwise be unresponsive to their efforts. By causing change to occur in the astral plane, which by its very nature is less substantial and more plastic than its physical counterpart, the material analogues of astral images are also changed.

Occultists believe that each person is possessed of a number of "subtle bodies" (the actual number vary according to the school) and that each of these bodies will operate effectively only in its own discrete sphere. Thus, to work on the astral plane in a manner that will allow for direct manipulation rather than passive viewing, it is necessary to develop a functioning and controllable vehicle, which in this case we could term the "astral body" but which is often called a "Body of Light".

Likewise, to explore planes other than the physical or astral further specialised vehicles would need to be developed.

Whilst this is not the place for an extended discussion of such matters, which deserve a book, or better a whole library, to themselves, it can be seen how important Yesod, as the focus of the astral plane, is to the practical magician.

A brief word of caution would not go amiss here. Though there are undoubtedly universal verities that apply throughout the planes, each one of these levels has its own laws and modalities which result from its unique internal structure. It is well for the magician to remember that actions or attitudes appropriate to one plane may not be appropriate to another, indeed may be positively dangerous.

A great deal of grief awaits those who confuse the planes, or do not sufficiently banish the one before entering the other.

It is important therefore not to "confound the space-marks", and to do in Rome what the Romans do, but to do that only in Rome and not in Corinth or Mitylene, at least if one would hope to see Heliopolis.

The name of God in this sphere is Shaddai-el-Chai, which means the "Almighty and Ever-Living God" or "Supreme Lord of Life".

The name Shaddai, literally the "Almighty", was a term favoured by some early Jews as a substitute for the most holy name of AHIH before being supplanted in common usage by the Tetragrammaton of IHVH, which itself became the subject of taboo by virtue of the third commandment.

As with the name Elohim, Shaddai signifies far more than a purely masculine generative impulse. This powerful aspect of the creative deity has rulership over the reproductive principle as it manifests in the material world. It encompasses both the male and female potencies in balanced expression for *ShD* signifies the female breasts and nipples just as much as it does the masculine reproductive drive.

By gematria "Shaddai" adds to 314 and is the numerical equivalent of the name of the Archangel of Kether, Metatron, the "Great Angel of the Covenant" who we will meet again in Malkuth. By the rules of Qabalistic numerology these two names may be considered equal and indeed the Almighty warned Moses against offending his angel with the words, "My Name is in him", (*Zohar*), while the *Talmud* says "His name is like the name of his master".

In some early works Metatron is addressed as though he were in fact Shaddai Himself; while the *Zohar* describes him as the "Garment of Shaddai".

Yesod's mundane chakra is *Levanah*, the sphere of the Moon.

With the exception of Shemesh, the Sun, the Moon is certainly the most visible object in the heavens, and the one whose effect on the life of Earth is most marked. With its regular periodic cycle of waxing and waning it has long been identified with woman's mysteries, the ebb and flow of the tides, and the strange passing humours of the mind.

Every culture has its Lunar lore regarding such matters as the right and proper season in which to plant, tend, or lift the fruit of the earth, and equally every culture has at one time or another used the Lunar calendar to determine its holy, and perhaps not so holy, observances. Although the phases of the Moon and the Lunar calendar itself are embedded in the traditions and observances of Christian churches it is within the pagan tradition that the major body of Lunar lore is to be found.

The Moon has long been associated with the sea whose very tides are caused by its gravitational pull. Both the sea and the Moon represent remembrance; the sea our racial memory and earliest origins, the Moon, our personal and family history.

She has both a light and a dark side to her nature. Works of

184

destruction and purgation are traditionally carried out during the waning phase, whilst beneficial works and works of positive construction are presided over by the waxing Moon.

It is common-place to equate the periodicity of the Moon with that of woman, bound as she is for half a lifetime to the same monthly rhythm, physically expressed through her menstrual cycle. On a more subtle level, men too are subject to cycles which echo those of the Moon and of woman. The Moon is primarily the sphere that rules and regulates the mystery of womanhood, but it can also call forth the feminine in the man. Acts of worship directed towards the Moon are not exclusively in the domain of women; men also must be prepared to work with the Lunar forces, as women must likewise be prepared to work with the Solar current. Only in this way will it be possible to achieve true balance and harmony in both individual and society.

Our moon shines and illuminates the Earth not by its own luminosity but by the reflected light of the Sun. In the same manner Yesod reflects the light of Tiphareth down into Malkuth and the world of actions.

The Earth and the Moon are said by some occultists to share one etheric body, and that the Moon is the positive pole in this duad.

From the point of view of the Holy Tree much the same could be said of the relationship between Yesod and Malkuth, for here too the "Foundation" is the positive polarity in the circuit with Malkuth as its receptor. This concept of a shared etheric body is supported of course by the allocation of the seventh palace jointly to the Moon and Earth.

Astrologically, the Moon represents the principles of flux and response, assimilation and reflection. In a natal chart the position and relative strength of the Moon by sign house and aspect is said to determine the outward behaviour of the native, his habits, instincts and relationship with the mother figure. It rules the period of early childhood; before the infant child grows into the full light of its natal Sun, which is a physical analogue of the ineffable divine light. In much the same way we as adults must strive to grow into the light of Tiphareth, which is itself but a lower arc of the incomparable splendour of Kether.

The Moon and the great waters are both traditional and somewhat obvious images of conception and child-birth. The new Moon has often been used as a metaphor for coitus. The word "synodic", used to describe a period between two new moons has its root in the Greek, *"sunodos"* meaning copulation, the derivation of the image being clear when one remembers that the new Moon results from a Solar/Luna conjunction. Therefore the sight of the swelling waxing Moon, after its union with the Sun, has given rise to its use as an image of pregnancy.

Before leaving the subject of the Moon it is worth turning again to the collects from the Gnostic Mass in which our satellite is described and petitioned thus:...

"Lady of night that turning ever about us art now visible and now invisible in thy season, be thou favourable to hunters, and lovers, and to all men that toil upon the earth, and to all mariners upon the sea". *(3rd Collect)*

Yesod's archangel is Gabriel, the "Mighty", the "Man-God",

"that stand(s) in the presence of God". *(Luke 1:19)*

Gabriel guards the western quarter, the station of the down-going Sun. His colours are predominantly green-blue shot with silver, as befits one who is of the nature of water.

As the angel of the Annunciation and the Resurrection, Gabriel is one of the few such beings admitted by the modern established churches, although nowhere in the Bible is he actually described as an archangel, being referred to only as an angel, and even, (in *Daniel 9:21)* as "the *man* Gabriel". The only entity specifically described as an archangel in either the Old or New Testaments is Michael, traditionally the archangel of Hod but more fittingly placed in Tiphareth.

Although Gabriel's correct weapon is a chalice, in the popular imagination he will be forever associated with the trumpet, whose shape is anyway an attenuated form of chalice. The "Mighty Angel's" horn is however no common musical instrument but a stylised phallus symbolising his powers of fecundation and generation.

The trumpet which is both phallus and chalice underlines Yesod's position as the point at which the differentiated current is re-united in one sphere. It symbolises the masculine and feminine potencies conjoined and refers to the magickal weapons of Chokmah and Binah, the level of the Tree at which the unity of the primal impulse was first divided.

Although it will be found that some authorities give the appropriate order of Angels for the ninth Sephirah as the *Kerubim* this is an error for the proper place of the "Angelic Cherubs" is in Malkuth.

The correct angelic hosts for Yesod are the *Ashim*, the "souls of fire". This name is developed from the Hebrew *Aish* which carries the meaning of a "justified" or "just" man. In spite of the male connotation of the name Yesod's host exhibits both masculine and feminine traits.

The choir of *Ashim* carry forward the generative process initiated by Shaddai and further developed by Gabriel into the astral realm which precedes final concretion in Malkuth.

They are much concerned with the penultimate sphere's function as the Holy Tree's propagation centre, facilitating germination and reproduction on both the subtle and the physical planes.

In Yesod are found the basic sexual drives; it is the root of the emotions of sex and the sphere that corresponds with the generative organs on the physical body. The gods and goddesses of the path reflect this sexual element, as they do Yesod's other attributes.

They may be roughly divided, albeit with considerable over-lapping, into the categories of specifically Lunar deities, which would include the "Lords and Ladies of Magick"; gods and goddesses of fecundity and sexuality, and those who are held responsible for supporting the sky or the globe of earth.

It may come as something of a surprise to find included amongst the deities of Yesod and its mundane chakra a goodly number of male gods, some of them very male indeed. It has to be remembered that we are dealing here with basic principles and that these principles are not always gender specific in their natural manifestation but only seem so in their corrupted social form.

Each human being is a microcosm containing all the potencies and potentials of the Holy Tree, regardless of their presenting sex. Yesod is after all not only the focus and synthesis of the final triad, it is also heir to the combined Sephirothic influence. As such it is to be expected that the polarities will be found manifested in perfect harmony.

It is largely because of Yesod's generative capacity and its association with human sexuality that Crowley suggests all exclusively phallic gods belong in Yesod.

However few gods are "exclusively phallic" and those that most nearly approximate that condition may perhaps be more accurately assigned to alternative Sephiroth by virtue of their other characteristics.While one is always well advised to consider Crowley's suggestions most carefully, the phallic gods have not automatically been included here unless they also qualify by other criteria.

Of all the Lunar deities, Diana the Huntress is possibly the one who springs most readily to mind. Diana, the Roman form of the Greek Artemis, although best known as a goddess of the Moon, was originally an Indo-European sun goddess. She became particularly associated with the Moon in the popular mind as the "goddess of the pagans" during the dark centuries of the "burning times" in Europe.

Diana developed into a major goddess of the embattled pagans who had perforce to worship her at night in wild places or hidden groves. Some traditions assert that Diana was originally the supreme female deity, the consort of Lucifer "The Light Bringer" and mother of Aradia who descended to earth in order to impart her mother's mysteries to the witches.

Artemis was a nature and moon goddess of ancient Greece and the model for Diana. She was the daughter of the all-father Zeus and Leto the Hyperborean and was the twin of Apollo, the Sun god. Interestingly, although the twin of Apollo she was a day older than her solar sibling, reflecting the relative positions of Yesod and Tiphareth on the journey of ascension up the middle pillar.

She was mistress of magick, protector of youth and patron of hunters, who also ruled over all the mysteries of women from menstruation to childbirth. In Sparta she was worshipped in her dark aspect with annual human sacrifice. She has been known by a variety of different names including; Callisto, Cynthia, Delia, Phoebe and Pythia.

A complete model of the phases of womanhood as it relates to the periodicity of the Moon is found in the figure of the Triple Goddess.

Here is described the stages of womanhood; Virgin, Mother, and Hag or Crone. The goddesses who fall most readily into these categories are; Selene, the virgin; Aphrodite, voluptuous lover and symbol of fertility; and Hecate, popularly perceived as barren and destructive. These stages represent the new, full and waning moon respectively.

Khons, or Khonsu, an Egyptian Moon god, may also be attributed to Yesod. At one time he was considered to be a functional aspect of the twin god, Horus; and as the son of Amun and Mut was himself the divine child of a holy triplicity. His name means "traveller", which presumably refers to his nightly journeys across the sky in his lunar guise. In common with many female Moon deities, at certain periods in his development Khons, like his father, was worshipped as a Sun god. He was however primarily a god of healing and a protector against malevolent animals.

Khons also had a ghostly manifestation which is particularly apt for Yesod and in this subtle form was considered to be the joint guardian, with the *ka* or etheric double, of the monarch's physical and psychic health.

Thoth, Lord of Magick, was also worshipped as lord of the Moon and was called the "silver Aten", Aten being the visible manifestation of the Sun god, Ra. Although Thoth is also assigned to Hod his attribution here is entirely appropriate, for Yesod is both a lunar and a magickal sphere.

Shu, also from the Egyptian pantheon, was born as breath from the nose of the primal creator. He was the god of air, who, along with his sister-wife Tefnut, goddess of moisture, brought forth the sky-goddess Nuit, and Geb, the god of earth. It was Shu, who, by lifting the body of Nuit above his head, separated the vault of the sky from the earth. In numerous mythologies we find men or sacred animals performing the office of Shu and supporting the vault of heaven or, alternatively, holding aloft the material globe.

These figures represent both Yesod's function as the Foundation of the physical world, and as a bridge from one kingdom to another.

The aspect of the Christian God that is most appropriate to the ninth Sephirah is that of "God the Holy Ghost", who comes upon the Virgin Mary, in effect as an incubus, to impregnate her with his seed; a dramatic scenario that is part of a long tradition of unorthodox conceptions and a common motif in mythology and folk-tale throughout the world.

The third component of the body of the "Archetypal Man" is termed *Nephesh*, and is located in the sphere of Yesod. Here we encounter the unredeemed "animal soul" of man, which is often compared to the psychoanalytical concept of the subconscious mind, but which might be better related to the "collective unconscious", for we must not forget that Yesod is the "Treasure House of Images" and the great repository of forms and archetypes.

Nephesh consists of two principle areas or elements; the first is the astral self of the individual, already briefly discussed, while the second is akin to "Prana", the breath, or life-force, of the Eastern tradition.

In the book of Genesis (2:7), that most instructive of Qabalistic documents, we may read a graphic account of man's acquisition of the "vital principle" of *Nephesh* through the agency of the breath of IHVH Elohim, imparting the gift of life to Adam, the "Man of Dust".

Qabalists have termed *Nephesh* the "lower soul" to distinguish it from the *Neshamah* the upper or "precious" soul.

The *Zohar* says:..."The *Nephesh* is the awakening from below and she is a support (Foundation) to the body"; and further, that;.... "This *Nephesh* forms and is made a throne for the *Ruach* to rest upon", which becomes in its turn a throne for the support of the *Neshamah*.

The chakra corresponding to Yesod is the *Muladhara*, said to be subtly located between the genitalia and the anus. This area of the body, termed the perineum, is an important plexus both in occult and in physical terms. It is considered the root or "hiding place" of the Kundalini Serpent, and is the seat of sensual pleasure. The perineum is also one of the most powerful of the "G-jo" or acupressure points, the correct stimulation of which is claimed to be highly efficacious even in cases where the patient is near death.

The *Muladhara* chakra functions as the sexual centre of the subtle body and is visualised in the form of a four-petalled lotus.

Amongst the most important of Yesod's symbols are the rich variety of lunar images, particularly those based on the apparent shape of the Moon in her changing phases; full, crescent, balsamic, and gibbous, each conveying a particular aspect of her nature.

It must be emphasised that the Moon images described here are only to be considered as being symbolic of aspects of the Sephirah of Yesod, and are a means of more closely approaching the sphere. Their usage in this context should not be confused with that of "pure" planetary workings where the same symbolism may be used but with the specific intention of invoking the lunar current itself.

The virtue of Yesod is Independence, whilst its vice is given as Idleness. The Qliphothic attribution is *Gamaliel*, the "obscene ass", a reference to the perversion or exaggeration of Yesod's sexual function.

The magickal weapons are three in number; the Sandals, the Altar, and Perfumes. Taking them in reverse order, the perfumes represent a link between heaven and earth; to quote Crowley, "This link is material by virtue of the substance of the incense, and spiritual by virtue of their action through the olfactory sense upon the consciousness" (*Liber 777*). Incense has long been used as a sacrificial offering to the deity and as a medium of communication with the "spirit world" who may use the fumes as an aid to manifestation on this plane. Perfumes are also extremely powerful psychological agents which are capable of profoundly influencing the sub-conscious mind, as the vast fortunes amassed by the worlds great perfumeries testify!

The particular perfume which most accurately corresponds with the level of consciousness expressed by Yesod is Jasmine, by reason of its supposed effect on the generative process.

Ginseng, the Chinese tonic, stimulant and all round wonder-plant (*Panax*, one of its botanical names, means "all-healing") can perform the office of both a drug or a perfume in Yesod, which is itself the "sphere of perfumes".

The altar represents the foundation of the work in a temple and provides the base upon which the structure of a ritual is built, mirroring the action of the ninth Sephirah.

Although the generic altar belongs to the sphere of Yesod, there are specific types of altar which, by virtue of their design, position, or specialised functions are more aptly assigned to other Sephiroth.

Sandals provide both the "holy ground" on which the magician treads and his "mode of going". The Ansate Cross (Crux Ansata or "Ankh") often used to symbolise the divine in ancient Egypt, was developed from the pictogram of a sandal strap and signifies the power to move forward, becoming thereby a symbol of life in its fullest sense.

This form of cross, implicit in Yesod, becomes explicit in the sphere of Tiphareth where it is elevated to a major symbol in its own right.

Yesod's Magickal Grade is Zelator $2° = 9^{\square}$, whose principle duties, as recorded in *"One Star in Sight"*, are to "achieve complete success in Asana (yoga meditation postures) and Pranayama (yogic breathing)". He is also expected to begin his studies of the formula of the Rosy Cross of which the ankh or Crux Ansata is an important form.

For a comprehensive account of the whole subject of meditation and yoga from a western magickal standpoint the interested student is strongly recommended to study Crowley's *Book Four part 1*.

The Magickal Image of Yesod is a beautiful naked man, powerful and well muscled. The classical depiction of Atlas supporting the world is an excellent form upon which to construct an appropriate image.

The colours in the four worlds are as follows; in the world of Atziluth, the indigo of the etheric plane, which in Briah becomes a rich violet, as if the colours of Chesed and Geburah were mingled together. In Yetzirah we find, as always, a combination of the Atziluthic and Briatic scales here producing a deep dark purple; and in Assiah, citrine (a pale greeny-yellow) flecked with azure, which is possibly derived from Chesed via Netzach.

The animals assigned to Yesod include the elephant and the tortoise, both of which are found in mythology as supporters of the sky or globe. Also given is the toad, which was once thought to have hidden in its skull a precious jewel of great virtue, this being symbolic of its fabled generative power, a power well demonstrated by its copious spawn.

The plants include the aphrodisiac, Damiana, also assigned to Netzach as a vegetable drug; and Mandrake, which, with its man shaped root, has always been considered a strongly phallic plant.

The Banyan tree, also referred to Kether, is placed in Yesod for, to quote *Liber 777;* "It is, so to speak, the foundation of a system of trees as Yesod is the foundation of the branches of the Tree of Life".

The orchid root is the vegetable drug of the sphere, again due to its reputation as an aphrodisiac and is a good example of folk-lore based firmly on the "doctrine of signatures". In this case it is the characteristic testiculate shape of the root which suggests a possible use, for it is strongly reminiscent of a human testicle and it is in fact from the Greek word for testicle that the plant's generic name comes.

Although the orchid root is especially appropriate here all roots are sacred to Yesod by reason of the sphere's role as the "root and foundation of the Tree".

As well as the inevitable attribution of Moonstone, the crystalline varieties of Quartz, which are much used in healing, are also said to correspond with Yesod, most particularly with its Foundation aspect.

According to Crowley the gold that is sometimes found in quartz is suggestive of the concealed glory of the sexual process and also suggests a reflection of *Shemesh*, the mundane chakra of Tiphareth.

There are a great number of different forms of quartz, some of which are attributable to other Sephiroth, but the quartz group as a whole belongs in Yesod. Apart from the occasional piece with golden inclusions it is probably the clear variety, known as Colourless Quartz or Rock Crystal, which is most appropriate for the ninth sphere although Crowley places it in Malkuth as it superficially resembles the diamond of Kether.

Rock Crystal's birefringent, or "twice refracting" property reminds us that the ineffable light of Kether has itself been twice refracted through the spheres of Daath and Tiphareth before it illuminates the ninth emanation, and that being crystallised directly from the primal magma its origins are to be sought at the very beginning of the creative process.

The cards of the Book of Thoth are, of course, the four nines these being; The nine of Wands, "Strength"; the nine of Cups, "Happiness"; the nine of Swords, "Cruelty"; and the nine of Disks, which is titled "Gain". As Crowley puts it:

> "Each of these cards gives the full impact of the elemental force, but in its most material sense; that is, of the idea of force, for Yesod is still in Yetzirah, the formative world".
>
> *(The Book of Thoth)*

15

Malkuth

THE KINGDOM   THE QUEEN

The Tenth Path is the Resplendent Intelligence, because it is exalted above every head, and sits on the throne of Binah. It illuminates the splendour of all the lights, and causes a supply of influence to emanate from the Prince of countenances" *(The Yetziratic Text)*

Malkuth is the final Sephirah of the Holy Tree and the ultimate stage in the sequential emanation of the Godhead. It occupies the basal point of the Middle Pillar, pendant to the sphere of Yesod.

It is positive in itself but negative to all the other Sephiroth on the Tree and is the junction for only three paths, which connect it to each of the Sephiroth of the Triad of *Olam-ha-Mevethau.*

The tenth Sephirah does not represent any new attribute or principle; it is the final phase of concretion of the primal impulse, for here the influences of the preceding Sephiroth come at last to the place of manifestation.

The *Zohar* says of Malkuth; "It is the sum total of the permanent emanating yet immanent activity, of the totality of the entire Sephiroth, and is Elohim's presence in Its creation".

Malkuth is the sphere of the concrete, the realm of the physical world. It represents the Sabbath day, the day of rest and repose, passivity after the strenuous labours of the Sephiroth of Construction.

Malkuth encompasses more than just the perceived world of matter however, for contained herein is what has been described by Dion Fortune as, "the subtle, psychic aspect of matter; the underlying noumenon of the physical plane which gives rise to all physical phenomena". (*Mystical Qabalah*) This aspect of Malkuth's compass exists in the upper-reaches of the emanational area of activity, the highest level of its operations. The psychic aspect of matter occupies a midpoint in the vital and reciprocal relationship existing between Malkuth and Yesod. The basis of phenomenal reality lies in Yesod's astral forms, which in their densest aspect begin to impinge on Malkuth. Likewise, the more rarefied manifestations of the power of Malkuth reach up to contact the penultimate sphere.

Although the *Sepher Yetzirah* states quite clearly that Malkuth should be "exalted above every head", it does not say that it should be exalted above every Sephirah. As the realm of the physical world, Malkuth has always been in danger of being considered inferior or less holy than the preceding Sephiroth. By now it should be clear that this is far from the case, for the sequence of emanation does not in any way represent a dilution or deterioration of "spiritual quality" but is rather a process of increasing specialisation and concretion of its expression.

Malkuth represents the culmination of this process, for here is God made visible by His works, glorying in His creation.

All the Sephiroth of the Tree are holy, the last even as the first, for they are not scaled or graded in any way. As we are constantly reminded by Qabalistic doctrine; "Kether is in Malkuth, though after another fashion".

The *Sepher Yetzirah* also makes a specific reference to Binah, the third Supernal, stating that Malkuth "sits upon its throne". Binah is the first Sephirah in which the idea of form becomes apparent, albeit in a archetypal manner. Malkuth, being the quintessential sphere of form in which is evinced the final development of that concept, rests firmly upon the pioneering work done in the Supernal world.

Malkuth is termed by the Qabalists "The Lower Shekinah", while Binah is called "The Upper Shekinah". Reference has already been made to the doctrine of the Shekinah in the chapter dealing with Binah, so we will confine ourselves here to that part of the concept which specifically relates to the tenth Sephirah.

It will be recalled that the Shekinah, whose name means "dwelling", "brightness", or "Bride", can be loosely described as "the Holy Spirit conceived as feminine in essence". The Lower Shekinah of Malkuth is a concretion of the Spirit of Binah, exercising, as it were, the executive power of the Supernal in the material world and is the spirit of God revealed in the plane of action, "the Glory of the Presence of the Deity" made manifest.

Whilst the Shekinah appears in Binah in her ineffable glory, she moves across the face of Malkuth as a tangible influence. The Shekinah as she appears in Malkuth is distinguished by the fact that her dark and potentially malevolent aspect is far more in evidence here than in the worlds above the Abyss. She may even on occasion be possessed by that power of stern judgement operational in the sphere of Geburah.

The *Zohar* tells us that; "At times the Shekinah tastes the other, bitter side, and then her face is dark". This dark and terrible aspect reflects the dual nature of woman, implicit in the twin mother figures of Binah, the bright fertile form of AIMA, and the dark barren form of AMA; it also suggests the waxing and waning of the Moon with its light and dark phases.

Some Qabalists have claimed that the destructive aspect of the Shekinah in Malkuth arises from her separation from the body of God, and consider this condition to be one of "exile". They say, in effect, that there is an element of God which is divorced from the whole, and that therefore a part of Him is exiled from Himself. The Shekinah is said to represent His feminine component, which has become detached through the sinful and destructive actions of His own created beings.

The biblical history of the wandering children of Israel is taken to be one of several allegorical accounts of a process which has caused a deep rift to appear between God and man, spirit and matter, and man and woman. It is part of man's redemptive work to heal the breach between "God and His Shekinah", and restore thereby the harmony of the original creation.

The first stage of this ambitious task must be to reconcile the fragmented elements of our own psyches, and in particular to come to accept and embrace the woman in man and the man in woman.

The Hermetic axiom "As above, so below", means not only that the breach between God and His Shekinah is mirrored in the human condition, but that by celebrating our own "alchemical marriage" we have an immediate healing effect on the condition of the Deity, for it is equally the case that what occurs below effects what occurs above.

One classical method of applying the "ineffable name" of IHVH to the Tree which throws additional light on the relationship between Malkuth and Binah is to assign the initial *Yod* to Chokmah, the first *Heh* to Binah, the *Vau* to Tiphareth and *Heh final* to Malkuth.

The letter *Heh* is then taken to signify the feminine principle in the formula; as Queen/Great Mother in Binah, and as Princess/Daughter in Malkuth. An alternative attribution, which has the letters applied to the four worlds, with Malkuth as *Olam-ha-Assiah*, may also be used in this context, although the assignation of the first *Heh* to Briah must necessarily include Chokmah as the joint tenant of the Briatic world.

We can see how the formula of Tetragrammaton highlights the close relationship between the two spheres, the higher octave of the feminine principle being applied to the third emanation, the lower octave to the tenth.

The *Zohar* says of the third Supernal; "Thou shalt call Binah by the name of Mother", and in *The Lesser Holy Synod* describes Malkuth as the "Mother of all living things". This is quite literally so, the ideal forms of all subsequent manifestation reside in Binah, but it is in the sphere of Malkuth that they are born into the light of day.

Several of Malkuth's subsidiary titles emphasise its relationship with Binah, and reinforce its position as the lower form of the Supernal Mother. Although clearly referring to the crudest possible manifestation of the maternal principle, the "Inferior Mother" is one such title recalling the Zoharic descriptions of both the third and final spheres.

The title "Virgin" can be said to refer both to the "pure" condition of Binah prior to its devolution to the material world, and to the status of that world before its eventual "marriage" to Tiphareth. "Kallah, the Bride" and "Malkah, the Queen" may be taken to refer to union with Tiphareth as the Son and King, or alternatively to Malkuth as the Bride and Queen of Tetragrammaton.

Other titles use the image of the "gate" (usually, but not always, as a prefix), these include: "Gate of Justice", "Gate of Death", "Gate of the Garden of Eden", "Gate of the Daughters of the Mighty Ones", "Gate of Tears" and simply "The Gate". The reoccurring motif of the gate suggests that there is some traffic through Malkuth and that the sphere does not represent a cul-de-sac or a terminus as such.

These titles plainly refer to a two way movement, both into the sphere and away from it. The "Gate of Death" can be seen as referring to both the spiritual essence leaving a physical body, (a death in our plane of consciousness, but a birth in another) or to an incarnation on this plane of a new spirit. We enter into life via the gate of the womb, but a condition of that life is the existence of death, for life and death are complementary states, two sides to the one coin. The gate therefore, even as it initiates into life condemns to certain death. There is implicit in incarnation the fact of death, but it must be remembered that each death is also a re-birth, even as each birth represents a death on another plane.

"The Gate of Justice" recalls the fact that Malkuth is the world in which karmic burden is accrued, whilst the "Gate of the Daughters of the Mighty Ones", and "Gate of Tears", refer us once again to Binah as the first feminine sphere, whose power is the "Vision of Sorrow".

The name of God in Malkuth is given as either Adonai ha Aretz, or Adonai Malekh. The first name means "Lord of the Earth", and the second, "The Lord who is King" and both are facets of the God made manifest in His created world. Not only is the God-form of Malkuth manifest in the world of matter there is a sense in which that very world is generated entirely out of His own substance. At the Atziluthic level of the god-name is found the point at which matter as we know it is originated, formed as it were from the very body of God in His most tangible aspect. The "Lord of the Earth" is then at one and the same time both ruler and originator of the physical realm. It is He who takes the perfected images of Yesod and compresses them into solid form, and who animates and sustains those forms in the world at large, aided by His willing workers the archangels, hosts and elemental spirits.

The Archangel of Malkuth is usually given as Sandalphon, and although he is now accepted as such by most modern Qabalists it is arguable that the traditional assignment of Metatron is perhaps more valid, especially for the totality of the sphere.

As we know from our study of Kether, Metatron is the "Great Angel of the Covenant", and the sum of all the angelic forces. He was the first of all the creatures created by the God, "The oldest of His house", the servant given governorship over the angelic forces of the entire Tree.

Although vested with universal authority, he is particularly associated with the Middle Pillar, the column of balance and harmony.

His attribution to the sphere of Malkuth confirms his rulership over the whole material universe, demonstrating the insoluble link between spirit and matter. His presence is implicit in all the Sephiroth, but is explicit in Kether as the "first servant" of the Most High, and in Malkuth as the "Angel of the Presence".

As Metatron has rulership over the entire physical realm he of course has rulership over the elements (in all their aspects) of which that realm is largely composed.

Sandalphon however is specifically the Archangel of Earth, his realm being confined to this one planet, although it is true to say that one is likely to experience his influence most strongly in the continuum between Malkuth and Yesod, an area of activity which encompasses both the ninth and the tenth spheres.

A distinction must be made here between Earth as a planetary body and earth as an element. Sandalphon is strictly the Angel of the planet, while Uriel is the angel of the element, although above them both stands the mighty figure of Metatron.

It is possible to view Metatron and Sandalphon as two aspects of one entity. The great angel of Kether being, traditionally, "The Light Angel" and the angel of Malkuth his "Dark Twin".

In some pictorial representations of the OTz ChIIM, the angels are depicted standing either side of the Tree with their right hands jointly grasping the hilt of the flaming sword, which then becomes the lightning flash of the descending power on its journey from the unmanifest to Malkuth. Sandalphon is the "Dark Angel" of the duo by reason of his realm being one of physical incarnation, with all that is implied thereby; and the realm also of karmic accretion.

The order of angels in Malkuth is often given as the *Ashim*, "the souls of fire", but this designation is incorrect for the proper hosts of the final Sephirah are the *Kerubim*, "The Strong", "Angelic Cherubs of the four ways, winds and forms". This is clear when one realises that the Kerubim are a supermundane but relatively dense expression of the *Chayoth-ha-Qadesh*, or "Holy Living Creatures" of Kether and that, under the governorship of Metatron, they exercise control over the sphere of the elements which is the mundane chakra of Malkuth.

Although some early Qabalistic writings assign the Moon to Malkuth on the grounds that it, like the final emanation, reflects the glory from on high, most authorities now agree that the correct placement of the Moon on the Tree is in Yesod and that the proper mundane chakra of the tenth Sephirah is indeed *Cholem ha-Yesodoth*, the "Sphere of the Elements".

The early alternative, although inaccurate for a mundane chakra as such, should not be dismissed out of hand for as we have already seen Earth and Luna are said to share a single etheric body while Malkuth and Yesod reside in the same palace and to a certain extent function as a duo. It may well be that the power of Yesod's mundane chakra penetrates further into the succeeding sphere than is the norm elsewhere on the Tree and that it therefore has an invisible but not inconsequential influence on the world of form in general and the "subtle psychic aspect of matter" in particular.

Although Malkuth has no assigned planetary correspondence some rituals do use Saturn for the sphere, but this is specifically a "Saturn viewed as earth", and not the celestial Saturn which is properly applied to Binah.

The four elements of Earth, Water, Fire, and Air, represent states and modalities of being or reacting rather than actual phenomena.

The physical material of earth for example is the densest, least abstract form of the element, and would be described by Qabalists as "earth of Assiah", "earth of Malkuth" or even "earth of earth".

The same principle applies for each of the remaining elements, which can then be assigned a degree of abstraction from their material form by reference to one of the four worlds. For example, water, in its most rarefied state, what might be termed the "spiritual condition of water" would be assigned to the archetypal world as "water of Atziluth", whereas the densest form of that liquid, designated by the formula H_2O, would be called "water of Assiah".

The variable nature or quality of one element may also be further defined by reference to another. Therefore the fluid, malleable part of earth would be termed "water of earth", and the dynamic initiatory aspect "fire of earth". (Of course, "water of earth" and "earth of water", "fire of earth" and "earth of fire" etc, although having some relationship, are actually very different states and one must be careful to distinguish between them). Each element then may be subdivided into four levels or degrees of manifestation, the purest expression of which is described as "air of air", "fire of fire", and so forth through the elemental sequence.

Classification according to elements is found in every area of the esoteric sciences from healing to astrology, and is an extremely useful method of organising attributes and comparing the nature of dissimilar things.

The basic principles of the unmodified elements may be summarised as follows:

EARTH	WATER	FIRE	AIR
supportive	flexible	initiatory	mobile
static	receptive	aspiring	communicative
functional	sensitive	active	intellectual
restrained	intuitive	assertive	connective
cautious	emotional	ardent	excitable

Possibly the most obvious example of this four-fold division is to be found in the Tarot suits, which are assigned as follows:

EARTH	WATER	FIRE	AIR
Disks	Cups	Wands	Swords

While in psychological terms the elements may be disposed thus:

Sensational	Intuitive	Feeling	Intellectual

One could go on to classify virtually all phenomena in terms of elemental and sub-elemental categories, but the above examples should suffice to illustrate the general principles.

Before leaving the *Cholem ha-Yesodoth* we should remember that behind the four traditional elements there lies a fifth, Spirit, the upper-most point of the pentagram, which permeates the entire structure of the Tree, and therefore all creation.

To help develop a real understanding of all five of these elements the serious student is recommended to study *Liber Samekh sub figura DCCC*, "The Bornless One", and its accompanying scholion, which may be found in a number of places, including the invaluable *Magick in Theory and Practice*.

The Egyptian god Geb (sometimes written as Seb or Keb), in his capacity of "Lord of the Earth" is an obvious Malkuth correspondence. The offspring of the sibling deities Shu and Tefnut, and sister of Nuit, he emulated his parents' incestuous relationship by mating with his sister, producing Osiris, Isis, Set, and Nephythys.

With his impressive generative power Geb was considered ruler of the world and was usually depicted in his ithyphallic form, or occasionally as a goose, an ancient symbol of sexual potency.

His successors to the mantle of earthly authority were; first his son Osiris, then his grandson Horus, and finally the line of the kings of Egypt, among whose many titles was to be found "heir of Geb".

Unusually for a deity so closely connected with the earth Geb was very much a male god, in contrast to so many others with similar power and authority who are almost always female; the earth conceived as both virgin and mother.

Crowley gives several alternative Egyptian attributions; The Lower Isis and Nephythys as virgins "imperfect until impregnated", and the Sphinx.

The Sphinx is a most interesting correspondence in the light of Malkuth as it displays all the characteristic features of the Kerubs, who themselves represent the four elements, so strongly featured in the tenth Sephirah.

The Greek goddess Persephone, the virgin earth, is another major Malkuthian deity. She in fact predates the Greek civilisation with which she is most associated but was said to be the daughter of Zeus and Demeter. She was known to the Romans as Proserpina and it is under that name that most references to her will be found in classical works. Persephone was also known, in her aspect as the maiden, as Kore. Her story tells how she was abducted by Hades and forced to spend one half of the year underground, being allowed to return to the surface only during the spring and summer months. This is a particularly apt myth for Malkuth as it plainly refers to the cycle of vegetable growth, with its spring rebirth and summer glory; her six subterranean months of imprisonment being the winter period of no apparent growth.

The story of Persephone has been a favourite subject of classical painters and poets, changing gradually over the centuries to an allegory of death with Swinburne in particular showing a fascination for the tale's more morbid aspects.

The goddess Persephone may be regarded as a lower form of Demeter, with whom she was associated in the fabled Rites of Eleusis, in the same way that Malkuth may be considered a lower arc of Binah.

Ceres, the Roman goddess of Corn, is fairly typical of the multitude of earth fertility goddesses found in all parts of the globe and was worshipped until relatively recently in the temples of the Aventine hills of Italy.

Lakshmi, the Hindu goddess of love and beauty, and wife of

Vishnu, in her aspect as a symbol of sensuality and fertility, is another appropriate image for the tenth Sephirah.

The Christian correspondence is that of the Virgin Mary, again on a lower arc than the aspects seen in Binah which are "Mary mother of God" and the "Mater Dolorosa".

Nephesh, the last category of the three-fold division of the archetypal man, was assigned to Yesod, completing the traditional classification. In Malkuth, at least according to the writings of Rabbi Azariel ben Menahan, there is yet another component; that of the material body itself.

The physical vehicle is termed by the Qabalists *Guph* and strictly speaking is not part of the body of Adam Qadmon, being but a temporary "lodging" of the immortal self. The specification, characteristics and usages of this vehicle hardly need be rehearsed here as it is presumed that the majority of those reading this text will have an example in their possession, or at least close at hand!

There is a good deal of confusion to be found amongst occultists regarding the assignment of a chakra to the sphere of Malkuth. Indeed there is a school of thought which argues that there is no justification for making any assignment at all, given that Malkuth is the Sephirah of the physical world itself and therefore the place where the subtle actions of the power centres have their ultimate effect.

One suggestion, from Dion Fortune amongst others, is that the correct chakra for the sphere is the *Muladhara*, with the *Svadisthana* then transposed from Hod to Yesod. This system of correspondences is less than satisfactory however when one looks at the attributions that are necessarily forced upon the preceding Sephiroth if the *Muladhara* is applied to Malkuth rather than Yesod.

The system adopted throughout the present work is based on Crowley's researches and has, by and large, been found to be both logical and practical. In this system of attribution Malkuth does not relate directly to any individual chakra but is considered to be subsumed into the sphere of Yesod and therefore is only indirectly attributed to the *Muladhara*. (The *Muladhara* chakra itself is touched on in the chapter dealing with the ninth sphere).

Although in some Qabalistic traditions Malkuth is related to the anus and buttocks, it is more practical in ritual usage to consider the sphere as being approximately on the level of the feet. In both the Middle Pillar exercise and the Qabalistic Cross Malkuth is visualised as a sphere whose zenith covers the feet and whose nadir is in contact with the earth; but for aesthetic reasons it is usual to touch the groin, or point to the ground, when making the sign of the cross rather than risk an undignified injury by attempting to reach the feet.

The feet are actually not an inappropriate physical correspondence for Malkuth as they constitute a major plexus of subtle energy channels, which radiate throughout the body. Practitioners of Reflexology, or therapeutic foot massage, claim that an individual's internal organs are mirrored in the soles of the feet and that pressure manipulation of specified areas can effect changes in the function of these organs. The parallel with Malkuth can readily be seen; where in the feet is found the "mirror" of the body's vital organs, in Malkuth is discovered the "totality of the entire Sephiroth".

The Spiritual Experience or Magickal Power of the tenth Sephirah is the "Vision of the Holy Guardian Angel". The HGA has already been discussed under the heading of Tiphareth, to which sphere belongs the achievement of its "Knowledge and Conversation".

The power of Malkuth however should not be confused with that of the sixth Sephirah. In Malkuth the work is preparatory to Tiphareth's achievement, a foreshadowing of the full experience, being an increasing awareness of the presence of the angel, but without any immediate possibility of genuine communication.

The Virtue assigned to Malkuth is "Discrimination"; the ability to assess and act upon perceived differences.

The characteristic vices are Avarice and Inertia. Malkuth is the ultimate sphere of form and stability and avarice relates directly to its form aspect, being a pathological need to acquire and retain. It will be recalled that avarice is also the vice of Binah, and is in fact the first of all vices to be applied to the Tree. This double attribution emphasises Malkuth's close association with the third Supernal, which between them span the whole range of possible expressions of the concept of form, from the most rarefied to the most tangible. It also warns against the distracting glamour of the material world and reminds us that even at the level of the Supernal kingdom it is possible to be deflected from the work by the bright baubles of the lower paths.

The second of Malkuth's twin vices, inertia, clearly results from an overemphasis of the sphere's essential stability, negating any possibility of change and growth.

The Qliphothic attribution is Lilith, "lady of night", traditionally the first wife of Adam, and supposed mother of a race of demons. Lilith, although sharing the same numerological value as Samael, her mate in Yesod, relates us back again to Binah which is the fount of all feminine attributes. The *Zohar* goes so far as to state that she "was a maid-servant to the Matrona", a title which is applied to both the Shekinah and Malkuth itself and which may also on occasion be used to describe Binah.

Although popularly considered to be a creature of unmitigated evil she is perhaps better considered as a version of the Kali/Androphonos figure met with in both Binah and Netzach than a typical Qliphah. Probably the main reason for her banishment to the infernal realm is the fact that, as Adam's first wife, she refused to submit to her husband's will and, equally damning in the eyes of the pious, was rather indiscriminate in her choice of sexual partners.

Malkuth's symbols include the equal-armed cross, representing the elements in equilibrium; and the double cubed altar.

The altar is generally speaking a symbol referred to Yesod in its capacity as the "Foundation", but the altar of the double cube is specific to Malkuth. This structure, usually occupying a central position in the temple, is constructed to the approximate height of the main ritualist's navel and is painted black externally and white internally. The two cubes, one placed above the other, symbolise the maxim "As in the macrocosm so in the microcosm", or more directly "As above so below". It is by reason of this symbolic function that the altar has been included under the category of magickal symbol rather than that of magickal weapon.

The magick circle and the "Triangle of Art" are the two major weapons of Malkuth. The circle delineates the magician's sphere of operation, offers a degree of protection and "announces the nature of the Great Work". (777)

The triangle, which must be placed outside the protective ring of the circle, is the place of manifestation for an evoked entity, where form is conferred upon the formless, and is clearly reminiscent of the sphere of Malkuth itself.

A few words regarding evocation might be in order here as it is often confused with invocation which is quite different in both purpose and technique.

During invocation the magician calls down a specific aspect of cosmic power which, having made himself a fit vehicle for its reception, he allows to consume and intoxicate him. The adept at this time takes on the nature of the force invoked and for the duration of the ritual becomes the embodiment of that force. Invocation may be described as a species of possession, although that possession is (or should be!) willed and controlled.

Whereas invocation requires that the adept attunes himself fully to the desired force and allows, indeed welcomes, its influx, the practice of evocation requires that every precaution is taken to avoid such contact. Traditionally evocation has been used to summon up those unbalanced lower forces commonly referred to as demons or spirits. Modern interpretation tends to classify these entities as dissociated elements and complexes of the magician's subconscious mind. Whichever view the student takes the fact remains that in either case it is well to treat these energies with the greatest respect. To that end evocation demands that there be provided a safe place of manifestation, outside the circle and away from the body of the magician, where the evoked entity may be summoned to vision and properly restrained. It is usual to provide a triangle for this purpose. The being may then be safely questioned until such time as the adept gives it licence to depart.

Elemental spirits and demons of all persuasions have on occasion, by virtue of superior strength or guile, overcome the magician and escaped from their confinement causing considerable psychic, or even physical harm to the ritualist. It is fair to say that although evocation is a valuable magickal skill it is well to avoid its practice until sufficient magickal experience has been gained and the magician is absolutely sure of his abilities.

In spite of evocation's attribution to Malkuth such skill is unlikely to have been accumulated as yet by holders of its magickal grade, which is Neophyte $1° = 10°$.

The Neophyte's task is to obtain mastery of the astral plane prior to entering Yesod via the Tau or Universe Path which links the ninth and tenth Sephiroth. Below the grade of Neophyte lie two others which are not related to the Sephiroth as such. The first of these preparatory grades is Probationer $0° = 0°$ whose task is to begin to practice those disciplines that most appeal and to write a detailed record of the same for the one year prior to his admittance to the grade of Neophyte. Before reaching even the acknowledged level of Probationer the aspirant is considered to be a Student and expected to study the various systems of attainment "as declared in the prescribed books", which are detailed in the curriculum of A∴A∴ published in the *Equinox* and *Magick in Theory and Practice*.

Malkuth's Magickal Image is a young and beautiful woman, crowned and enthroned. She is a representation of Malkah the Queen, but is also the Virgin, and Kallah the Bride.

The Atziluthic colour is yellow, of which Crowley writes; "The yellow indicates Malkuth as the appearance which in our senses attach to the solar radiance. In other words, Malkuth is the illusion which we make in order to represent to ourselves the energy of the Universe". (777)

In Briah the colours are Citrine, Olive, Russet, and Black; each a combination of the colours of the preceding triads. The four Briatic colours are those which are seen quartered on the Disk, one of the elemental weapon of earth. In Yetzirah the colours remain the same but the black is now flecked with gold, while the colour in Assiah is a black rayed with yellow, representing Malkuth upon the throne of Binah, touched by the yellow rays of her bridegroom, Tiphareth.

The animal assigned to Malkuth is the Sphinx, also considered a "god" of the sphere, and which is included here as an animal for precisely the reasons given under the first category, namely the elemental correspondences expressed in its composite body.

Plants include the Willow, Lily, Ivy, and all cereals. The Willow is a tree that has a particular association with the virgin, here considered as "Malkuth unredeemed"; whilst the Lily symbolises that maiden's essential purity and at the same time reminds us of the eternal presence of death.

The Ivy suggests another aspect of Malkuth, namely its tenacious and rather clinging nature.

Cereal crops and wheat in particular are also assigned to Malkuth as they represent the "staff of life" both actually and symbolically. Crowley also suggests the Pomegranate which is both sacred to Proserpina and suggestive of the "feminine symbol", although it may also be assigned a place in Yesod or Netzach, or for that matter in Binah.

Malkuth's vegetable drug is corn, which may be rendered into a spirit by distillation, or act as a base for the growth of ergot, a powerful hallucinogenic fungus.

The perfume is "Dittany of Crete", much used in ceremonial magick in classical times.

Crowley gives Rock Crystal as the preferred precious stone of Malkuth, for the reason that it reminds one of the aphorism "Kether is in Malkuth and Malkuth is in Kether, but after another manner". However the resemblance is somewhat superficial and the stone is better placed in Yesod for the reasons given under that heading.

One unconventional, but apposite, stone, though hardly a "precious gem", is coal. This material is composed of the countless minute bodies of our planet's early inhabitants and the vegetable matter through which they moved and on which they often fed. It is in a sense a distillation of the attributes of Malkuth. Coal also reminds us that there is a close connection between the first and the last Sephiroth for both it and diamond are carbon based although each has been subject to different formative process.

The four tens of the Book of Thoth relate to the final Sephirah, and have the following rather gloomy titles:... Ten of Wands, "Oppression": Ten of Cups, "Satiety": Ten of Swords, "Ruin": and the Ten of Disks, "Wealth".

These cards are all rooted in form, the fluid energetic nature of the elemental forces are stilled and brought to stasis, only for the earth suit of Disks is there here an appropriate environment. Crowley says of the Ten of Disks, the final card of the sequence:

"There is another view to consider, that this is the last of all the cards, and therefore represents the sum total of all the work that has been done from the beginning. Therefore, in it is drawn the very figure of the Tree of Life itself". (*The Book of Thoth*).

Thus in the most material and "earthy" of the seventy-eight images which comprise the Tarot we see the entire Tree shining forth in its ineffable power and glory, completed as it were in the arena of manifestation.

This then is the culmination and fulfilment of the primal impulse initiated by the establishment of Kether and the start of a new creative cycle as the divine energies and potencies prepare to return to their source.

"Tumult and peace, the darkness and the light -
Were all like workings of one mind, the features
Of the same face, blossoms upon one tree,
Characters of the great Apocalypse,
The types and symbols of Eternity,
Of first, and last, and midst, and without end."
                    (William Wordsworth, *Prelude, "Crossing the Alps"*)

16

The Literal Qabalah

The Literal Qabalah is divided into three major areas. These are termed; "Gematria", "Notariqon", and "Temurah", and each involves some manipulation of letters or their numerical equivalents. Of the three it is Gematria which is most widely practised today and which offers its exponent the most immediately practical benefit.

Gematria

It has long been held by theologians and philosophers of many different cultures and traditions that numbers represent the purest possible expression of cosmic truth. Thinkers such as Pythagoras, Plato, Augustine, Origen, and Bede, quite apart from innumerable specifically Qabalistic writers, have extolled the virtue of numbers and their relationships as a means of better understanding the structure of the universe. Indeed Pythagoras went so far as to claim that "all things are numbers", and St. Augustine that; "God made the world in measure, number and weight: and ignorance of number prevents us from understanding things that are set down in the scripture in a figurative and mystical way".

Today, many of the more adventurous scientific speculations are only expressible in mathematical terms, which, although they might appear to the layman to have little to do with numbers as such, ultimately owe their existence to the pioneering work of those early scholars.

As numbers are the most abstract of symbols they are considered to be the most fitting to represent the least tangible of structures, and that being, as it were, unconfined to any one plane or dimension, are equally and consistently applicable to all. They thus provide a universal language which is not confined by cultural and temporal barriers, and which may yet prove to be the principle mode of communication between different species.

The American scholar K.J.Conant expresses this well when he says:

"The philosophers perceived that number, being perfectly abstract, can therefore be shared by all three worlds: physical, spiritual and mystical. Beautiful patterns of spiritual thought are elaborated by the adepts in symbolic numerical studies - patterns which give pure joy because they are entirely uncontaminated by mundane or temporal things. The philosophers considered that the beauty, order and stability of the universe depended on number".

(Medieval Academy excavations at Cluny: 1963)

One could go on to fill page after page with quotations from both classical and contemporary scholars regarding the value and variety of numbers, some exceedingly erudite, others frankly little more than rank superstition. But for our present purposes we need only accept that any given number has its own individual significance and that it carries a weight of symbolic meaning which has been accumulated over thousands of years. These symbolic correspondences show a remarkable consistency throughout the ages and a surprising unanimity of meaning across the cultural spectrum; suggesting that numbers do indeed represent profound universal verities.

Of course numbers do not exist in isolation, they relate to each other in a variety of ways, the most obvious being by addition, division, and multiplication. Any number above the unity of one can be divided into constituent parts which increase in complexity and permutation according to that number's value. In the same way that Malkuth can be said to contain the essence of the nine preceding Sephiroth, so the number ten can be said to contain all of the preceding numbers. And, in accordance with our favourite aphorism that "Kether is in Malkuth, though after another fashion", we find that the first element of the figure ten is one, referring us back to the original unity.

Staying with our example of the number ten for the moment, we can see that it may be constructed in a number a different ways, each of which throws a different light on its character. We might for instance view it as a combination of the two significant numbers of seven and three, with all their multitudinous correspondences and references, or alternatively, as the result of adding four, the number of solidity and power, to the solar number, six. It is clear then that each number not only has an arithmetical and a symbolic value, it is also composed of other numerical elements which are themselves the products of meaningful sets of relationships.

211

Although many Qabalists would argue, along with Pythagoras, that numbers have an inherent virtue it is not necessary to subscribe to this view in order to practise Gematria. It is quite possible to use numbers simply as reference points in the comparison of words and phrases without investing them with any intrinsic quality. But we should always be aware that numbers have historically been held in the highest esteem, and that many of the terms used in Qabalah have been selected with special regard to their numerological significance.

As we have already learned, Hebrew, like Greek, has no numerals. Therefore each of the twenty-two letters of the alphabet doubles as a number. (see table in appendix). It follows from this that any given word will also have a numerical value derived from the addition of its constituent letters. This also applies to phrases and even whole scriptural passages.

A brief look at the table of numerical equivalents will show that the first nine numerals are assigned to the letters from *Aleph* to *Teth*; the tens from *Yod* through to *Tzaddi*, and the the first four hundreds to the remaining letters of *Qoph*, *Resh*, *Shin*, and *Tau*.

It should be noted that in most cases combinations of numbers are written with the greater symbol preceding the lesser. So in the case of number eighteen the combination is ten plus eight, or *Yod* plus *Cheth*, bearing in mind of course that Hebrew is written from right to left. There are however certain exceptions to this rule as in the case of the numbers fifteen and sixteen which are not, as might be expected, written as *Yod* plus *Heh* and *Yod* plus *Vau* because both are fragments of the divine name IHVH, and therefore may not be written down by the orthodox. Here the solution is simply to arrange a different combination of letters to add to the same value, *Teth* plus *Vau* (nine plus six) for fifteen, and *Teth* plus *Zayin* (nine plus seven) for sixteen.

In Gematria certain of the letters may take on a different value when they appear in their *final* form at the end of a word; for example *Mem*, which has the value of forty in the primary or medial position, becomes six-hundred when placed at the end; while *Peh* is multiplied by ten to become eight-hundred in its *final* form.

Another point to remember is that when a Hebrew letter is written large its value is increased a thousand-fold, thus *Gimel* which has a normal value of three becomes three-thousand, and *Daleth* increases from four to four-thousand.

Do not be too alarmed if all this seems rather complicated, the practice is very much easier than the theory, and in any event a quick reference to the letter table in the appendix will give sufficient information for most work.

In Gematria each word is considered to possess a numerical value which is derived from the sum of the values of its constituent letters. Any other word or phrase which has the same number value is held to be identical with, or in some manner explanatory of, that word.

Personalities, concepts, and objects which are at first sight utterly dissimilar may be shown by Gematria to have meaningful relationships. Often the relationships thus exposed are somewhat startling; one classic example, mentioned earlier in this book, is the correspondence between the Hebrew words *Nahash* ("Serpent"), and *Mashiah* ("Messiah"), whose numerical values are both 358. Other examples might be the name "Adam", which shares the value 45 with "The Fool"; "Son of God" which adds to 138, the same value as "He shall smite", "divide" and "to leaven or ferment"; and the number 228 which encompasses "First-born", "Blessed", "Ruler of Earth" and "Tree of Life".

Occasionally it may be found that two words share not only a common number value but are also composed of the same letters, although of course in a different arrangement. In such cases we may assume that the bond between them is especially strong. One such relationship occurs with the Hebrew word for "Nothing" or "Negative Existence"which is usually transliterated *Ain*, and the word for "I", the personal identity, which is *Ani*. Taking *Ain* as the condition obtaining before the creative process begins, and *Ani* as the end result of that process, the showing forth of God's "personality" in His creation, we are presented with what Gershom G. Scholem describes as

"a dialectical process whose thesis and antithesis begin and end in God". *("Major Trends in Jewish Mysticism")*

Another example may be found with the word *AL* and its reflection *LA*. The first is a title of the *Book of the Law* and means God; while the second has the meaning "Not", which refers to a condition or modality of being rather than to absence or negation.

Our understanding of the traditional concepts associated with some of the individual letters of the Hebrew alphabet may be enlarged by comparing their numerical values with full words and phrases.

A particularly good example of this is found with the letter *Shin*, which refers to both fire and spirit. As can be seen in our table, *Shin* has the value of three-hundred, which is also the value of the phrase *Ruach Elohim* or "The Spirit of God". This is the spirit that appears in the midst of the four elements, expanding IHVH to IHShVH, Yahweh to Yeheshuah, bringing the Saviour forth into the world.

Before we go on to consider other aspects of Gematria it might be well to look at some more examples of how this technique may be used to expose unsuspected relationships between seemingly dissimilar concepts.

We have touched on the Messiah figure twice in this chapter, once relating the word itself to the serpent by reason of common numerical value, and once referring to Yeheshuah, or Jesus, the Anointed One of the Christians.

In Hebrew the name of Jesus has a Gematric value of 326, an increase of 300 over the value of the Tetragrammaton. However according to the *Sepher Sephiroth* (which counts *Mem final* as 40 rather than 600) the phrase "The name Jesus" adds to the interesting total of 666, "Six-hundred three-score and six", the number of the Beast in *Revelation*. At first sight this might seem an unlikely combination, but surely no more so than that of the Messiah and the Serpent.

Tiphareth, the "Christ-centre" and "Sphere of the Sacrificed Gods", is the sixth Sephiroth in the order of emanation, whose mundane chakra is Shemesh, the Sun. The number six is therefore considered to be a solar number, but it is also the number of man for he was created on the sixth day. We can see the number 666 as being the number of man raised by virtue of the trinity to the highest degree; as *Revelation* tells us it is not only the number of the Beast, but also the number "of a man". The triple six suggests that here all aspects of the triune deity are activated and the three Supernal Sephiroth are now concentrated in Tiphareth. This is the ultimate solar number. Addition of all the figures contained in the solar square, or "Kamea", which comprises thirty-six numbers arranged in six rows of six, gives us the total of 666. Amongst many other Gematric correspondences this number includes that of Sorath, the spirit of the Sun, and embraces the concept of "Ommo Satan", the "evil" trinity composed of Typhon, Apophras, and Besz.

The complex of ideas which may be cross-referenced through 666

214

is enormous, those given above being but a selection of the better known (or perhaps more notorious) examples, but they should be enough to demonstrate just how useful the practice of Gematria can be to Qabalists.

Another good example of the usefulness of Gematria, this time using the Greek Qabalah, is found when we look at the number 93, which is of special importance to Thelemites. Numerical correspondences include; *Thelema* and *Agape*, Greek for Will and Love respectively; an expanded form of the Gnostic name of God, *IAO*; *LA-AL-LA*, a formula of emanation within the Supernal Triad; the formula *LAShTAL*; and a version of the name *Aiwass*, the disincarnate entity who dictated the *Book of the Law* to Crowley at Cairo in 1904. In fact so numerous are examples of this number in Thelemic literature that the magickal current of the new aeon is frequently referred to as the "93 current".

Although the "order and value" of the English alphabet is known it is probably better for the novice to translate English words and phrases into Hebrew or Greek before using Gematria, at least at first. This is for the reason that both these tongues use letters to represent both phonetic and numerical values, which is not the case with English, and have a considerable body of tabulated Gematric conversions available for study and comparison. The most useful of these is the *Sepher Sephiroth (sub Figura D)* (Hebrew), often found published as an appendix to *Liber 777*; and *Liber MCCLXIV* (Greek) which is rather harder to find but has been published under the auspices of the O.T.O. in a number of countries in the last few years.

It is of course essential that the student invests in a comprehensive Hebrew lexicon and English/Hebrew dictionary and becomes familiar with the forms of Hebrew letters, both script and printed.

It is important also that the basic rules of Hebrew grammar are committed to memory, and in this regard an introduction to Biblical Hebrew, such as a "Teach Yourself" book, is invaluable.

Greek presents fewer difficulties for western student. We are more familiar with its symbols, and its structure is closer to English than is Hebrew. Also the fact that it is written from left to right and uses vowels, unlike the north-western Semitic languages, makes it an altogether less intimidating proposition.

Along with much other information the Greek alphabet as used in Gematria may be found tabulated in *Liber 777*.

There is one final point worthy of note, neither the vowel points in Hebrew or the accents in Greek serve any purpose in Gematria and both may be safely ignored.

Notariqon

The term Notariqon is derived from the latin word *notarius* which means shorthand writer. It is a technique of exegesis used to great effect by evangelising Christian Qabalists in their attempts to convert Jews by radical re-interpretation of the Scriptures. We have seen in our introduction how successful their efforts were with the notable physician Paul Ricci and John Stephen Rittengal, the translator of the *Sepher Yetzirah*, both converted by this means.

There are two forms of Notariqon, the second being the exact reversal of the first. In the first form every letter of a given word is taken as the beginning of another, so that from a sample word a phrase may be built up. A word four letters in length will generate a sentence of four words, each one of which starts with one of those letters.

A word which much exercised the imaginations of medieval Qabalists, and which was one of the principle Christian weapons in their evangelising efforts amongst Jewish Qabalists was the first word of Genesis, which in Hebrew is *Bereshith*. So much work has been done on this one word, usually taken to mean "In the Beginning", that it is frequently used to illustrate this form of Notariqon. Indeed it is such an excellent example that no apologies are offered for citing it once again here.

MacGregor Mathers, in his introduction to the *Kabbalah Unveiled* gives several examples of the manner in which this single word may be made to offer up a variety of instructive sentences.

The first, and from the orthodox Jewish point of view, the most acceptable of these phrases is;

BRAShITH RAH ALHIM ShIQBLV IShRAL ThVRH,
"In the beginning Elohim saw that Israel would accept the law".

The following examples are the work of the Christian convert Prosper Rugere (whose name before abandoning the faith of his fathers was Solomon Meir Ben Moses) and are primarily aimed at demonstrating that the Messianic nature of Jesus; the doctrine of the Holy Trinity; the Immaculate Conception; and the principle of Tran-

216

substantiation, are all detailed, albeit somewhat obscurely, in the Pentateuch.

BN *RVCh AB ShL VShThM IChD ThMIM..*
"The Son, the Spirit, the Father, Their Trinity, Perfect Unity".

BN *RVCh AB ShL VShThM IChD ThOBVDV*
"The Son, the Spirit, the Father, ye shall equally worship Their Trinity".

B *KVRI RAShVNI AShR ShMV IShVO ThOBVDV*
"Ye shall worship My first-born, My first Whose name is Jesus".

B *BVA RBN AShR ShMV IShV ThOBVDV*
"When the Master shall come Whose Name is Jesus ye shall worship".

B *ThVLH RAVIH ABChR ShThLD ISh VO ThAShRVH*
"I will choose a virgin worthy to bring forth Jesus, and ye shall call her blessed".

BO *VGTh RTzPIM ASThThR SHGVPI IShVO ThAKLV*
"I will hide myself in cake (baked with) coals, for ye shall eat Jesus, My Body".(The Hebrew transliteration follows MacGregor Mathers' scheme.)

It is clear that with a modicum of imagination any word whatsoever may be expanded in this way to produce the result of choice.

It is good practice to experiment with strictly secular words and see what may be developed from them. For example one may take the word "Match" and make of it "Mighty Art Thou, Cunning Hunter", or thinking of a football match rather than a "lucifer";"Many Are The Crazed Hooligans"!

There is really no end to the possibilities, and therefore to the nonsense, that can be derived using this technique.

The second form of Notariqon is, as we have said, exactly the reverse of the first. Here the initial, medial, or final letters of each word in a phrase are taken to construct one composite word.

An example quoted else-where in this book is the God-name AGLA, *Aleph, Gimel, Lamed, Aleph.* This is constructed from the Hebrew phrase *Ateh Gibor Leolahm Adonai,* which has the approximate meaning of "To Thee be the Power unto the Ages, O my Lord".

With this example it is also possible to take the final letters of each word and produce the construct "HRMI", *Heh, Resh, Mem, Yod,* or either of the two available middle letters and arrive at another two variants.

Each of the possible constructions will of course have a different numerical value in Gematria and therefore a change in emphasis. This form of Notariqon is actually quite useful to the practical magician. In effect we are producing a distillation of the power of a given phrase, rendering it down into a more convenient and concentrated form.

Again the student is advised to play around with sentences, using any of the letters of each word to construct a single word of great power. All that needs be remembered is that one must be consistent in which letters are chosen; that is to say if you decide on using initial letters you must use those and no other from each word. Likewise if a medial letter is chosen it must from the same position in each word. It also helps if the word developed is pronounceable, with a bonus point for it also being an appropriate proper word.

Unlike Gematria, Notariqon is easy to practise in English, without the need for translation. Careful study of "books of ancient and half-forgotten lore", namely older Qabalistic texts, will reveal a number of examples of this form of Notariqon.

Temurah

Temurah, the third and last technique of the literal Qabalah, means "permutation" and involves replacement of each letter in a word for another according to certain arcane rules. This is in effect a simple substitution code which is initially derived by folding the Hebrew alphabet in two, thus producing eleven columns of two letters each; for example:

11	10	9	8	7	6	5	4	3	2	1
K	I	T	Ch	Z	V	H	D	G	B	A
M	N	S	O	P	Tz	Q	R	Sh	Th	L

By rearranging these letters it is possible to produce a total of twenty-two different combinations. These arrangements are called the "Table of the Combinations of *TzIRVP*" (Tziraph). The example given above is that known as *ALBTh* (pronounced "Albath") as each of the tables derives its name from the first two letter pairs on the right. The other variants are: *ABGTh, AGDTh, ADBG, AHBD,*

AVBH, AZBV, AChBZ, ATBCh, AIBT, AKBL, ALBK, AMBL, ANBM, ASBN, AOBS, APBO, ATzBP, AQSTz, ARBQ, AShBR, and *AThBSh.*

It is really quite easy to use these tables; each letter of a given word is simply exchanged for that above or below it in each column. A very simple example should suffice to illustrate the principle.

In the Table *ALBTh* we can see that the entries under column one are *A* and *L*, so that when *A* appears in a word we would substitute it for *L*, and when *L* appears it is substituted for *A*. If we take the word *AL*, meaning "God", as our sample word and transpose the letters as above we find that we have the word *LA*, which as we already know means "Not", and is both the reflection of *AL* and a profound comment on the condition of such a being. Of course were we using one of the other twenty-one tables the results would have been quite different, with each new permutation offering varying degrees of sense, and very often, nonsense.

As if these twenty-two tables were not enough Temurah also offers two more modes of permutation called *ABGD* and *ALBM*; the so-called "Rational Tables of *TzIRVP*", of which there are another twenty-two combinations!; three "Tables of Commutations", in their "Right", "Adverse", and "Irregular" forms; and finally, "The Qabalah of the Nine Chambers".

Actually the last is quite important, especially when it comes to working with magick squares or *Kameas*, and is therefore much more frequently encountered in general occult texts than are the other forms of permutation.

The "Nine Chambers" are produced thus:

Shin	Lamed	Gimel	Resh	Kaph	Beth	Qoph	Yod	Aleph
300	30	3	200	20	2	100	10	1
Final Mem	Samekh	Vau	Final Kaph	Nun	Heh	Tau	Mem	Daleth
600	60	6	500	50	5	400	40	4
Final Tzaddi	Tzaddi	Teth	Final Peh	Peh	Cheth	Final Nun	Ayin	Zayin
900	90	9	800	80	8	700	70	7

This arrangement is sometimes referred to as *AIQ BKR* (pronounced Aiq Beker). It takes its name from the first six letters of the table, which are (from right to left) *Aleph, Yod, Qoph, Beth, Kaph*, and *Resh*.

Aiq Beker allows for the reduction of a letter's numerical value to tens or units. For example; in the case of the Hebrew for Israel, *Yod* (10) *Shin* (300) *Resh* (200) *Aleph* (1) *Lamed* (30), the total value amounts to 541; by applying AIQ BKR we may reduce the values of *Shin* and *Resh* to 30 and 20 respectively, thereby arriving at a total of 91. It is also possible to eliminate the zeros altogether and produce a final total of 10 or even 1.

As another example we may take the biblical name *Aaron* which is composed of the letters *Aleph* (1), *Heh* (5), *Resh* (200), and *Nun* final (700), a total of 906. Using *AIQ BKR* we reduce *Resh* to 20 and *Nun final* to 70 giving a new total of 96. Reducing these further by disposing of the zeros, we produce a total of 15. It is possible to take this reduction one stage further and add 1 to 5 to produce 6, the solar number and one perfectly appropriate for Aaron the High Priest.

As these formulations are mostly used in developing sigils and magickal designs based on traditional magickal squares the level of reduction will be determined by the size of the square to be used. Hence that of Saturn, being composed of three rows of three letters, ranging from one to nine, will require elimination of all zeros, while the solar square of thirty-six letters will not.

AIQ BKR has a number of other uses, including that of a crude cipher, but as these are somewhat specialised and are of doubtful value to the modern Qabalist they have not been included here.

One other form of Temurah deserves to be mentioned. This is the mode called *ThShRQ* (Thashraq), which is simply writing words backwards.Crowley provides us with an excellent example of this technique in the title of the book called *"THISHARB"* (sub figura CMXIII). This title is simply his transliteration of *Bereshith* reversed, extremely appropriate for a document that gives instruction for the development of magickal memory and which contains exercises involving speaking, writing,reading, and even walking, backwards!

Appendix One

THE LESSER BANISHING RITUAL OF THE PENTAGRAM

Next to the Qabalistic Cross, which forms part of this Banishing, the LBR Pentagram, as it is commonly known, is the most simple of all magickal rituals. Its uses are legion however, as are its variations. Indeed it is no exaggeration to say that it forms the basis of virtually all other ritual workings, including the Thelemic "Star Ruby": *Liber Reguli*, or "The Ritual of the Mark of the Beast"; and *Liber Samekh*, a ritual leading to knowledge and Conversation of the adept's Holy Guardian Angel.

It is infinitely adaptable to any occasion and to any use, from a simple daily performance of "psychic hygiene", to a preparatory ritual used before a major magickal undertaking. It is strongly recommended that the student use the ritual to open and close all magickal work, even something as seemingly innocuous as a Tarot divination or a scrying.

In this section we will be concentrating on the ritual in its simpler form and solely as a banishing technique, although students should be aware that there exists a more complicated variant, called, perhaps not surprisingly, "The Greater Banishing Ritual of the Pentagram", and that all the Pentagram rituals may also be used for invocation.

It is important that the student masters the "Lesser" form before even contemplating the "Greater", and that on no account should any invocation be attempted before proficiency is gained in the basic ritual.

The student should be prepared to devote long hours to this work and to practice assiduously until the required degree of competence is reached. This is not to say that the ritual itself is especially long or complicated, for it is not, but it is vital that the required visualisations are firmly established in the mind and eventually imprinted on the deepest level of the unconscious mind.

Given sufficient study and practice the ritual may be expanded and personalised to suit the situation and the ritualist concerned.

The LBR Pentagram is open to endless experimentation and elaboration, but only to the degree that the basic paradigm is understood and assimilated.

LBR Pentagram

We will now look in detail at the basic ritual and some of its more common variations and elaborations but in order to help the student in the early stages of practice a step-by-step description is also appended at the end of this chapter.

The ritual itself comprises three separate elements, one of which, the Qabalistic Cross, is repeated to close. These elements are:...

A) The Qabalistic Cross
B) Inscribing the Pentagrams / Vibrating Godnames
C) Invoking the Archangelic Powers
D) The Qabalistic Cross

The ritual is always commenced while facing east and the gestures are usually performed with the right hand. Some occultists prefer to use an empty hand, while others are happier with an appropriate weapon.

If using the hand it is best in the beginning to form the traditional sign of benediction by extending the first two fingers whilst covering the remaining two with the thumb. It is also possible to use a "phallic gesture" which many Thelemites prefer as being more appropriate to their belief-system. In this case the thumb is pushed through the first and second fingers and extended as far as possible.

With some practice it should be possible to detect a slight difference in effect or a change of emphasis in the feel of the ritual by alternating between these gestures.

As with the hand gestures the use of weapons of various descriptions can radically change the feel and effect of even this most elementary of rituals but for every day use it is probably best to use a simple steel dagger, at least to begin with, and that as plain as possible.

Having placed himself in the centre of a clear space, facing east, the ritualist starts with a performance of the Qabalistic Cross. The effect of this is to draw down the divine energy from above and then seal and stabilise it in the body.

First visualise a glowing sphere composed of the pure white light of Kether immediately above the head, imagine that as you start to intone or vibrate the first line of the ritual this spiritual force, the *Mezla* of the Holy Tree begins its descent into the body.

Touch the forehead and say or vibrate: *ATEH*
("Thine")

Touch the groin area and say: *MALKUTH*
("Kingdom")

At this point imagine that a brilliant shaft of light is now piercing the body, from the crown of the head to the soles of the feet.

Touch the right shoulder and say: *Ve-GEBURAH*
("and the Power")

Touch the left shoulder and say: *Ve-GEDULAH*
("and the Glory")

The brilliant white light has now formed the horizontal axis of a great cross which defines the body's outer limits.

To end this section of the ritual clasp the hands as in prayer or interlock them over the heart-centre and say:.. *Le-OLAM AMEN* ("Forever, So Be It", or, alternatively, "Forever - Truth")

It is possible to transpose the points Gedulah (Chesed) and Geburah, and some ritualists do use this form as a matter of course. Much depends on the way in which the practitioner visualises the Holy Tree for one can of course either face or back on to it. Both courses are legitimate and the final decision is left to the individual. Remember that the macrocosmic Tree is usually depicted with the Pillar of Mercy on the right and the Pillar of Severity on the left and that in the microcosmic Tree that is the human body these positions are reversed.

In the Thelemic version of the ritual there is an additional point which may be incorporated. This covers the Tiphareth heart-centre and refers to the adept's Holy Guardian Angel.

As the vertical axis of the cross is being drawn touch the breast and say *AIWASS* continuing as above.

Aiwass, it will be recalled, was that "praeter-human entity" who dictated "The Book of the Law" to Crowley over a period of three days at Cairo in April 1904ev.

Much later Crowley came to recognise that Aiwass was in fact his own HGA, and in a sense the Guardian Angel of the Aeon of Horus. The Thelemic ritualist should therefore use the name Aiwass until such time as he or she attains to full Knowledge and Conversation of their own Holy Guardian Angel after which that exalted entity's name may be legitimately substituted, although not in public.

The second section of the ritual concerns the inscription of the protective circle of pentagrams and the simultaneous vibration of the appropriate god-names.

A word about pentagrams:...

Each of the five points of a pentagram refers to one of the traditional elements but with the added dimension of Spirit.

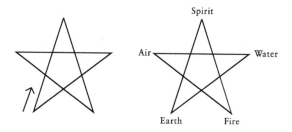

As Spirit naturally occupies the uppermost pinnacle of the star the pentagram is usually inscribed as shown above.

There are other types of pentagram, such as the inverted and averse forms, but these have a very precise technical function and are not to be used in the type of ritual described here.

Note again that pentagram rituals may be used to invoke as well as to banish, the main difference being in the manner in which the symbol is traced. The rule is; to invoke an element one moves towards the angle concerned, while to banish one moves away. Hence, in the earth pentagram used in this ritual, to invoke elemental earth the symbol is started at the uppermost point, the point of spirit, and moves towards the lower left which is the point of earth. To banish the reverse is the case and the pentagram is inscribed from the earth point moving towards spirit.

It is a good idea to practice drawing pentagrams in the air, using a variety of different gestures and weapons, before going on to the next stage of the ritual. Do make the symbols big and bold and as consistent as possible, devoting as much time as is needed to perfect the visualisation. It is important to be able to sustain in the mind's eye four distinct blazing symbols linked by a circle of white light.

A possible modification might be to visualise each pentagram in the appropriate colour for its elemental quarter; blue for west, red for south and so forth. Once again, after some experience has been gained such experimentation can offer considerable insight both as regards the ritual itself and the powers which it is designed to represent.

To trace a full size pentagram in the air extend the right hand away from the body and, starting from a position which corresponds with the left hip, traces a line up to a point in front of and above the head.

From this position the hand is brought down to a point before the right hip. The next movement is to the level of the left shoulder, still in front of the body, followed by a horizontal line across to a point before the right shoulder.

The final movement is from the right shoulder back to the starting place before the left hip.

Still facing east, the direction in which was performed the Qabalistic Cross, begin to inscribe the pentagram whilst at the same time vibrating the name *IHVH*, "Jehovah", pronounced "Yah-ho-wah" or "Yah-ho-vay".

Having drawn the pentagram extend the hand or weapon into the centre of the figure and visualise the God of the Israelites in His appropriate form (which will vary from ritualist to ritualist and also from performance to performance) standing as a protector against all evil and harm which may approach from the east.

After a moment, with the arm still extended turn to the south and repeat the performance but now using the name *ADONAI* - Lord.

A visualisation of the one God as Lord of all creation is appropriate here. Again the intention is to petition for protection from any harm emanating from this direction.

After a momentary pause to build up the image and reflect upon its particular potency, turn - hand still extended from the centre of the southern pentagram - to the west.

The pentagram is drawn as before, while the name *AHIH*, "I AM", the God who spoke to Moses from the burning bush, is vibrated.

This name is a difficult one for many people, at least at first, as its correct pronunciation involves a perfect balance between inhalation and exhalation. It is important not to get too obsessive about this as hardly anybody does manage to pronounce it properly, most being content with something along the lines of, "Ee-he-yay".

Try a number of different forms of pronunciation and breath control and see what best suits. As always there are no hard and fast rules in this, what is more important is intention and commitment, although as in all magickal work aesthetics count for something too.

Finally, turn to face the northern sector and trace the fourth and final pentagram whilst intoning the word "AGLA", pronounced "Ah-ga-la". It will be recalled from our preliminary studies that this is not a proper name but a notariqon constructed from the initial letters of the Hebrew phrase *Ateh Gibor Leolahm Adonai* which means "To Thee be the Power unto the Ages, O my Lord", or "Thou art mighty for ever O Lord".

This is the God, mighty and everlasting, who stands as a bulwark of strength against any evil which might approach from the north.

After vibrating this last name and inscribing the final figure turn back to face east, and with the right hand still held away from the body complete the protective circle by finishing at the centre of the eastern pentagram.

A brief note on Archangels and their images:...

At this point begins the third stage of the ritual, the invocation of the four Archangels who rule the quarters.

With the Archangels it is particularly important that the ritualist should have spent some time building up a good visual image for each, preferably in their appropriate colours and wielding the correct weapon.

Having said that, these images are, or rather they soon become, very personal, so the suggestions offered below are to be treated only as models and not as definitive descriptions.

Some people prefer to develop their images in a traditional manner using the classical representations of the angels as a basis. Others are drawn to a minimalist approach, visualising columns of bright vibrant air coloured in the correct hue for the cardinal point. Both these approaches work and both are entirely legitimate; and as with many facets of ritual work thoughtful experimentation can only broaden our knowledge and understanding.

The ritualist continues to face east while spreading his legs and holding his arms parallel to the ground, forming thereby a giant pentagram somewhat after the manner of the famous da Vinci illustration.

Say: "Before me Raphael"; vibrate *Raphael* - "Rah-fay-ell" - whilst visualising a mighty being robed in pale yellow and carrying a fan or yellow handled dagger.

Alternatively, imagine a vast pillar of yellow light rising out of the ground before you.

Say: "Behind me Gabriel"; vibrate *Gabriel* - "Gab-re-ell" - whilst envisaging a great being clothed in blue and holding aloft a chalice of the purest water.

Alternatively, visualise a shimmering blue column appearing behind you.

Say: "On my right hand Michael"; vibrate *Michael* - "Mik-ay-ell" visualising a flame-wreathed figure in blood red robes holding a blazing scarlet wand.

Alternatively, a great pillar of flame or a red column.

Say: "On my left hand Uriel"; vibrate *Uriel* - "Oo-re-ell" whilst calling forth an image of a tall powerful being in robes of an earthen hue, combining russet, citrine, olive and black. This figure holds aloft a disk, the weapon of elemental earth.

Alternatively, visualise a towering column, either plain black or a combination of the four colours listed above.

Still facing east and standing with arms and legs outstretched.
Say..."For I am the flaming pentagram in the column of the six-rayed star" (the Hexagram of the Shield of David and, amongst other things, the symbol of the universe) visualise the archangelic forms inclining to the centre of the circle so that they touch above and below - forming an inviolable protective shell within which glows the human pentagram.

After a few moments of sustained visualisation the ritualist performs the Qabalistic Cross in exactly the same manner as in the opening.

Summary Of Ritual

1). Stand facing east and perform Qabalistic Cross -

Touch forehead and say:..	*ATEH*
Touch Breast and say:...	*AIWASS* (optional)
Touch groin and say:...	*MALKUTH*
Touch right shoulder and say:...	*Ve-GEBURAH*
Touch left shoulder and say:...	*Ve-GEDULAH*
Clasp hands in front and say:...	*Le-OLAM AMEN*
Bring hands back to sides.	

2). Trace eastern pentagram while vibrating   *IHVH*

3). Trace southern pentagram while vibrating   *ADONAI*

4). Trace western pentagram while vibrating   *AHIH*

5).Trace northern pentagram while vibrating   *AGLA*

6). Face east. Assume shape of pentagram and say:... "Before me Raphael - Behind me Gabriel - On my right hand Michael - on my left hand Uriel.For I am the flaming pentagram in the column of the six-rayed star".

7) Qabalistic Cross to close.

Appendix Two

TRANSLITERATION TABLE
HEBREW   ENGLISH

Letter	Figure	Value	English
Aleph	א	1	A
Beth	ב	2	B
Gimel	ג	3	G
Daleth	ד	4	D
Heh	ה	5	H (E)
Vau	ו	6	V (U)
Zayin	ז	7	Z
Cheth	ח	8	Ch
Teth	ט	9	T
Yod	י	10	I (Y or J)
Kaph	כ ך	20 500	K
Lamed	ל	30	L
Mem	מ ם	40 600	M
Nun	נ ן	50 700	n
Samekh	ס	60	S
Ayin	ע	70	O
Peh	פ ף	80 800	P
Tzaddi	צ ץ	90 900	Tz
Qoph	ק	100	Q
Resh	ר	200	R
Shin	ש	300	S - Sh
Tau	ת	400	T - Th

Where there are two numbers given the second (larger) value is only used at the end of a word, e.g. *Nun* is 50 but *Nun final* is 500.

When a letter is written large its value increases a thousand-fold, e.g. *Aleph* is then increased from 1 to 1000, and *Vau* from 6 to 6000.

Bibliography

Qabalah and Magick

Fr. Achad *QBL or The Brides Reception*, Weiser, N.Y. 1972

Bligh Bond and Lea *Gematria* (1917) R.I.L.K.O. London 1981; *The Apostolic Gnosis, Part II*, R.I.L.K.O. London 1985.

W.E. Butler *Magic and the Qabalah* Aquarian Press, Northants 1972.

Aleister Crowley *The Holy Books of Thelema*, Weiser, Maine 1983; et al. *The Equinox, Vol.1 Nos.1-10 (1909-13)*, Weiser, N.Y. 1972; *The Book of Thoth (Equinox Vol.3 No.5 1944)*, Weiser, N.Y. 1973; *Book 4 (Part 1 and 2, 1911-12)* Sangreal, Dallas 1972; *Magick in Theory and Practice (Book 4 part 3) (1929)* Castle Books, N.Y.; *The Qabalah of Aleister Crowley, (1907-9)* Weiser, N.Y. 1973, (Also published as *777 and other Qabalistic Writings of Aleister Crowley* Weiser, Maine 1977); et al. *Liber MCCLXIV*, Albion Lodge, OTO, London 1989ev; / Marcelo Motta *The Commentaries of AL*, R.K.P. London 1975; / Israel Regardie *The Law is for All*, Falcon Press, Pheonix 1986.

Dion Fortune *The Mystical Qabalah* (1935) Ernest Benn, London 1976.

Solomon Ibn Gabriol *The Fountain of Life* (c1050) Philosophical Library, N.Y. 1962.

W.G. Gray *The Ladder of Lights*, Helios, Glos. 1968.

Zev ben Shimon Halevi *Kabbalah*, Thames and Hudson, London 1979.

Bill Heidrick *Magick and Qabalah No.1*, OTO, Berkeley 1976.

Aryeh Kaplan *Meditation and Kabbalah*, Weiser, N.Y. 1982.

Gareth Knight *A Practical Guide to Qabalistic Symbolism, Vol.1-2.* Helios, Glos. 1972.

Eliphas Levi *The Book of Splendours*, Aquarian, Northants 1975; *The Mysteries of the Qabalah* (1886) Thorsons, Northants 1974.

S.L. MacGregor-Mathers *The Kabbalah Unveiled* (1887) R.K.P. London 1981.

Adam McLean (Intro) *A Treatise on Angel Magic (Harley ms. 6482*

230

1699-1714) Magnum Opus Hermetic Source Works, 1982.

Issac Myer *Qabbalah* (1888) Stuart and Watkins, London 1970.

Israel Regardie *A Garden of Pomegranates* (1932), Llewellyn, Minnesota 1986; (Ed.) *The Golden Dawn. Vol. 1-2* (1937-40), Llewellyn, Minnesota 1971; *The Tree of Life* Weiser, N.Y. 1969.

Gershom G. Scholem *Major Trends in Jewish Mysticism* (1946), Schocken, N.Y. 1974; *On the Kabbalah and its Symbolism,* Schocken, N.Y. 1965.

James Sturzaker *Kabbalistic Aphorisms,* Theosophical Publishing House, London 1971.

Doreen and James Sturzaker *Colour and the Kabbalah,* Metatron Publications, London 1986.

R.G. Torrens *Secret Rituals of the Golden Dawn,* Aquarian, Northants 1973.

A.E. Waite *The Holy Kabbalah,* Citadel Press, undated.

William Wynn Westcott *Sepher Yetzirah* (1887), Weiser, N.Y. 1975.

Mythology and Gods

Richard Carlyon *A Guide to the Gods,* Quill, N.Y. 1982.

Janet and Stewart Farrar *The Witches Goddess,* Robert Hale, London 1987.

Pierre Grimal (Ed.) *Larousse World Mythology,* Paul Hamlyn, London 1971

Veronica Ions *Egyptian Mythology,* Newnes. 1986.

Manfred Lurker *The Gods and Symbols of Ancient Egypt,* Thames and Hudson, London 1986.

Betty Radice *Who's Who in the Ancient World,* Penguin, London 1973.

Alan W. Shorter *The Egyptian Gods,* R.K.P. London 1983.

Astrology

Stephen Arroyo *Astrology Karma and Transformation,* CRCS Publications, California 1978.

Aleister Crowley *The Complete Astrological Writings,* Ed. John Symonds and Kenneth Grant. Star/W.H. Allen, London 1987.

Liz Greene *Saturn, A New Look at an Old Devil,* Aquarian, Northants 1977.

Margaret E. Hone *The Modern Text Book of Astrology,* L.N. Fowler, Essex 1980

P.I.H. Naylor *Astrology, An Historical Examination*, Robert Maxwell, London 1967

Vivian E. Robson *The Fixed Stars and Constellations in Astrology*, Weiser, N.Y. 1979

General

Reuben Alcalay *The Complete English-Hebrew Dictionary*, Massada, Jerusalem.

Richard I. Evans *Jung on Elementary Psychology*, R.K.P. London 1976.

Wallace K. Ferguson *Europe in Transition*, Houghton Mifflin, Boston 1962.

Shyam Sundar Goswami *Laya Yoga*, R.K.P. London 1980.

Carl G. Jung *Man and his Symbols*, Aldus Books, London 1964.

Bertrand Russell *History of Western Philosophy*, George Allen and Unwin, London 1961.

R.C. Wren *Potter's New Cyclopaedia of Botanical Drugs and Preparations*, Health Science Press, Sussex 1970.

Glossary

ADEPTUS EXEMPTUS   Magickal grade of CHESED. $7° = 4^\square$

ADEPTUS MAJOR   Magickal grade of GEBURAH. $6° = 5^\square$

ADEPTUS MINOR   Magickal grade of TIPHARETH. $5° = 6^\square$

AGAPE   Love, numerical value 93 in the Greek Qabalah. See THELEMA.

AIQ BKR   "The Qabalah of Nine Chambers". System of reducing the numerical value of letters to tens or units using a table which is divided into three columns of nine letters each. See TEMURAH

AJNA   "Brow Chakra", the "Third Eye" - situated at approximately the level of the pineal gland. Corresponds to Chokmah in Crowley's system although Dion Fortune and others give Daath.

ANAHATA   "Heart Chakra" - situated in the thorax. Attributed to the combined Chesed-Geburah-Tiphareth triad in Crowley's system; Fortune gives Tiphareth alone and J.F.C.Fuller assigns it to Chesed.

ANSATE CROSS   Ankh, or Egyptian Cross.

ARIK ANPIN   "Long in Face" or "Vast Countenance" - Macroprosopos. Title of Kether, occasionally applied to the Supernal Triad as a whole.

ASANA   Any Yoga posture.

ATU   Alternative name for a tarot trump.

BODY of LIGHT   Usually refers to the "astral body".

BOOK of THOTH   Tarot Pack.

CACADAIMON   "Noisy spirit".

CHAKRA   Subtle power centre on human body.

CHAYOTH ha-QADESH   "The Holy Living Creatures" - Bull, Lion, Eagle and Man.

CHIYAH   Sub-division of NESHEMAH representing the creative impulse and supreme will of the individual.

CHOLETH ha-YESODOTH   The "Sphere of the Elements", mundane chakra of Malkuth.

DIN   "Judgement" Secondary title of Geburah. See PACHAD

FYLFOT CROSS   Swastika or Solar Cross.

GEMATRIA   Sophisticated form of numerology.

GEOMANCY   As used in the west, a form of divination which involves interpreting marks made in fine earth or sand.

GUPH   The physical body.

IPSISSIMUS   Magickal grade of Kether. 10° = 1□. Effectively a god.

KAMEA   A "magickal square", used in constructing talismans.

LAMEN   Design worn on the breast of a magician symbolising the forces with which he is currently working.

LEVANAH   The Moon, mundane chakra of Yesod.

LINGAM   Phallus, male sexual organ

MACROPROSOPOS   "Vast Countenance" - see ARIK ANPIN

MADIM   Mars, mundane chakra of Geburah.

MAGUS   Magickal grade of Chokmah. 9° = 2□

MAGISTER TEMPLI   Magickal grade of Binah. 8° = 3□

MAZLOTH   The "Sphere of the Zodiac", mundane chakra of Chokmah.

MEZLA   The "influence of the Most holy Ancient One" which flashes down the Tree from Kether.

MICROPROSOPOS   The "Short in Face" or "Lesser Countenance" the sixth Sephiroth below the Abyss, excluding Malkuth. See ZEIR ANPIN.

MIDRASH   Commentary, glosses and expansions of sacred texts.

MULADHARA   "Root Chakra", situated around the area of the perineum. Location of the coiled Kundalini force. Attributed to Yesod by Crowley and Malkuth by Fortune and Fuller.

MUNDANE CHAKRA   Physical correspondences of the Sephiroth, usually planetary bodies.

NEOPHYTE   Magickal grade of Malkuth. 1° = 10□

NEPHESH   Third and final division of the "Archetypal Man". "The unredeemed animal soul", found in Yesod.

NESHEMAH   "The Triad of the Immortal Man." That part of man which may be considered divine and immortal. Comprises three distinct elements: YECHIDAH, CHIYAH (see elsewhere) and NESHEMAH proper which corresponds to Binah.

NOGAH   Venus, mundane Chakra of Netzach.

NOTARIQON   Technique of exegesis used in Literal Qabalah of which there are two forms. In the first, every letter of a word is taken as the beginning of another so that a complete phrase is generated. The second method reverses this process and takes a letter from each word in a phrase to construct a new word.

PACHAD   Fear. Secondary name of Geburah. - see also DIN.

PAROKETH   "The Veil of the Temple"; placed between Tiphareth and the spheres of Netzach and Hod in the Golden Dawn scheme, although others place it above the sixth sphere, separating Tiphareth from Chesed and Geburah.

PATH OF THE ARROW   The combination of paths which make up the Middle Pillar. Also known as "The Way of the Mystic".

PHILOSOPHUS   Magickal grade of Netzach. $4° = 7^\square$

PRACTICUS   Magickal grade of Hod. $3° = 8^\square$

PRANA   Life-force (Hindu), closely associated with breath.

PRANAYAMA   "The Breath-way", yoga breathing technique.

PRIMUM MOBILE   "First Swirlings", mundane chakra of Kether. Signifies the first movement of the creative impulse as it emerges from the void. see also RESHITH-ha-GILGULIM.

QESHETH   "The Rainbow", considered by some Qabalists to be a veil situated above Malkuth. Takes its name from the letters of the three paths which it bisects; Qoph, Shin and Tau; QShTh or "rainbow".

QLIPHOTH   "Shells", "Rinds" or "Harlots" - singular Qliphah. The Demons of Qabalah

RAHAMIN   "Compassion", alternative name for Tiphareth, rarely found outside of the Zohar.

RESHITH-ha-GILGULIM.   See PRIMUM MOBILE

ROS   "The Heavenly Dew", a mystical fluid collected in some subtle manner from the aether and which is said to seep down from the brain into the spinal column and thence to the genital region.

RUACH   The intellect. Composed of five elements; Memory, Will, Imagination, Desire and Reason - one for each of the Sephiroth below the Abyss excluding Yesod and Malkuth.

RUACH ELOHIM   Spirit of God. see below

RUACH-ha-QADESH   The Holy Spirit. See SHEKINAH

SAHASRARA   "The Thousand Petalled Lotus". Chakra located at the crown of the head, associated with the thalamus. The final chakra in the system. Said to be the collecting point of the ROS. Attributed to Kether.

SEPHIROTH-ha-BENYIN   "The Sephiroth of Construction" - refers to the Sephiroth from Chesed to Yesod and symbolises the "six dimensions of matter".

SEPTUAGINT   Greek version of the Old Testament, composed circa 270BC by seventy-two translators, all working independently. It is said that when the translations where compared there was not one error or point of disagreement between them.

SHABATAI   Saturn. Mundane chakra of Binah.

SHAOLIN BROCADES   Meditation technique developed by Shaolin priests in China. Often used as preliminary exercises before T'ai Chi or martial arts practice.

SHEKINAH   "Brightness" or "Dwelling". Feminine form of the Holy Spirit. Has an "upper" and "lower" form which dwell in Binah and Malkuth respectively.

SHEMESH   The Sun. Mundane chakra of Tiphareth.

SHEVIRATH-ha-KELIM   "The Breaking of the Vessels". Theory developed by Issac Luria (1534-72) to account for the presence of evil in the created world.

SOPHIA   Greek concept of wisdom viewed as female in character.

SOTHIS   Sirius, or Sept - the "Dog Star". First magnitude binary star, situated in Canis Major. Possible mundane chakra of Daath

SUPERNALS   The three Sephiroth above the Abyss.

SVADISTHANA   Hypogastric Chakra. Situated just above the genital area and associated with the prostate gland in men. Attributed to Hod by Crowley but to Yesod by others. See TAN T'IEN

T'AI CHI   "Supreme Ultimate", the Chinese "Yin/Yang symbol. Also a martial arts based system of movement and meditation, the "inner form" of Kung Fu.

TAN T'IEN   "Cinnabar Field". Chinese power centre located just below the midriff and equated with the SVADISTHANA chakra (see above).

TARGUM   Rabbinical interpretation of scriptures. See MIDRASH.

TEMURAH   Complex Qabalistic technique involving permutation and substitution of letters. see AIQ BEKER

TETRAGRAMMATON   "The Four Lettered Name". IHVH, The name of God in the sphere of Chokmah.

THRASHRAQ   Form of TEMURAH (see above) which involves writing words and phrases backwards.

THELEMA   Will. In the Greek Qabalah numbers 93. see AGAPE

TSADIKIM   "Righteous Ones", or "saints".

TZEDEK   Jupiter, mundane chakra of Chesed.

VERSICLE   Mantra-like phrase or incantation. Magickal weapon of Hod.

VESICA PISCIS   "Fish Bladder". An ovoid shape often containing additional symbols. A symbol of Binah.

VISHUDDHA   Chakra located at about the level of the larynx. Associated with the thyroid gland. Corresponds with Binah in some systems and with Daath in others.

YECHIDAH   "The Unique One". Subdivision of NESHEMAH (see above) corresponding with Kether. "The supreme self of the aspirant", immortal and eternal.

YEYA   Aramaic form of IHVH.

YONI   Female sexual organ.

ZEIR ANPIN   see MICROPROSOPOS.

ZELATOR   Magickal grade of Yesod. $2° = 9^{\square}$

SKOOB BOOKS PUBLISHING

Titles by Kenneth Grant

REMEMBERING ALEISTER CROWLEY

The memoir of the personal relationship
between Kenneth Grant and Aleister Crowley
in Crowley's later years contains much hitherto
unpublished material and illustrations. A subtle
humour informs Kenneth Grant's commentary
on their mutual correspondence which
illuminates Crowley's magical mentality
from unsuspected angles.
ISBN 1 871438 22 5   hbk   £24.99

The Typhonian Trilogies

THE MAGICAL REVIVAL

"The most authoritative history of 20th century magic that now exists."
ISBN 1 871438 37 3   hbk   £18.99   *Books and Bookmen*

ALEISTER CROWLEY AND THE HIDDEN GOD

An exhaustive and critical study of Crowley's system of sexual magic.
ISBN 1 871438 36 5   hbk   £18.99

CULTS OF THE SHADOW

Aspects of occultism often wrongly confused with 'black magic'.
ISBN 1 871438 67 5   hbk   £18.99

NIGHTSIDE OF EDEN

A previouly rare exposition of the 'left-hand path'.
ISBN 1 871438 72 1   hbk   £19.99

HECATE'S FOUNTAIN

Magical contact with alien intelligences, through rites of strange beauty.
ISBN 1 871438 96 9   hbk   £24.99

OUTER GATEWAYS

Examines the influence of the 'alien' upon the 'human', and the attainment of undivided consciousness.
ISBN 1 871438 12 8   hbk   £24.99

AVAILABLE FROM ALL GOOD BOOKSHOPS
OR ORDER FROM SKOOB TWO WITH A CREDIT CARD, TEL 071 405 0030 DELIVERY POST FREE IN UK.
A DISCOUNT OF 20% IS AVAILABLE WHEN YOU ORDER TWO OR MORE, DIRECT FROM SKOOB

further titles from
SKOOB BOOKS PUBLISHING

THE MIND OF THE DRUID   *Dr E Graham Howe*

Dr Howe draws from his many years as a practising psychiatrist and from the elemental world of fire, water, trees and rocks, to question and challenge the religious and material values of contemporary society.

'Many influences of astounding variety have contributed to shape (Howe's) philosophy of life which, unlike most philosophies, takes its stance "in" life, and not in a system of thought.'   *Henry Miller*
ISBN 1 871438 75 6   Pbk £6.99

THE TRIUMPH OF PAN   *Victor Neuburg*

Facsimile of the first edition published by Aleister Crowley's Equinox press in 1910.

'There is in these deep and richly evocative poems the great power and sensitivity of a Shelley, along with the visionary incisiveness of a Blake. They are marked by the almost voluptuous sense of visual imagery common to the Symbolist school... A marvellous collection.'
ISBN 1 871438 55 1   (hbk, limited edn) £39   *Gnosis*

SKOOB DIRECTORY OF SECONDHAND BOOKSHOPS IN THE BRITISH ISLES

Fifth edition

The best informed, best organised most affordable guide to secondhand bookshops. Full details of stock, opening hours, location and specialities of 1000 bookshops.
Compact and accessible *The Skoob Directory* now includes national route maps for motorists, a set of helpful articles on the book trade and terminology, and a specially written preface by A. N. Wilson.

'Skoob have produced an accessible and manageable directory ideal for the pocket.'   *Antiquarian Book Monthly Review*
ISBN 1 871438 52 7   Pbk £6.99